To Dad

Happy Father's Day

From your loving
daughter Clare.

It is wonderful
to have such a good
21/6/98' father as you.
Thanks for everything.
Love.
Clare.

In the

HALF
LIGHT

JACQUELINE KENT

In the

HALF
LIGHT

Life as a child in Australia
1900-1970

ANGUS
& ROBERTSON
PUBLISHERS

For Kenneth

ANGUS & ROBERTSON PUBLISHERS

Unit 4, Eden Park, 31 Waterloo Road,
North Ryde, NSW, Australia 2113, and
16 Golden Square, London W1R 4BN,
United Kingdom

First published in Australia
by Angus & Robertson Publishers in 1988
First published in the United Kingdom
by Angus & Robertson (UK) in 1988

Copyright © Jacqueline Kent 1988

National Library of Australia
Cataloguing-in-publication data.

Kent, Jacqueline, 1947–   .
  In the half light: Australian childhood 1900–1970.

  ISBN 0 207 15663 8.

  1. Children — Australia — Social life and customs.
  2. Children — Australia — History.   3. Australians.
  4. Australia — Social life and customs — 20th
  century.   I. Title.

994

Typeset in 11pt Baskerville
Printed in Singapore

The rocking horse days of my childhood
Are slipping and sliding away.
And, though I lived well in the half light,
I welcome the coming of day.

From a poem by an unknown
Queensland boy, 1950s.

Acknowledgments

The following list includes those people and organisations to whom I owe a special debt of gratitude.

The Literary Arts Board of the Australia Council; the staffs of the Mitchell Library (Sydney), La Trobe Library (Melbourne), State Library of South Australia, Battye Library (Perth), W.A. Museum of Childhood; New South Wales Government Printer; News Limited; Fairfax Magazines; Lisa Allen; Jennifer Isaacs; Richard Walsh; Sue Phillips of Angus and Robertson Publishers.

I must also thank those friends and acquaintances who helped me find some of the people whose words appear in this book and finally I am extremely grateful to the contributors themselves. Without them this book would not exist.

J.K.

Contents

Introduction

The rocking-horse days of my childhood
Are slipping and sliding away.
And, though I lived well in the half light,
*I welcome the coming of day.**

The child is the same person as the adult, but they live in different worlds. This book is about the way adults remember the other world of their childhood.

Material for the book was obtained by taping interviews with hundreds of people throughout Australia over a period of almost two years. Much of this material was later discarded as repetitive or uninteresting. The people whose memories are recorded here were chosen because they had very clear recollections of their childhoods, and because they were as representative as possible of Australians — rich and poor, country and city dwellers.

They came from many backgrounds and spoke of varied experiences — some haltingly, as though their memories were painful or difficult, some with happiness and affection. Because what they said was often self-revealing, most people chose to remain anonymous, so I decided that all contributors should be anonymous. This means that names have been changed, though physical descriptions have not.

Obviously, recollections of childhood needed more words than have been used here. Moreover, memory is rambling and frequently fails to follow a coherent sequence, and people often do not finish their sentences. These interviews, then, have been condensed and reassembled to make them coherent and readable. Where part or inaccurate quotations were given (of poems or songs, mainly), the original has been checked and reproduced accurately. Reported speech has been made into direct speech for immediacy and greater impact. Otherwise, the memories in these pages are what the people who were interviewed believed to be true.

The contributors' words give new colour and new perspectives to events we have been accustomed to see as flat sentences in history books about Australia in the twentieth century. (Of course, where obvious facts contradict memories, correction has been made.) From their memories has been drawn a typical selection of

*From a poem by an unknown Queensland boy, broadcast over the ABC Argonauts Children's Session in the late 1950s.

Australian childhood, designed to evoke the most significant as well as the most common experiences.

A boy or girl who grew up during the Depression does not remember statistics of the unemployed or details of government social welfare programmes. He or she remembers going down to the corner shop and asking for 'specks' or spoiled fruit that was given away for nothing, or hiding shoes in a culvert on the way to school because the poor kids in the class beat up the richer kids who wore them. War is not presented as a matter of battle statistics: it is a small girl cowering in terror as the guns went off over Sydney harbour in 1942, or a boy coming to terms with a father who went overseas before his son was old enough to remember him.

There are also the ordinary things, the events that are a normal part of growing up in Australia. An eighty-year-old can still describe the bright taste of water from a bush creek on a summer day when she was only seven years old. Other people recall the pride of wearing a white dress at a Christmas party, or making a catapult out of rubber bands and twigs, or the bliss of being warmly tucked up in bed, wearing clean pyjamas while it poured with rain and blew a gale outside.

People sometimes say that when they were children summers were longer and hotter, cicadas sang more loudly, food tasted better. Statistics meteorological, zoological and agricultural tell them they are wrong, but nostalgia has very little to do with facts. The difference is that the small joys of being alive — the smells, colours, textures — are at their freshest when we are children, and we still remember them. And such things as birthday parties and Empire Day pageants have a sheen and a glory that adult celebrations never match.

This has been the fastest-changing century in human history. Australians born in 1900 have been through two world wars, major and minor economic depressions, the monstrous threat of annihilation by nuclear weapons, and they have seen miracles of technology that were unknown only two generations ago. People who grew up before World War I often look at today's children in some perplexity: how can these confident, noisy kids understand what life was like without refrigerators or radios or television or computers? Today's kids have never seen a brother or sister die of diphtheria, never rushed into the street awestruck as a Model T Ford whirled past at a giddy twenty miles an hour.

There are so many differences. Bread from a supermarket comes in neat polythene-shrouded slices; it is not delivered from the back of a horse-drawn cart. Once-common characters such as the bottle-oh, rabbit-oh and clothes-prop man have disappeared and are now found as footnotes in social histories or noted as 'obsolete' or 'colloquial' in today's dictionaries. School compositions used to be written with pens dipped in inkwells, the letters carefully formed and correctly angled with the help of slope cards; now some eight-year-olds type impressions of their holiday in Bali on a keyboard and see their words flicker up on a small screen. Once telling the time was a matter of concentrating hard to see the relation between the big and little hands on a watch face: now the information is slapped out in sloping black numerals on the face of a digital watch. The 'left over right, loop under and pull' method of tying shoelaces is unnecessary for a small child whose shoes are fastened by Velcro strips. Decimal currency has made redundant the laborious addition, subtraction, multiplication and division of pounds, shillings and pence; in fact, measurements of all kinds have become very simple now that calculators are common.

Many of today's children are more familiar with fast-changing technology than their parents. But they are still dependent creatures because of their youth — and because of this, children have always been spectators, sometimes tossed around by events they don't understand, at the mercy of adults who manipulate these events for their own incomprehensible reasons. The great ambition of most children has always been to grow up, to have power over their own destinies instead of being at the mercy of adults. Events through which people live during their childhood, no matter what their social status and expectations may be, often seem chaotic and disconnected.

Most people seem to feel, looking back, that their childhood selves have little to do with the people they have become. One middle-aged woman quoted in this book said, 'I feel as though everything that happened to me before the Depression really hit us — I was ten — happened to somebody else. I feel like one of those caterpillars that's been chopped in half and regenerates.'

The things that happen to people when they are young and vulnerable often have a profound effect on them. An eighty-year-old man faltered only once in his matter-of-fact recital of a hard childhood — when he described his father leaving his family. 'I was only eleven,' he said, 'and you know what? The worst of it was, I *liked* my dad.'

Memories freeze time: they are the reality of the past for all of us.

1900—1914

We always had people to do things for us

We always had people to do things for us

The yellowed photograph in the album has a caption in ink that has faded to grey: 'C. and me in garden, 1911'. 'C', who is Caroline Howard, is standing next to her mother. Both squarely face the camera, both have straight black eyebrows, small mouths and firm chins.

This is not a casual snapshot: the clothes look too stiff and starched, with an obvious look of 'Sunday best' about them. Caroline, who is aged seven, wears an elaborate Alice-in-Wonderland outfit: a long-sleeved, white dress frilled at the wrists and knees, white pinafore, white stockings and black shoes with a single strap across the instep. Her dark, loose hair spills over her shoulders, restrained only by a headband. Her mother, who looks to be in her late twenties, has the pouter-pigeon look we associate with the Edwardian period: her high-necked blouse has leg-of-mutton sleeves and a cameo brooch pinned to the bodice, while the narrow-waisted skirt she wears sweeps to the ground. Her hair is pulled back from her face in a loose, soft topknot.

The 'garden' in which they are standing is obviously far from the usual suburban plot of ground: it seems to consist entirely of lawn rising smoothly behind them to a large house. A flight of shallow stone steps leads up to an imposing front door and a wide verandah. The style of house, which is called 'Federation' in Sydney, is 'Edwardian' in Melbourne, where this photograph was taken.

It seems an ordinary photograph of a very prosperous mother and daughter early this century. But a closer look reveals a few interesting things about it. Neither Caroline nor her mother looks at ease. The limitations of Edwardian photography may be responsible for the

3

strained, set poses; perhaps the summer sun has made both Caroline and her mother frown and screw up their eyes. Then again, perhaps not. Caroline's mother looks tense and uncomfortable: the arm around her daughter's shoulders does not seem to fall there by nature or by force of habit. And there is the slightest suggestion of flinching in the angle of Caroline's neck and shoulder.

Caroline looks the more commanding of the two, levelling an imperious stare at the camera, her hands clasped loosely in front of her. She is controlled, like an actress who has just finished performing: at any second, you think, she will bow to acknowledge applause. It is an oddly adult pose for a little girl of only seven.

When I was small I thought my name was far too imposing and important: Caroline Eleanor Macmillan Howard. I felt it was up to me to do something to grow into it. But I couldn't think of anything until my seventh birthday. On that day in 1911 I was taken to Her Majesty's Theatre in Melbourne to see the woman my Aunt Nettie described as the 'greatest singer in the whole world', Dame Nellie Melba.

In honour of my first visit to a theatre, I wore my best brown velvet dress with the white lace collar. My hair, which was usually dead straight, hung down my back in glossy ringlets — even though my scalp ached from the rag curlers the housemaid had twisted mercilessly through my hair the previous night. With Auntie Nettie and Uncle Norman, I climbed what seemed a million stairs and sat behind a curved, golden balcony. All around were more people than I had even seen in my life: men in dinner jackets and neatly trimmed whiskers, women in bare-shouldered dresses with stoles and long, white gloves, their hair piled high. Many of the women, I was thrilled to see, wore *lipstick* and *rouge*. I was squirming round, trying desperately to see everything, the soft gas lights, the brilliant cream and gold proscenium, the glamorous people in the little curtained boxes near the stage that reminded me of a Punch and Judy show. 'Keep still!' hissed Auntie Nettie, poking me in the back. 'Pay attention!' The gas lights went down, the huge, gold-fringed curtain with a crown on it parted, everybody was quiet.

Then applause started, wave after wave of it. I couldn't understand why: all I saw was a bright light on the stage and way down there, far below me, was a dumpy little woman who looked like the picture of Queen Victoria in my school history reader. She bowed, and bowed again. Auntie Nettie and Uncle Norman were applauding vigorously by this time, and I thought I should clap too, out of politeness. But at the back of my mind was the thought: Is *this* the wonderful Nellie Melba? She's old and fat!

I was so disappointed and disgruntled that I didn't hear a note she sang — not that it would have meant much to me, for I didn't come from a family of musicians. I cannot remember what her voice sounded like, though I've heard records since, of course. Frankly, I was rather bored. But at the end of the concert, when the last note from her and from the orchestra had died away, the whole theatre erupted. A roar went up from the stalls, from the boxes, from the balcony. Men jumped to their feet, beaming and clapping; women dropped gloves in their eagerness to applaud. Dame Nellie stood there, bowed her head meekly, spread her hands and accepted all the homage.

That really impressed me. As the applause went on and on, I thought how wonderful it must be to have people like you so much just because you stood alone on a stage and sang. As we joined the queue shuffling down the stairs and into Exhibition Street to look for a horse cab, I decided I would be a famous opera singer. All that attention would be wonderful.

For months after that I sneaked shawls, sheets and blankets from our enormous linen press, draped them around myself and practised being Dame Nellie Melba in front of a mirror. Mostly I bowed and accepted the roars of applause; the illusion was shattered the moment I opened my mouth. I croaked away earnestly for days on 'Lo, hear the gentle la-ha-hark' and 'Home sweet home', but it was no use pretending that my singing voice was any better than a crow's. I realised sadly that I'd have to find another way of being adored.

I never told Mother or Dad that I wanted to be an opera singer; I knew they would not have approved. Singers, even opera stars, ranked a small step above actresses in their estimation, and that was very low indeed. Such women, I knew, were regarded as deeply immoral (the only evidence for this seemed to be that they went to public houses with men to whom they were not married), and wore lipstick and rouge during the day as a matter of course. When I named my favourite little bantam Grace Palotta, after a famous vaudeville star, Mother said, 'Surely you could have thought of a better *name* for her, dear!'

My parents were not more snobbish than others of their set; theatrical people were 'not our sort', that was all. I knew who 'our sort' were from a very early age. They were the women who came to Mother's 'at homes' and charity tennis parties in their wide hats and long coats and dresses, drinking China tea and eating the crumbly, yellow cake the maid served them; they were the men, their husbands, who drove glossy De Dion Boutons and Model T Fords, wearing leather-lined tweed motoring coats and jaunty caps and goggles, smoked huge, smelly cigars in the house and laughed too loudly after dinner. *My* sort of friend was not Henry Riley, the son of the clothes-prop man, who came to the back door with his father where cook or the housemaid received them; a good friend for me was Louise Marriner, whose mother worked with mine on charity committees and who was always coming to visit. Louise and I sometimes sat cross-legged on the flagstones inside our enormous living-room fireplace, with an old sheet tacked across the front as a curtain, and peered over the top with our dolls, just like the Punch and Judy man who used to come to all my birthday parties.

Ours was one of the largest in a suburb of big houses. It was a formal home, as were most others I knew, and parts of it were out of bounds to children. The reception room and dining room were for the adults, used only for entertaining: they seemed to me dark and gloomy and full of massive furniture. I much preferred the living room, which I thought extremely elegant. I loved the golden rose-patterned wallpaper and the pictures on the walls: my favourites were *Stag at Bay* by Landseer, a highly romantic one showing a young couple and called *Wedded*, and *The Sea Hath Its Pearls,* in which a beautiful girl, wearing a white dress, gathered shells on the seashore.

Between the horsehair sofa and the corner whatnot was Dad's pride and joy: the phonograph, in its heavy, walnut case that stood almost as high as I did. After dinner sometimes he would lift the needle, carefully place a huge record on the turntable, wind the handle, and the thin, clear voice of Galli-Curci or Melba would come out through the horn.

One of my jobs was to arrange the roses in tall, brass vases on the side-table by the door. This was a responsibility I took very seriously when I was small, mainly because of Uncle Michael: Dad's brother, who had been killed in the Boer War, smiled out of a silver frame next to the vases. I had a very vague idea of what had happened to him: I believed that he had been galloping over some hills that looked like the Dandenongs and the Boers, who must have been like Indians, shot him dead. Nobody talked much about Uncle Michael except at Christmas, when Granny never failed to say how he would have enjoyed being with us all, and Dad looked sad.

In the living room, before bed, Dad sometimes told me stories about Ned Kelly and read me Kipling's *Just So Stories* and *The Jungle Book*. I had a very good, parrot-like memory, which he used to encourage: once he gave me two whole shillings, a fortune, for learning Gray's 'Elegy' by heart and repeating it perfectly. I must have needed the money badly; Gray's 'Elegy' goes on forever. When he didn't feel like reading to me, Dad would sit in his armchair by the fireplace, with the large, pink-paged paper called the *Bulletin* (which bored me because the print was so small and I couldn't understand any of the jokes), or chuckle over the Steele Rudd books, puffing away at his pipe.

Apart from being read to, I didn't have much to do with Dad while I was small. He was an imposing figure with glossy, black shoes and a high, starched collar on his suit who went to work every morning with great ceremony. He was an importer who worked in the city and who always took the train with his other businessmen friends. Trains were very genteel then, particularly after the factory workers had finished their journeys and it was time for the city gents. Dad seemed to me to work very hard: often he looked at figures after dinner in his study, at the high roll-top desk.

Mother, too — never 'Mummy' or 'Mum' — was a comparative stranger to me. She spent her days organising charity affairs, going to lunches or teas, attending dinners and balls in the evenings. She didn't seem to belong to me: she was more like a magnificent, glamorous guest who stayed with us for a long time. And I was a little afraid of her, mainly because I felt she would have chosen a different daughter from myself. She would have preferred a girl who never made any noise, never fought with her brothers and sister, always walked and never ran.

Mother liked ceremony, organisation, order. I remember when I was about four she and Dad came in to say goodnight before going out for the evening. The ritual was always that I would be in bed, my hair brushed and my teeth cleaned, and Mother and Dad would pat me on the head and say goodnight. For some reason, on this particular evening, Mother looked more than usually magnificent in a low-cut lace ball dress and a diamond fillet in her dark hair. I thought she looked like a fairy princess. 'You're *lovely*, Mother!' I said, bouncing up out of bed enthusiastically. She moved back, afraid, I think, I was going to hug her. 'Darling, don't spoil my dress,' was all she said, but I had seen the look on her face and I knew not to attempt to hug her again.

This sounds as though Mother was cruel, inhuman. She wasn't — but I now know that she had been brought up as the only child of a wealthy family, with nurses and governesses and remote parents. She had never learned how to talk to her own children, and I think she resented us because we were sometimes rowdy and uncontrollable and got in the way. She had four children in the end, and I'm convinced she never intended to have so many.

Grandfather and Grandmother, Mother's parents, were not comfortable people either. They seemed immensely tall and thin to me: I never saw Grandma's spine touch the back of a chair. (As she suffered from arthritis, she must have held herself upright by sheer force of personality.) They lived in Sydney, so visited us very seldom: being summoned to talk to them was rather like attending an audience at the court of King Edward and Queen Alexandra. I always turned into a wooden little girl in my white pinafore, and when Grandfather announced graciously, 'You look very well today,' I could say only 'Yes,' not even 'Thank you.' I was always pleased when they left — and so, I found out years later, was Mother. Grandma had a habit of comparing Mother's upbringing with ours, seldom in our favour.

The most important person in my daily life was Miss Craig, who was my nurse for many years. This is not to say that I liked her: far from it, because she was severe. A scowling Scotswoman with a body like a bolster, currant-like eyes and sandy hair that never stayed up at the back, she controlled my life. I thought she was immensely old, though she must have been only about forty. Miss Craig's mother had come out to Australia in the 1860s as a governess under the auspices of the Female Emigration Society; she had found the country inhospitable and the people badly educated, and had eventually drifted into a job as a housemaid for a grazing family in western Victoria, where she married a local lawyer and had a daughter. Miss Craig had been luckier than her mother; she went to a good Melbourne girls' school and, though unmarried, came to us. I found out these details about her much later: when I was small I knew nothing about her, not even her Christian name.

Miss Craig's duty, as she saw it, was to Mould my Character. She was relentless about this. If I did some sewing that wasn't perfect — and I rarely took the trouble to make my stitches tiny and straight — she declared, 'Every stitch of this will have to come undone!' In vain I protested that it would look better when it was pressed: No, shoddy work had to be corrected as far as Miss Craig was concerned.

On the very rare occasions that Miss Craig allowed herself a day off, I was delighted and relieved. I much preferred to be looked after by one of the housemaids, who were timid young girls. They wore black dresses and white aprons and frilly lace caps, which looked very pretty, I think — though heaven knew how they kept them clean. We always got on very well. They didn't consider that little girls had to be boiled red when they had their baths, and controlled the flow of water from the chip heater much more conscientiously than Miss Craig did. And they didn't consider that children were like horses: needing a brisk rubdown with a rough towel at the end of the bath.

I remember that we never had fewer than three housemaids, rather shadowy figures who appeared and disappeared regularly. They worked from dawn to dusk, cleaning the silver, dusting the heavy furniture throughout the house, polishing the wooden floors of the living and dining rooms, scrubbing the kitchen flagstones and blackleading the stove, boiling the water for the copper and just about breaking their backs as they hauled the sodden clothes to the wringer.

Apart from the housemaids, the person who appeared to work hardest around the house was the cook. Or at least, if you listened to her, nobody else in the place did a hand's turn. Mrs Grainger, her name was, and she stayed with us for years. She was a grudging woman who presided over the kitchen and woe betide any child who wanted to come in. The kitchen was completely out of bounds.

Mrs Grainger obviously terrorised the household, and why she wasn't sacked I shall never know. She was diligent and served all meals on time, but could never be accused of excessive imagination. I remember a mournful procession of Sunday dinners, the same for years. We all sat up together in the dining room, whether it was freezing cold or the temperature was over the century, and we always had roast beef and Yorkshire pudding with pumpkin and beans and baked potatoes. All the milk, meat, fruit and vegetables were delivered in those days, and when I saw the carts coming down the road, the food all looked wonderfully fresh and interesting. Not when Mrs Grainger had finished with it. The beans were boiled to a meek mush, the potatoes were bluish and swimming in fat. I swear Mrs Grainger roasted the whole meal in lard. We hacked our way through it, and then came the pudding. In summer this was always apple snow, which Dad called 'deceptive pudding' because you could never eat as much as you planned, and, in winter, apple pie or rolypoly pudding with raisins.

When I think of the food we ate, it really is a wonder we survived childhood without succumbing to scurvy or beri-beri. Evening tea or nursery dinner consisted of Arnott's Milk Arrowroot Biscuits or sugar-covered bread soaked in milk; breakfast was usually porridge (with some of the blue lumps left over from the Sunday potatoes, I think) and toast and jam; during the week we had shepherd's pie (minced roast beef from Sunday's joint), chops with watery gravy or boiled tripe. Fresh fruit was rare, and we never tasted a raw vegetable as far as I can remember. Yet we thrived.

Until I was seven I was an only child: loved, protected,

secure. Then I began to realise that something peculiar was going to happen to Mother. There were no signs — like many women of her time, Mother wore wide bandages bound around her stomach during pregnancy to ensure she remained nice and flat — but people kept asking me questions like, 'What will it be like to have a little brother or sister?' I didn't know why they bothered to ask. Then Mother started being quite ill, and I vaguely understood that her illness was concerned with the appearance of this mythical being. Still not very interesting, I thought. For no apparent reason I was sent to stay with Uncle Norman and Auntie Nettie for a few days; when I returned the house was changed. People were quieter, tiptoeing around, and thin wails came from Mother's room. 'You have a new brother,' said Miss Craig, who had remained to help with the birth. 'His name is David.' She took me upstairs to see a tiny, red-faced, gulping, mewing creature in a basket covered in white lace. Horrible, I thought, and nothing to do with me. 'Where did *that* come from?' I asked Miss Craig, who said, 'They found him under a gooseberry bush,' with a wink at Mother, who was lying in her big bed. I was disgusted because I knew Miss Craig was lying. Gooseberry bush! There *weren't* any where we lived.

David didn't have a great deal to do with my life: nor did Jennifer, who was born about eighteen months later. But when Neil, the last one, arrived, I was old enough — about eleven — to be much more curious about where babies came from. Nobody discussed such things, of course, and I knew better than to ask questions. But at that stage I had become convinced that *anything* could be discovered from books, even how babies were made. In the glass-fronted bookcase in Dad's study I came upon a thick, black book called *The House We Live In*. I opened it to discover that it was a textbook about the human body, apparently written for women, with lots of illustrations of dreadful things like pus-filled legs and children disfigured by smallpox. Ugh, I thought, but flicked over to a chapter called 'The Joys of the Nursery'.

It didn't take me long to realise that I'd been cheated. Furiously I read the writer's bland assumption that everybody knew how babies were made; he started off the chapter with a lot of stuff about the arrival of a 'bonny, bouncing infant to bring happiness to the home'. The whole chapter was about feeding, cleaning, bathing and looking after this wonderful new creature — and contained useful medical hints for the mother, such as, 'If your blood is deficient in iron, soak two nails in a glass of water overnight, remove them in the morning and drink the water.' That was all. I had never been so disgusted and disappointed in my life.

Many things we took for granted then are now considered dreadfully unhygienic. For instance, we never washed our hands after going to the toilet or before sitting down to a meal, and the water we drank was not very clean. When we went into town we had to be very careful of where we stepped on the streets; not only did people sell fruit and vegetables in fly-blown heaps, but all kinds of rubbish, from decayed vegetable peelings to newspaper, ran down the gutters. Dad told me that in 1902, just before I was born, rats from the ships had brought bubonic plague to Melbourne and many people had died.

Sometimes I wonder where television advertisements get their pictures of happy childhood at the turn of the century, with pretty little girls and boys in sailor suits. So many photographs you see now show us as sweet demure children — but life was often desperately uncomfortable.

I never smiled in photographs when I was a child, being very ashamed of my teeth, which were crooked and brownish. Their condition was partly my fault: even though I wasn't a brave child, I would put up with agonising toothache for days rather than go to Mr Gillies, our dentist. After all, I thought, toothache will probably go away.

Mr Gillies' surgery was full of stained wood panelling and frosted glass, and smelled of chloroform. Mr Gillies was a tall, florid man who wore a white coat and his hands, which peeled from dermatitis, had red hairs and freckles on the backs. His nurse stood beside the table which held a large jug containing a fearsome array of instruments that looked like different-sized crochet hooks; in a tiny annexe off the surgery was the dental mechanic who made false teeth all the time. His table always had pink rubber moulds and sets of false teeth all over it.

I would shrink into the chair, put my head on the padded headrest, close my eyes and wait while Mr Gillies made his decision. This took a long time because he had to peer earnestly into my mouth: those little mirrors on sticks weren't used then. He would pick up one of the crochet hooks from the jug, wipe it on a towel, and start picking at my teeth. When I jumped, as I always did when he found the sensitive tooth, he said: 'Ah, you should have come to see me before, shouldn't you?'

I asked, 'Do I have to have it out?'

Mr Gillies was progressive for his time, I think. 'No,' he said, 'not this time.' Oh the relief! 'But I'll have to fill it.' Even more than the nitrous oxide that he used when I had a tooth out, I hated the drill. It could mean sitting in that chair for an hour while Mr Gillies excavated; it buzzed mercilessly and hurt like mad. While he was doing his work, I couldn't think of anything but the pain. Having an anaesthetic was unthinkable; after all, it was only a filling, not an extraction.

After what felt like hours, I staggered out to the waiting room and Miss Craig, the receptionist handing me a boiled sweet on the way. The most horrible part of the whole episode was knowing that the same tooth would probably have to be drilled again fairly soon: Mr Gillies did not always drill properly.

Apart from going to Mr Gillies — and that as seldom as possible — I was basically a healthy child, with the usual illnesses. When I had my tonsils out, Miss Craig and I journeyed over to the doctor's surgery by train. I didn't go to hospital, simply lay down on the doctor's table in my stockings and petticoat while he put an ether-soaked pad on my nose. When I woke up hours later, feeling very sick, he patted me on the shoulder, said the tonsils were out, and I could go home. So Miss Craig and I caught the train back. I remember sitting on the station feeling as though I was going to die: my head ached and my throat was so viciously sore that I was unable to swallow for days.

When I had mumps, David, Neil and Jennifer were moved into my room with me, even though Neil was only about two at the time. The theory was, of course, that they too would get the disease and have it over with. Over the door of the room the gardener tacked a sheet with big black blobs of carbolic on it. This was supposed to sterilise the area.

My most traumatic and painful childhood illness was swollen glands when I was about twelve. My face and neck puffed up so that I looked evil and oriental, and I could neither swallow nor speak. Finally our doctor decided to operate, and he came to our house to do it. He and the gardener brought the nursery tea table into my bedroom and covered it with sheets; I got out of bed and clambered up onto the table and the doctor put a chloroform-soaked pad across my nose. I came out of a swirling mist much later to find that he had cut my neck open just below the right ear: I still have the scar. I couldn't turn my head for days, and had to have yards of lint packed into the wound every day. This was supposed to sterilise it.

How did we react to illness? I think we were fairly stoic about it, on the whole. I wasn't the sort of child who complained, anyway. And I always had the consolation of thinking: I'm not as badly off as poor Louise.

Louise Marriner was supposed to be my best friend, although we didn't get on very well all the time. According to her mother, Louise was 'delicate', somebody to be cosseted and spoiled. I think that's why Louise and I weren't entirely soulmates: it's hard when you want to play cowboys and Indians with a girlfriend whose most common sentence is, 'Mummy won't let me do that.' All games Louise and I played had to be quiet, and I found her boring.

I never really knew how 'delicate' Louise was, but as she was an only child she was very spoiled indeed. And again, Mrs Marriner was a real ghoul: never in my life have I met anybody who knew so many stories of dreadful railway accidents, or babies who were born with two heads, or grisly illnesses in which the sufferer died within three days. I remember that she taught Louise and me a rhyme that went: 'Why mother dear, what is that here/That looks like strawberry jam ?/Tut tut my dear, 'tis your papa/Run over by a tram.'

Louise was the perfect daughter for Mrs Marriner: she was tall, with sharp elbows and knees, whitish hair, pale skin and brimming, pale-blue eyes. She *never* looked well, and I suspect she quite enjoyed all the attention. Certainly I have never known anybody who took as much medicine as she did: Hottentot Punch for indigestion after meals, a hop cordial as a pep-up, Condy's crystals if a sore throat looked remotely like attacking, mustard plasters for bronchitis. When she was eleven, she suddenly grew an inch or so, and smelled very strange for a while; her mother used to rub her skinny legs with eucalyptus oil for growing pains. To me, a child who never had to swallow anything more exotic than castor oil, syrup of figs and perhaps honey and sulphur as a general tonic, all Louise's medicine was unnecessary.

One day I thought Louise was overacting as usual when she turned dead white, swayed and announced she had to go home because she had a dreadful headache. I might have been more sympathetic if it hadn't been her turn to ply the skipping-rope attached to the linden tree in our back garden; being a good hostess, I had held the rope for hours while she skipped, instead of going first. And now she was going to deny me my go! I was annoyed. 'Oh, all right,' I said crossly, and flung down the rope. 'I'll take you home.' She lived nearby and I stomped up the street ungraciously while poor Louise staggered along behind. When we arrived at the huge Marriner house — nearly as big as ours — Mrs Marriner wasn't home. What was I supposed to do? I looked at Louise again; she had a strange, greenish tinge to her skin and for the first time I panicked, thinking that maybe she was going to die.

'You'd better go to bed,' I said, grabbing her skinny arm and dragging her up to her bedroom. The poor girl had stopped speaking by then. I made her lie down on her bed, and hovered, not knowing what to do. I had never seen anybody look quite so dreadful.

'I'll get you some water,' I said, rushing to the bathroom where there was a basin and ewer. When I came back, she still looked the same — horribly pale — but as I approached she whispered, 'I...feel...' and was promptly and violently sick all over her nice, white counterpane. Wanting to be sick myself, I cleaned her up as well as I could and — thank heavens — I heard the front door slam downstairs. It was Louise's mother.

'Mrs Marriner,' I shrieked. 'Help! It's Louise!'

Mrs Marriner bolted up the stairs, took one look at Louise, clutched her chest in horror and told me to go home. Offended, I marched home, vowing that that would be the last time I did anything for *anybody*.

The next day I learned that Louise had typhoid fever, and was extremely ill. She wasn't expected to live, but she did, though she stayed in bed for weeks. She wasn't the only person in the district to catch typhoid, either: it seemed that a man who carried the deadly germ had delivered infected milk to the local dairies. I wondered whether I would catch typhoid, but I escaped — we all did.

When Louise emerged, she looked exactly the same as before, though her pale, blonde hair had been cut very short. ('I had my head *shaved*, Caroline!' she said, and I was impressed.)

I suspect that Mrs Marriner could have been more regretful that fate had given her a chance to say 'I told you so' about Louise's indifferent health.

Louise always wore clothes that were a little too old for her; they were her cousin Leonie's hand-me-downs. Leonie was what my Auntie Nettie called, disapprovingly, 'a gay girl', who went in for lots of frilly blouses, dresses with low necklines, and lace camisoles. Louise didn't inherit these: just useful garments which were far too large for her. Her combinations (the woollen under-suits with a split between the legs that we all wore mainly in winter) came down far below the knee so she wore dresses much longer than those that the rest of us did. They were so long, in fact, that she looked as though she had let her skirts down, something you were not supposed to do until you were eighteen. I think Louise was miserable about the lengths of her dresses, because she was afraid that people might think she was 'fast' like Leonie, who rouged her lips to go to parties and danced too close to men. 'Soon ripe, soon rotten,' muttered Miss Craig about Leonie.

I was passionately fond of good clothes, something I inherited from Mother. When her bodice tops came back from the laundry every week, I enjoyed threading ribbon through the eyelet holes of the neckline. Once Mother's dressmaker made me two summer dresses, one white, one pink, with *no sleeves*. My arms felt naked and awkward, and when Dad saw me wearing the pink one, he said, 'Take that off the child!' Even a dress without a collar was less indecent than a sleeveless one. Mother argued, Dad gave in, and I continued to wear my sleeveless dresses, and became the envy of Louise. But most of my good clothes were starched and ironed and scratchy in summer. I still remember the feel of lisle stockings under a froth of petticoats when the temperature was almost ninety; the nearest petticoat always stuck to the back of my legs. But I never wore breeches or trousers, except for riding. Trousers felt very uncomfortable to me, as I was used to the feel of skirts and petticoats. The only pants I wore were pyjamas, one-piece affairs, rather like combinations. They were hardly becoming garments, but at least they were warm if it was necessary to trek across acres of freezing floor to the bathroom during the night.

When I was fourteen, Mother permitted me to come shopping with her. I really enjoyed these expeditions, going into town in our good clothes: Mother in a silk dress with a wide-brimmed hat, me in a knee-length, woollen dress and black stockings. Mother had just learned to drive our car, a Delauney Belleville; she was the only woman I knew who could drive, and I now think that refusing to employ a chauffeur and driving herself was one of her ways of asserting her independence.

We climbed majestically up into the leather seats and set off. Going in the Delauney was exciting. We sat inside the dark cabin, trying to peer through the side curtains made of mica that distorted almost everything. The cabin smelled of leather and varnish, and being in it was rather like travelling inside a wallet. When it was wet my job was to work the windscreen wipers, pushing the little knob above the dashboard that made the tiny blades move back and forth. If I forgot this, Mother would say sharply, 'Caroline, I cannot see a *thing!*'

Driving was difficult enough without any problems I might have caused. How Mother managed to change gear in that car I will never know. Every time she wanted to do so, she had to double-declutch and judge when the engine note was exactly right to push the gear lever. She often didn't do this properly, and the engine went 'Weeeeeeaahaa', a sound that could not be ignored. I generally looked the other way and pretended some other driver was responsible.

We rattled and jolted our way into town, avoiding the horses and carts and carriages that still formed a large part of Melbourne's traffic. By the time we pulled up in front of Myer's, my back was always aching: because the Delauney's springs were so stiff, it was impossible to avoid swaying around whenever we jostled over the wooden blocks that often made up part of the road surface then. Though cars were becoming more popular, the roads of Melbourne were still built for horses.

Shopping before the war was a gracious affair. A man, waiting at the door of the store, would park the Delauney for us, and we would glide into the foyer. A floorwalker, dressed in striped trousers with a swallow-tailed coat that had a red carnation in the button-hole, respectfully directed us to the department we wanted — which was often the ladies' dress department. Though Mother had her own dressmaker, as did most women then, she occasionally patronised dress shops or department stores that sold ready-made clothes. The dress department was most elegant: we sat in tall chairs with Austrian cane seats surrounded by marble floors, plants in shiny brass jardinières, and velvet-draped windows. Once Mother had told the shop assistant what she required, she always said, 'Enter and send.' Like everybody else, the department stores delivered everything. We never carried parcels.

I was gradually being 'trained' for my station in life — as the wife of a well-to-do or wealthy man. Sometimes I hated this idea: women didn't have careers then, but I dimly felt that there *had* to be more to life than domestic or social responsibilities. I was quite good at practical things and I think I could have studied science, perhaps become a doctor, but women doctors were considered 'fast' and unfeminine in our circles, so I kept this ambition to myself. But when I was sixteen I met Walter. I married him two years later...and life went on.

Growing up was bloody hard work

Arthur Dwyer doesn't move fast now, but his face is grasshopper sharp, the face of a bush kid who was good at running and other sports. He's not much of a wordsmith: ideas come rapidly, but he has trouble expressing them in complete sentences. Nevertheless, he speaks fast, jerking his head and nodding while he makes a point.

Oddly enough, he does not use his hands in conversation. They are folded in front of him as if they are on a school desk, and they are surprising hands for a small, quick man: large, heavily veined, with spatulate fingers and short, blunt nails. They seem too heavy for his thin wrists; they are hands that make, push, bend objects into shape. They are workman's tools, never used unless needed.

Arthur frowns down at his hands, turns them over, examines the thickened palms. 'My mother had big hands, too,' he says thoughtfully. 'Now, she was a worker. I reckon you always know what sorts of lives people have had by their hands.'

I was born in western Queensland, little place called the Forty Mile. You won't find it on any maps! That was in 1902, the year The Victory won the Melbourne Cup. My middle name's Victor, and Dad named me after that horse: my birthday's at the end of November.

The first thing I remember was my little sister dying of the croup. Her name was Lilian Mary and she was only three months old. I was the eldest, and I remember seeing a tiny wax doll with its eyes closed, wrapped in a cloth. Dad took her with him on a horse and rode to the cemetery in town to bury her, about forty miles away. I stood outside with Mum and waved them goodbye. I must have been about two. It was a boiling hot day in the middle of summer.

Growing up was bloody hard work

The Forty Mile was pretty isolated. Dad worked as an odd-job man for sheep station owners, which meant he was away for long periods of time. A few families besides us lived at the Forty Mile, in little, wood-and-corrugated-iron humpies like ours. The great event every now and again was the arrival of Fred Harrison the carter, who brought nails, flour, timber and mail. We didn't get any letters. Mum's family lived in Charters Towers, Dad came from Victoria. I didn't meet my grandparents or any uncles or aunts or cousins till I was almost grown up. Nobody had any money for travel. And Mum and Dad didn't come from families who had much to do with writing words.

When I was six we moved to a place called Emu Creek. By then I had a sister, Alice, and a brother, Stanley. I liked the idea of living in a town, with buildings in rows, and maybe real electric light, and buggies, and people.

Emu Creek was a real disappointment. The creek was just a trench in the red earth, winding through scrub and eventually drying up. There were no proper roads, just cart tracks, and only a few shops: one general store, a butcher, a blacksmith and a saddler. The biggest building in town was the Commercial Hotel, much more elaborate than the Catholic and Protestant churches. There were only a few houses.

The best thing about Emu Creek was the railway siding, and the line that stretched over the plain for miles and miles. That line fascinated me. I used to just gaze at it, wondering where it went to and if it ever ended. Sometimes I lay down and put my ear against the tracks and listened for the humming through the metal that meant a train was coming. I'd hear that for a long, long time before I saw smoke in the sky. Then there'd be a black dot getting bigger, and finally we'd hear the chuffing and the clanking. By this time, there'd be about six or seven kids waiting on the siding platform, because the train only came by twice a week. When it stopped, there'd be Harry Roland, the stationmaster, waiting to help the driver and stoker unload timber, grog for the pub, flour and sugar, corrugated iron and tools.

I remember the great day when the train came in carrying the materials for our house.

When we first got to Emu Creek we lived in a tent — Dad, Mum, Alice, Stanley the baby and me — while Dad 'sorted himself out'. He got work around the place and was eventually highly thought of. 'If you want anything done, send for Roy Dwyer,' people would say. He wasn't an educated bloke, but a great bush carpenter who used to boast that he could fix anything. The pockets of his moleskins were always full of bits of string, tacks, nails and pieces of wire. Watching him and his mates build the house out of split timber was a real education.

Nobody drew any plans, just a rough diagram of the house: it had a kitchen with two bedrooms leading off it, one for Mum and Dad, the other for us kids. All the rooms had hard, earth floors which Mum covered with rugs made from corn sacks or kangaroo skins. The windows were holes in the walls covered with wooden shutters (which I thought looked very elegant) and white flour bags cut down to make curtains. No glass — it was too expensive and difficult to transport. Nobody had glass windows in the bush!

The kitchen was the biggest room. The fireplace was set in the split-timber wall and made of galvanised iron, sloping up to the chimney on the side of the house; it wasn't in the actual kitchen area itself, so there was less risk of fire. The hearth was made of earth closely packed down. Set to one side of the fireplace was an iron post with hinged bars that could be swung over the fire, and you'd hang the kettle or stewpot on them. In winter the law in our house was never to let the fire go out! Making it again took a very long time. Mum had a bush oven which was a tin box with a door which she'd stand on top of the embers. She managed to make wonderful bread with that.

When I was little I used to like to watch her prepare yeast for the bread. That was really something. She would boil hops down, add sultanas and potatoes and boil the lot together. Then she would pour off the mixture and put it into bottles and let it stand for a few days. When it was ready, the corks in the bottles flew off — pop! — and the hops started running out. It looked just like lemonade. Mum would pour that over the flour standing ready in baking dishes, add more water, ask me to knead the bread because she said I had strong shoulders, and put it into tins where it stood until it rose to the top. Then into the bush oven it went. It was the best bread I have ever tasted. Mum was a bonzer cook.

The kitchen table and chairs were log slabs. Dad made cupboards from kerosene tins or petrol box cases, stacked on top of each other with hessian nailed across the front. The kitchen shelves consisted of packing cases. We kept our flour and sugar in large bags placed on a kind of stool that stood in a tray of water to keep the ants away.

We all had our baths once a week in a galvanised-iron tub in front of the kitchen fire. Baths were luxuries: one of the first lessons I learned was never to waste water. It was my job to check the level of water in the iron tank at the back of the house. I'd tap it slowly with a stick from the bottom upwards, listening for the heavy thud that meant it held water. If I heard a sharp 'thk thk', that was bad; that part of the tank was empty. I remember times in summer when the sky was hard and blue and I heard 'thk thk' right down to the bottom of the tank. Then we wouldn't have proper baths for a few weeks. Even now I get upset if I see a tap dripping.

The bedrooms were small, especially the one for us kids. Dad showed me how to build my own bed: four sticks pressed into the ground with wooden crosspieces and wire netting on top. Mum made the mattresses from chaff bags stuffed with grass and old rags and sewn at the ends. She also made pillows out of flour bags.

We didn't have a bathroom; nobody did. The dunny was a corrugated-iron lean-to out the back, built over a six-foot-deep pit with a seat on top. Alice and I had to make dunny paper: Mrs Burton from the general store used to give us old magazines and newspapers which we cut into quarters and threaded onto a length of string. This was Alice's favourite job: she used to get in there with the papers and spend hours reading about horrible murders and divorce cases and accidents with runaway motor cars colliding with horses. Used to drive the rest of us mad! I used to like looking at the mail order advertisements, all the wonderful things that people with enough money could buy. For months I desperately wanted a clockwork train with an engine and three carriages. It cost three shillings and sixpence: an absolute fortune. But things like that were for rich people.

Mum and Dad worked terribly hard to build the house and to make sure we had everything they could give us. But even when I was a nipper I noticed that they did things differently from each other. Their attitudes weren't the same.

For instance, Dad was always cheerful. He could fix anything; nothing was too much trouble. And he enjoyed us kids. From the time I was small, I remember being grabbed by Dad and hoisted up on his shoulders, or being tilted upside down and tickled mercilessly while he roared with laughter. Though he must have got more than enough physical exercise by splitting rail fences or putting up walls, he liked doing keep-fit exercises. The three of us kids used to do them with him in the kitchen every morning, as he bent over in his combinations and boots to touch his toes twenty times. Then he stood up and punched the air, breathing very quickly. Lastly, he sat down on the dirt floor and lifted his legs in turn. Stomach exercises, he said. This used to drive Mum mad when she was trying to get breakfast in the mornings: 'Why can't you all go outside?' she said.

Mum was a real worrier, and she didn't seem to find Dad as much fun as everybody else did. 'Roy, you'll wake the baby,' she would say if he laughed too loudly at a joke. 'Come on, Em, what's up?' Dad replied , and to us: 'Hey, let's see if we can make your mother laugh.' But Mum seldom played, just went on with her work. As she got older her mouth turned down and a deep wrinkle came between her eyebrows. Unfortunately, she wasn't very pretty; short and dark with a button nose and brown hair scraped in a bun behind her ears.

I don't know how old I was before I knew that Mum and Dad didn't really get on. They never had fights — we would have known because the house was so small that privacy was almost impossible — and Dad never beat up Mum or anything like that. It's just that Mum said to Dad, 'Roy, I wish you'd be more careful where you put your boots,' and: 'Roy, I wish you'd told me you weren't going to be home for a couple of days,' more and more often. Dad didn't smile so much when Mum was around, either: but he was still great with us. Mum would have been, too, in all fairness, but I didn't have much to do with her because she was always busy cooking, or cleaning, or making clothes, or mending. Always something, there was.

Though Mum took little part in social life, we found that Emu Creek was quite a sociable place. We didn't live far from the Capel family — Mr Capel worked in the saddler's, so Mrs Capel and the three kids thought they were a cut above us, I think. Mrs Capel was always coming over with bits and pieces for us, from flour and sugar to her kids' cast-off clothes. Mum was always a bit short with her and said, 'No thank you, Mrs Capel, we don't need that,' to whatever it was. Mum didn't like accepting help from anybody.

Mum didn't like Irish Joe, either. He was the biggest man in Emu Creek, well over six feet tall, with huge arms and a curly, black beard and black hair on his chest. He worked as a fettler on the railways, and seeing him whacking a twenty-pound sledge-hammer was really something. Irish Joe wasn't married. He told Mum seriously one day: 'I'm a good Catholic like you, Mrs Dwyer, and I'm looking for a decent girl to come along.' There wasn't any chance of that, Mum said. Irish Joe spent all his free time in the Commercial Hotel. When he got stuck into the rum on Saturday nights, you could hear him all over town. Then he'd stagger out, roaring drunk, and say he'd fight anyone he met. When Mum heard him bellowing 'I'll take you home again, Kathleen', she always made us come inside.

His best mate was another drunk called Dave Patterson, a weak, spindly little bloke. When *he* rolled home from the pub of a Saturday night, his wife used to beat him up. Saturday nights in Emu Creek were quite something. If you didn't have old Joe roaring away, you'd hear Mrs Patterson calling her husband a drunken, thieving mongrel.

Mrs Patterson was a pinched little woman with a bitter face; we kids always kept out of her way. She had a daughter, Ella, from a previous marriage; a girl about sixteen who was a bit simple. She was always walking around the place in awful old clothes, looking terrified; she'd act like a whipped dog if you even said 'hello' to her. Once I saw her with a black eye. Mrs Capel said her mother had whaled into her with a rope because she spoiled a batch of bread.

Ella was the town disgrace. Dave Patterson was obviously terrified of his wife, so he didn't do anything about her. Eventually Mrs Capel and the publican's wife wrote to the police, saying how dreadful it was, and how they should do something about Ella. Some men wearing suits and gold watch-chains came into town for a meeting in the pub, and later Ella was taken into care. We never saw her again, and the Pattersons disappeared soon afterwards too.

Mavis Flood was also a bit mad. She was a very old lady who smelled horrible: she lived by herself in a humpy by the creek. Whenever she saw any of us kids, she would smile with her black teeth and ask, 'Do you know how I got my name?' We would say 'yes' and try to get away from her, but it was never any good. She said she came from down the Darling and was rescued when it was in flood one time. 'Sitting on a haystack, I was,' she said, 'and when they managed to grab me out of the river they didn't know who I was! I was a baby. Like Moses in the bulrushes, wasn't it? And then, because they didn't know who me parents were, or where I'd come from, they called me Mavis Flood.'

I started school not long after we got to Emu Creek. It wasn't much of a place: forty kids in one wooden room with one teacher, and a blackboard, some desks, a packing-case bookshelf and a map of the world on a nail on the wall. The place was freezing cold in winter and boiling in summer. None of us kids wore shoes, of course, so our feet were either hard and tough from the sun or swollen with chilbains.

I wasn't very good at school; I only went because Mum made us, and I think she only did it to get us out of the way! I can remember learning a few poems like 'The Boy Stood on the Burning Deck' and 'Excelsior', and doing arithmetic, but I left before we got to long division and compound interest. Alice was much keener on learning; she was a good reader. Stanley was like me; he didn't care.

When I was about eight, in second class, we had a pretty, blonde teacher called Miss Hall. She came from the city and was very young and sweet and I was in love with her. She didn't understand life in the bush much. She used to come to school and tell us that she'd seen an emu or a big red kangaroo just out of town. We'd just look at her blankly. There were dozens around: what was she getting so excited about? I wanted to tell her that there was a nest of emu chicks out the back of our place, and that we saw kangaroos or wallabies most evenings in the scrub. But those things were so ordinary it didn't seem worth it.

Once, on the way to school, I saw a black feather in the dusty street. I knew instantly that it came from a black cockatoo: we were having a dry spell and the cockies were everywhere, screaming their heads off. I thought Miss Hall would probably like that, so I picked it up and took it to school. She was really pleased. Thrilled. 'What is it?' she asked eagerly. 'A magpie's feather?' We couldn't believe that a teacher wouldn't know the difference between a magpie and a cockatoo!

Miss Hall used to get very angry with some of us, especially the older kids, because a few of them used to fall asleep in class. My friend, Ben Baker, was always in trouble. She'd come up to him, with his head on his arms over the desk, and tap him on the shoulder with a ruler. 'You are lazy!' she said. It wasn't fair. Ben was the eldest of nine kids and he had to get up before dawn every day, look after the four horses his parents had — they were quite well off — collect the wood for the kitchen fire, light it, sweep out and chop wood. Most of us had to do similar things, but Ben also had to ride about thirty miles every day, just to get to school. No wonder he fell asleep during the morning. Anyway, somebody explained to Miss Hall that some of the kids didn't have it too easy, so she let them go early. The moment he heard her say, 'Those who have to go home early can leave now,' at about half past two, Ben would be out of his seat like a shot, beating the others to the paddock where he'd tethered his old brown horse, Nancy, and tearing home as though a bushfire was after him! He didn't like school much, Ben didn't. They used to say that his sister would make a perfect wife for a bushman because she could shear sheep, milk a cow, ride a horse and kill a snake.

School was mostly boring, except when the district inspector came about once a year. We were terrified of him: we hadn't worked out that he'd come to inspect Miss Hall, not us! His name was Harry Weston and he came from Cloncurry, so he wasn't too pleased to spend most of the day in a railway dogbox just to get to us. He was a little bloke with a red face, and he hated everything about the school; ordered Miss Hall around and told us the map on the wall was crooked and we weren't learning our tables properly. He'd pick on us and ask us about river lengths and heights of mountains and try and make us recite poetry we should have learned. Poor Miss Hall! She was almost in tears when he had finished. If he caught anyone talking in class he would give them two full-sized cuts on the palm of the hand with the cane. That was for the boys. He used to hit the girls around the back and shoulders, so hard sometimes the buttons on their dresses flew off. He was another reason I didn't like school. None of us did.

My best friend, an Aboriginal boy called Billy Rowdy, didn't go to school, and I wished I was so lucky. Billy was about four years older than I was, and he and I used to mooch around together with his dog, Skipper. He was a great dog, Skipper was, a yellow bitzer who you'd swear knew what you were saying. Skipper lived with Billy and his family in the blacks' camp about eight miles out of town. Billy's mother was a half-caste, and nobody knew who his father was: some people said he was Irish Joe because you often saw him around there. Billy and his family had, I think, come down from their tribal lands because of the drought, and were staying around Emu Creek doing odd jobs. There were about six of them, including Billy, but he was the only one in work. He had a job as delivery boy for Mrs Burton in the general store. I used to see Billy's family a lot but I never told Mum because she didn't like blacks much. 'They're all filthy,' she said. Well, there were a few flies buzzing around the humpies, and the dirt floors weren't swept like Mum's was, but they always shared everything they had with you, even though that wasn't much.

Billy was a tall, skinny kid with a wide grin. Somewhere along the line a Methodist minister's wife had taught him to read and count a bit, and he was naturally very bright — and one of the funniest people I'd ever met. One day he said, 'Let's go to church,' so he and Skipper and I walked over to the tiny Methodist church on the edge of town. Billy marched in, making sure nobody was around, and climbed up into the pulpit. He bent over, pretending to be old and crippled, like the Methodist minister who sometimes came to Emu Creek on circuit. Billy pointed his skinny arm to the roof and said in a croaky voice: 'Repent, you sinners! Repent before God!' I was laughing so hard I couldn't stand up straight myself, waiting for God to strike Billy dead at the same time. Skipper's tongue was hanging out, and I swear he was smiling.

Not long afterwards, Billy and his family left. All Billy said was, 'You wanna look after Skipper for me?' I was puzzled. 'Why can't you take him with you?' I asked. Billy just shrugged. I led Skipper away from Billy's camp on a piece of string, and that's the last time I saw Billy or his family. Mrs Capel told me later that he and his three brothers and two sisters had been split up by the mission people, and nobody knew what had happened to Billy's mother. 'She might have gone back where she came from,' said Mrs Capel.

Skipper was a great dog, best one I ever had. He was always with me; used to follow me to school, go away during the day and I always knew that he'd be waiting when I got out. 'The Yellow Streak', Ron Cassidy in my class called him; but Ron was jealous. He could be a devil. Once Mum cut my hair in a terrible hurry, and she didn't make a very good job of it; it was in jagged steps on the back of my head. Ron used to follow me around the school yelling, 'Go to Dwyer's hairdressing salon to get your hair pulled out by the roots with a tomahawk, cut with a pitchfork and brushed with a yard broom!'

Ron and I were sports mad. It didn't matter what the game was, Mum said, we'd play it. The first prize I ever won was for a school footrace. We had to stand with our hands on the back fence of the school paddock and run to the school bell when Miss Hall said 'go'. It was a couple of hundred yards. My nickname was Skinny, and you'd think I'd be able to run, but I still came last! Ron was going to give me curry over that, but it turned out to be a donkey race, with the last one home the winner. I had a choice of prize: a pocket-knife or threepence. I wanted the knife very badly, but I knew that Ron would probably get it off me in a fight anyway, so I chose the threepence. I knew Mum could use it.

I wasn't bad at sport in the end, though I was no Snowy Baker. I didn't learn to swim or dive, like he did, because there was nowhere to practise around Emu Creek. But I represented the district at cricket when I was thirteen. Ron and I spent hours practising, using a piece of wood for a bat. When I got a proper bat I thought I was made!

Ron and I collected cigarette cards with pictures of cricketers on them: Grace, Fry, Blackham and all the others. Ron's Dad smoked cigarettes, so he was luckier than I; Dad just had a pipe and Three Castles tobacco. Ron's cigarette card collection was the best in the school; I didn't have a chance of competing.

The cards had boxers, too: Tommy Burns and Jack Johnson, even though the Burns—Johnson fight had taken place some years before. Dad, who had been pretty handy with his fists in his day, often talked about Johnson's tactics in beating Burns. I couldn't see why Johnson had been so smart — he looked about twice as big as Burns in the pictures I'd seen.

We had a kid at school who I swear was even bigger than Jack Johnson, though he wasn't black. His name was Fred

Connors and he was the school bully. Fred used to boast they'd let him into the Commercial Hotel when he was only twelve, and you could believe him. He had a voice that would strip the wool off a sheep, and arms like tree trunks. He used to pick on me a lot, because I was small and thin. I was ashamed, because I was no fighter, and I used to try and avoid him. I kept out of trouble by learning to run; I'd do anything rather than face up to Fred. I have a bit of a soft nature, I suppose, I'm a bit weak in lots of ways, and I didn't like fights.

Dad gave me boxing lessons. Every now and again, when I wasn't expecting it, he would come up to me and jab me in the stomach. Until I learned how to cover, he hurt — which he meant to do. 'Come on, boy, fight back!' he said. Mum always pleaded, 'Roy, leave Arthur alone,' but Dad would just laugh and say I had to learn. Though his lessons were sometimes painful, I didn't mind because I was determined to build myself up and stop being small and skinny. I wanted Dad to be proud of me.

Dad left Mum when I was eleven.

The day it happened I came home from school to see Mum standing in the kitchen, no expression on her face at all, just stunned. Mrs Capel was there, with her arm around her; I thought that was strange because Mum wasn't one for hugs and she didn't like Mrs Capel because she was a busybody. My feet were freezing — it was in July — and I headed straight for the fireplace to get warm. 'Go outside,' said Mrs Capel. 'Don't disturb your mother.' I didn't understand the look on Mum's face, but I walked outside and played with Alice and Stanley for a bit — they had been sent outside too — and hoped we'd be able to come into the warm.

Not long afterwards Mrs Capel left. Her last words to Mum were, 'You write to the government, now!' As she walked past us she said, 'You *poor* children.' I didn't know what she was talking about. What had Mum done wrong? Why did she have to write to the government?

Mum was still standing near the fire and big tears were rolling down her cheeks. The three of us stood and looked at her. Mum *never* cried. Eventually she wiped her eyes with the back of her hand and told me, 'Your father has left us. Gone away. Left his job. He's gone for good.'

Then she said, 'I don't know what's going to happen to us.'

Years later I found out that Dad had met a thirty-five-year-old widow on one of the stations where he did general fence mending, about fifty miles from Emu Creek. He'd been seeing her for years: lots of people in town knew about it, but nobody had told Mum. I think, now, that they hadn't told her because she kept herself to herself, didn't make many friends, and she wasn't all that easy to talk to. I never knew how she had found out about Dad. Maybe Mrs Capel had told her — but Mum never mentioned Dad to us again. She took Mrs Capel's advice and applied to the government for assistance — less than a pound a week, it was then — and set about finding herself a job. She must have been dreadfully bitter, but we never knew.

Mum couldn't do much. She hadn't been trained for anything, and there were no jobs going around Emu Creek. She eventually went around town, washing for other people. Occasionally she went out to a couple of the cattle stations in the district and did washing there, but more often she brought washing home. From seven in the morning until late in the afternoon she was crouched over the old scrubbing board and galvanised-iron tub, scrubbing, for something like six shillings a week. That wasn't bad money, and with the government handout we could just about manage.

I wanted desperately to get out and help: I was the eldest son, and I thought I had to help Mum. But she insisted I should stay on at school for a year or two, so I could eventually get a good job. So I looked after Alice and Stanley when Mum wasn't there, and cut their hair, and soled their boots, and tried to cook occasionally, though I wasn't much good at that, not being handy like Dad. I used to wish I could do the things with his hands that he could do: fix furniture, mend almost anything, even play a tin whistle. As I've said, we weren't a family who had much to do with words, and I never told anybody how I felt when Dad left the way he did. But it was like carrying a stone around inside me. I couldn't understand why he had left us. The worst of it was, you see, I *liked* my Dad.

A few months after Dad left, Mum got a letter from him. 'I'm moving away and I don't want to see you again,' he said. He wrote from a sheep station near Charleville, just a short note on a torn-off piece of paper. (I saw it lying around the house: Mum never mentioned it, but I think she left it around for me to find.) I gathered that *she* was with Dad. I always thought of the woman my father ran away with as *she* or *her*, because nobody ever told me her name.

I tried not to think about Dad at all after that. I hated knowing that people in Emu Creek gossiped about us, and I used to walk away whenever I heard anybody mention anything. But people were very kind: they turned up with extra meat or clothes their own children had grown out of. Mum always thanked them rather abruptly, but I'm sure she was grateful.

That was the last we heard from Dad. He and his woman just disappeared and we never heard about them again. I don't know any more than that: how long Dad lived, where he lived, how he died. There was never any question of divorce, and Mum never took up with another man. She'd had enough.

I turned thirteen in November, near the end of the school year, and didn't bother going back for the couple of weeks after my birthday. There didn't seem any point, and I had to find a job before everything closed down at the end of the year. So I moved away from Emu Creek and got a job as a plumber's mate right down in Stanthorpe, hundreds of miles away. I was paid seven and six a week, not bad money, and I sent most of it home.

The first thing I bought with my own money was a suit. All the little country towns had their own tailors then. It was grey tweed, pure wool, and it cost three guineas, with an extra pair of trousers. All hand made. I thought I was Christmas.

The Empire was something we were proud of

*T*he Empire was something we were proud of

Dorothy Smythe's exercise book has a shiny, black cardboard cover decorated with the Australian coat of arms. On a white label at the top she has written 'Dorothy Smythe: History', followed by '1911', the year she turned eleven. The capitals have been fashioned in ink with intense concentration: one sees a sandy-haired, round-faced child with pen in hand bending over her book, her tongue stuck out at the side of her mouth in the effort to ensure that the letters do not vary in length or thickness of nib stroke.

Inside the book is a neatly written list of the kings and queens of England, starting with William the Conqueror and ending 'George V, our king'. The penmanship is the same carefully beautiful copperplate as that on the front cover. The rest of the book contains essays and exercises. One headed 'Henry VII' begins, 'Henry VII was a fairly good king. But he got into the habit of placing taxes on the rich people more heavily than on the poor people, so that the latter began to think they should not be taxed at all.' The neat red ink '9/10' and 'very good, Dorothy' at the top of the page show how much her teacher approved such conventional and non-socialist sentiments, worthy of a good little girl.

The back of the exercise book deals mainly with Australian history. Sadly, Dorothy's elegant handwriting deteriorates; information about Wentworth, Governor Phillip, wool and explorers straggles across the page. Dorothy's margins suddenly sprout completed games of noughts and crosses. But her writing regains its symmetry for a paragraph entitled 'Robert Clive, Servant of the Empire'.

31

Empire Day was a highlight of the year at our primary school. All sixty of us, from babies to twelve-year-olds, lined up in our classes under the playground pepper trees: the girls wearing black boots and stockings and white pinafores, the boys in jackets and knicker-bockers, Blucher boots and thick grey socks. We saluted the Union Jack and the Australian flag that flew from the school's two flagpoles (donated by the mayor and town council). Miss Nelson, the music teacher, who had originally come all the way from Sydney across the mountains and was artistic, stood in front of us and waved her arms sternly as we sang 'God Save the King'. Then Mr Bates, the headmaster, made a speech.

When I was little, Mr Bates was the tallest man I knew. He was thin and grey, and stood up very straight like a sergeant-major. He looked his most impressive on Empire Day, because he always delivered his speech standing at the top of the school steps with the other teachers behind him, and we had to look up at him.

His speech was always the same. He told us that on Empire Day we honoured God, served the King and saluted the Empire, and that our task as members of the Empire was to be true and fair, to accept just correction in a manly fashion (girls were not caned at our school) and to labour in the vineyard of God. This always confused me. The only vineyards anywhere near the town were at Mudgee, which I'd hardly ever visited — and besides, vineyards were where people grew grapes for wine, and wine was wicked. Mum said so and had made me sign the pledge when I was five. How could you labour in the vineyard of God if God was good and wine was evil?

After Mr Bates finished, Mr Walton stepped forward to speak to us. Fred Walton was the town's only Boer War veteran, and we were told every year that he had been prepared to lay down his life for the Empire. People called him 'the man who burned Paul Kruger' because he had led a march through the streets to burn Kruger in effigy. This had happened during the Boer War when I was a baby, and when I looked at Mr Walton with his soft, pink face and blond hair, I couldn't imagine him attacking an enemy of the British. He was a teller in the bank where Dad was the manager and, except on Empire Day, he never said anything.

'Boys and girls of the Empire,' he began in a voice that always sounded as if he had a toffee wedged down his throat, 'we are gathered here to honour the greatest Empire the world has ever known.' His speech was always longer than Mr Bates's; it was always the same and he read it every year from notes. 'Girls, your task in keeping the Empire great is to be pure, noble and to love your home; boys, you must act fairly, squarely and justly at all times. The girls will keep you up to this; it is part of their duty.' When he had finished, he wiped his forehead and asked us to lift our voices in song. Miss Nelson came down the steps and conducted us again:

> *Regions east and west united*
> *All our empire knit in one.*
> *By the royal hearts defended*
> *Let it wave beneath the sun.*
> *We salute thee and we pray*
> *God to bless this land today.*

After this, Mr Walton vanished into the bank until 24 May next year, and Mr Bates told us to get ready for our march through the streets. This, too, was a ritual, part of every Empire Day. We shuffled into rows of four and linked hands, preparing to march in step through the school gate where Miss Nelson stood waiting, ready to hand each row two flags — the Union Jack and the Australian flag. Every year, we worried whether the flags would arrive from Sydney on the train in time to be used for the procession. Once we were lined up along the dirt road outside the school gate, Mr Bates, Miss Nelson and the other teachers stepped to the front, and we set off, Mr Bates chanting 'left, right, left, right', until the six-year-olds immediately behind the teachers got the idea. I always marched with my best friend, Alma Thurston.

Every year the route was the same. We went past Mrs Fraser's corner shop that sold sherbet balls, humbugs, licorice straps and toffee cakes, and wheeled left up the hill past weatherboard houses with gardens. Women sometimes leaned over their front gates to see us go past, and wave. David Ferris always called out 'Hello, Mum!' when we passed his house, whether his mother was watching or not. This never failed to annoy Alma and me; *we* kept our eyes straight ahead and marched left, right, left, right, not even glancing sideways to see if the other two in our row did the same. We went past the blacksmith's, the garage (which my father always said should be called the 'car-age' because cars were serviced there), the School of Arts, the doctor's office (noticing that Dr Wiston's shiny, black De Dion Bouton was parked outside), the butcher's shop, the saddler — and down past the dairy to the school again.

'Dis-miss!' called Mr Bates. The march was over, and we were allowed the rest of the day off. There was usually a picnic in the afternoon in Rouse's paddock — with egg and spoon, sack and Siamese races. I never enjoyed these because I was not good at running or jumping. My favourite part of the picnic was the bun-eating contest. Buns on strings bobbed from a clothesline stretched between two posts and we had to try and eat them with our hands tied behind our backs. I knew how to judge the distance and twist my head and bite at the right time so I always won. But my three brothers — Roger, Harry and John — spent most of the picnic fighting with the other boys in their class. When they came home with torn shirts and dirty faces and Mum demanded who had started it this time, they simply looked wide-eyed and said, 'We dunno, Mum — it just happened.'

After the picnic, when the races had been won and the prizes handed out, we waited in the paddock for the dark and the fireworks: Roman candles, catherine-wheels, bungers. 'Stand back!' Mr Appleton, the saddler, always said as he lit the grey touchpaper and swoosh, up the fireworks went.

When I was in fifth class, Mr Bates announced that we were putting on a pageant for Empire Day, in front of the mayor and council at the School of Arts. Everybody in the school would have a part, he promised. This was the first time we had presented a show, and we could hardly wait.

Miss Nelson, who knew about music and the stage (coming from Sydney and being artistic) was going to manage the whole thing. This was not good news. Miss Nelson was a small, breathless woman who wore brightly coloured scarves and blouses and was not a good teacher. None of us liked her; she had a habit of rubbing her hands together and saying brightly, 'Goodness, it's cold today!' as if it were somehow her own fault that the temperature hadn't risen. When I became a teacher later, I knew straight away what Miss Nelson had done wrong: she was *always* apologising. Sarah Doherty, the naughtiest girl in my class, who was Irish and whose father was the local butcher, used to bully Miss Nelson by pretending not to understand what she said. 'What do you mean, please, Miss Nelson, if two trains are approaching each other at thirty miles an hour? What if one of them breaks down or goes up a hill?' Miss Nelson always considered the question seriously, her head a little on one side. 'Well, Sarah, I think we will have to assume, for the sake of this problem, that the trains are approaching at the same rate. Do you understand?' Sarah only had to look puzzled and shake her head — and that was the end of that particular arithmetic problem, while Miss Nelson got herself into all sorts of tangles trying to explain *why* trains used steam and *why* they went faster than cars. It always worked.

Sarah also followed Miss Nelson around the playground, imitating her hen-like scuttle when she wasn't looking, as well as the way she held her head to one side and her rabbity way of moving her lips back from her teeth when she spoke. Sarah was brilliant.

I never liked her; she was not a friend of mine. I was afraid of her. Though I knew it was wrong to make fun of Miss Nelson behind her back, I always joined the other children when they laughed at her; I didn't dare tell Sarah how cruel I thought she was. Sarah had dark, curly hair and bold, blue eyes and a sharp tongue, and she knew how to hurt. When Miss Nelson held up the huckaback shoe bag I'd spent days embroidering in class, and said, 'This is very good, Dorothy,' Sarah muttered from three desks away: 'Little goody two-shoes, aren't you?' I never knew how to answer her; all I could do was follow my mother's advice and not lower myself to Sarah's level.

Miss Nelson announced that the pageant would be called 'Britannia Rules the Waves', and everybody in the school would represent a person or group from the Empire. Britannia would stand on the stage of the School of Arts while everybody else marched up to do homage. Who was going to play Britannia? Every girl in the school wanted the part. I knew I didn't have a chance: Britannia was traditionally noble and tall, with a beaky nose. 'You're too fat,' said my brother Roger spitefully. 'And anyway, what do you want to be Britannia for?' I was blonde and dumpy, but still longed to be chosen. In my class Mavis Appleton and Austral Ferris didn't speak to each other because Mavis had boasted to Austral that she was certain to get the part.

Miss Nelson made the great announcement at assembly. 'The part of Britannia will be played by — Sarah Doherty!' Sarah, of *all* people! Mavis Appleton blushed, Austral looked appalled. I glanced at Sarah, expecting to see her smug little smile, and couldn't believe my eyes: Sarah looked as though she were about to burst into tears. When Mr Bates said, 'Congratulations, Sarah,' she barely thanked him. It seemed that Miss Nelson had chosen the only girl in the school who wasn't delighted to be Britannia. Not until I overheard her asking Julia Caulfield, her best friend: 'How am I going to tell Dad?' did I understand why.

Jimmy Doherty kept the butcher's shop in the main street near the bank. It was always dirty, probably because he was much more interested in talking politics than in selling meat. When I went in with Mum to buy the chops or steak, there was Jimmy behind the counter, lecturing a customer about the wrongs of Ireland. It didn't matter that you could hardly hear him over the buzzing of the flies swarming in the shop (there was no glass in those days for shopfronts). Jimmy, who was short and fat with a straggly moustache and lantern jaw, wouldn't bother to chase the dogs out if he was *really* attacking the British. 'The murdering leaders of a nigger Empire,' he called them, in a thick Cork accent, hacking into a side of beef with his cleaver as though it were the body of William of Orange. I was afraid of Jimmy too; I thought he might start attacking *me*. And even Mum, who was very outspoken about Jimmy and the other 'bog Irish' in town, said nothing when he started raving. Mum had told me that the Dohertys were Roman Catholics and not as good as we were, but it still didn't do to answer any of them back. Jimmy Doherty could make you believe that the British army was riding down the main street at that very moment, armed with guns and swords and cannons with which to slaughter every honest Irishman they could get their hands on. So I could see that he would *not* be happy that his daughter had been chosen to represent the spirit of the English King's oppressive and Irish-hating empire. As I watched Sarah walk slowly home after school that day, knowing that she would have to face Jimmy Doherty's wrath, I felt sorry for her for the first time in my life.

Next morning, there was a sensation at rollcall. We were answering 'present' as our names were called by Mr Bates, when Jimmy Doherty appeared, wearing his blue-and-white-striped butcher's apron and clutching his cleaver; by his side was Sarah, still looking as though all the starch had been taken out of her. Jimmy always opened his butcher's shop at about six in the morning, so he could supply meat for breakfast to the town's five boarding houses, and he had obviously just marched out of the shop to bring Sarah to school. His eyes popped with fury. Tiny bits of meat clung to his apron and his cleaver; he was so angry he didn't bother to wave away the small army of flies buzzing around his head.

'Where's Miss Nelson?' he demanded, cutting right across Mr Bates, who stopped. In a fuss, Miss Nelson came down the school steps, and hurriedly moved with Jimmy Doherty and Sarah away from the assembly. With the occasional glance at them, Mr Bates finished rollcall. He had to raise his voice to be heard above Jimmy Doherty's angry rumble, but he managed, and ordered the school dismissed. We marched off into our classroom, all of us wondering what was going to happen next.

Mr Bates told us, 'Miss Nelson will be with you soon,' so we sat obediently in class and waited, for her and for Sarah.

Eventually both appeared, Sarah looking red-eyed and meek. Miss Nelson said brightly, 'Well! There has been a change. I shall tell everybody at recess, but Britannia will now be played by Austral Ferris.'

That was all we ever heard about the scene between Jimmy Doherty, Sarah and Miss Nelson. Her father forbade Sarah to take part in the pageant at all: she was the only one in the school who had nothing to do with it. This meant that rehearsals with Miss Nelson were very quiet and well organised, and nobody made any trouble at all. Sarah suddenly stopped making fun of

Miss Nelson; she became almost polite to her. I still don't know if Miss Nelson cast Sarah Doherty as Britannia out of confusion, misguided goodwill, or sheer malice.

As for Austral Ferris, she was delighted; nobody else was. Austral was thin and dark-haired, with stringy plaits and a whining voice: nobody could imagine why she had been chosen, if not because of her patriotic name. But up there on the platform of the School of Arts, with her cardboard trident and helmet (borrowed from Tom Hoskins, the smallest fireman in our fire brigade), draped in a white, linen toga, she looked surprisingly majestic. It helped, of course, that Britannia didn't have to say anything.

I was given the part of Ceylon — a strange choice for a fattish, blonde girl. I wore one of Mum's old curtains draped around me, and bare feet, and had to walk gracefully on to the stage clutching a white paper bag containing tea, as I sang Miss Nelson's words:

> *Precious tea from See-lon,*
> *Tea that tastes so sweet...*
> *Bring it to Britannia,*
> *Lay it at her feet.*

After that I curtseyed, deposited the tea at the sandalled feet of Austral, who was smirking, and stepped back to join all the other children in the school. They were dressed as Red Indians, Australian Aborigines (my brother Harry was one of these, wearing a paisley loincloth and carrying a sharpened stick; the brown bootpolish he wore didn't come off for several days), Chinese, South African blacks, and so on. When everybody had given a gift to Britannia, we all lined up behind Austral and sang 'Rule Britannia', conducted by Miss Nelson from the piano, while the audience stood and joined in. The mayor and council said they had enjoyed the show very much, and the local paper called us 'proud sons and daughters of Albion'. We were, too.

Mum always said that Australians didn't speak or write properly, not like people at Home. Like Dad, she had been born here, but she had very strict ideas about the way we should speak: we had to sound as English as possible. I think this was partly because she felt she had a position to maintain; she was the bank manager's wife, which gave her — and us — status.

She taught the four of us to 'speak properly' by making us read aloud the editorial from the local newspaper. She gave me the paper, with its tiny print, huge pages and words I didn't understand, and said, 'Read this. It will mean nothing to you, but your job is to make me understand it. If you can count in your mind one for a comma, two for a semi-colon, three for a colon and four for a full stop, I'll understand what you are saying even if you don't know what the words mean yourself.' I stumbled through passages with words like 'protectionist' and 'deficit' and *didn't* understand them. Mum corrected my vowels ('I don't want you children to speak badly, like all the others in this place,' she said; from a very early age I knew that Mum didn't like living in a country town). I can hardly bear to hear newsreaders on the ABC these days. They sound *so* Australian, and they don't give enough importance to punctuation.

Everything had to be done *right* for Mum. As the only daughter, with three brothers, I felt it was my job to please her, and I managed most of the time; I was not a naughty child by any means. Once Mum snatched a cloth out of my hand because I hadn't dusted the chiffonier properly, but that is the only time I remember that she was displeased with me for not cleaning as thoroughly as she would have done.

Mum wasn't very pretty: I inherited her dumpy figure and her pale, grey eyes, but I wish I had inherited her hair. It was beautiful — long, rippling and a deep chestnut red. We rarely saw it down: even when she went to bed at night she plaited it up tightly, and during the day she wore it in a twist at the back of her head. She had the kind of hair that never comes down. When I was very little I touched it and said, 'Your hair is so pretty, Mummy,' and she always laughed and told me I was encouraging her to be vain. I didn't know what she meant, but now I think that she was half-serious. Mum would have regarded being proud of her hair as the most terrible vanity.

Because of that I learned not to be proud of my complexion, which was about my own best feature. 'Such a lovely skin,' said my aunts, and I really couldn't believe they were serious. After all, God had given me my complexion, so I had no cause to be proud of it: nothing to do with me! 'Handsome is as handsome does' was one of Mum's favourite proverbs.

I think she felt that she had to make an effort to bring us up properly because we were in Australia, not at Home. I knew from an early age that she considered Australia a very second-rate place: so did I. I loved learning poetry, but all we ever heard about was snowdrops, daffodils, hills, clouds and meadows and skylarks — nothing to do with all the things I saw around me. Blackbirds were beautiful creatures with a lovely, warbling cry — not the demon birds who dive-bombed us every spring to grab our hair for their nests; snakes, the great worry of my life ('don't go near rotting logs or fallen branches'), didn't exist at Home. The people who wrote about English brooks, not Australian creeks, were real poets. You couldn't call Banjo Paterson a real poet, he was just somebody who wrote nice, jingly rhymes about Australia.

Mum was the one who brought us up, and she had an awful job with my brothers, particularly Harry and John. She never said much, just, 'Come here' and whack! — they got the edge of her wedding ring across the ear. That didn't happen to me more than twice, I recall — and I remember both times. Mum's thick gold wedding ring really hurt. I still don't know how she managed to get so much strength in her arm!

Dad didn't have very much to do with disciplining us. He was a quiet man, who seemed to spend most of his time at the bank, worrying about other people's money. When he walked to work every morning, I thought he looked serious and clever, with his brightly polished black shoes, gleaming watch-chain, dark suit and tie and shirt with a celluloid collar. On the hottest December and January days, his clothes were still the same, and he *never* looked red or sweaty, as most of the other men did. At home in the evenings, he usually read the paper or the works of Rudyard Kipling, sometimes smoking his pipe in the living room if Mum would allow it. Because Mum controlled the house, it was never a question of 'ask Dad' about anything, always 'ask Mum'. Even Dad said, 'You'll have to ask your mother,' if one of us asked about pocket-money or being able to stay and play with kids after school.

Only in the bank did Dad have any authority. I used to love visiting him there. It was one of the oldest buildings in town: built during the 1840s, it had grooved marble pillars at the entrance and a beautiful, coloured, semi-circular light over the door. Inside, tellers sat behind high desks in wire-covered cages, and they never looked up because they were so busily adding up columns of figures or counting brown, blue and green notes. They had so much money!

Dad's office was on the first floor, up the stairs at the back of the banking chamber. Outside the door sat his clerk, Mr Hargreaves, a sleek young man with hair like patent leather. Mr Hargreaves was a young man about town, and he always looked quite a swell. I didn't like him because he always said, 'And what would the Lady Dorothy like?' in a voice that made me feel that he really didn't like me, but was only pretending.

Also near Dad's office door sat a woman typing away on an old Remington. She was the typewriter: what she typed on was called the 'typing machine'. Dad always had trouble finding good typewriters. They usually came from Sydney, where women were trained to type, and they stayed in town only until they found somebody to marry them, or became too bored with country-town life. I don't remember any of them very clearly; they didn't stay long, most of them. I can recall only a succession of young women, heads down, tapping noisily at rows of black keys. Type-writers always wore paper or celluloid cuffs pinned over their sleeves; I remember them wearing long-sleeved, dark dresses, no matter how hot the weather was.

Dad's office was my favourite place in the world. It had a huge window behind the desk that looked right across the stables and the horses to the hills around town. To the left of the desk, on the wood-panelled wall, hung a coloured lithograph of a stern-looking Edward VII and Queen Alexandra (later replaced by an equally stern picture of George V and Queen Mary). I loved the desk most of all. It was enormous, with a green, leather-cornered blotter on it, a diamond-cut glass ink bottle, a very stylishly carved pen in a wooden penholder, a flat, round enamel box full of aspirins, and Dad's pride and joy: a flattish, brown leather case lined with purple plush, in which rested a heavy, silver letter-opener. Carved into a raised oval on the handle were the words: *To James A. Smythe for fifteen years' faithful service, September 22, 1909.* Dad never used it to open letters; he had an ordinary steel knife for that. I think he opened it only when I visited him and insisted on seeing it again, otherwise it lived in its case and shone against the plush, but nobody could see it.

Dad was a completely different person in the office. For a start, he spoke much more than he did at home, and he used a different language. He spoke quickly and gave orders like 'get the Harbutt ledger, please' and 'bring me the interest-rate figures'. I was always very proud to think that Dad could talk a foreign language and get people to obey him in it.

But at home he seemed to shrink, and hardly said anything. The man who could make Mr Hargreaves do his slightest bidding was incapable even of making my brother Roger stop teasing me. Dad said, 'Roger, leave your sister alone,' when I came sobbing to him the day Roger chopped off the long blonde ringlets of my favourite china-faced doll, Margaret.

'I just cut her hair to see how long it would take to grow back,' explained Roger, all innocent blue eyes and flossy fair curls. All Dad said was, 'Well, that was very wrong of you, and you're old enough to know that you've ruined Dorothy's doll.' I was still sniffing, and Dad promised to get me a new doll. Roger got off scot-free.

My other brothers, Harry and John, were much easier to cope with: they were four and three years older than me respec-tively, and they did everything together; they left me alone. But Roger, who was only two years older than me, tormented the life out of me. When I eventually did get a new doll to replace the ruined Margaret — a golliwog — and took it to school proudly, Roger led a group of his friends at recess in following me around and chanting: 'Black pudding! Black pudding!'

Roger got away with murder at school, all the time. For instance, Mr Bates the headmaster had three beautiful Muscovy ducks, of which he was very proud. Every child in the school had seen them waddling importantly around their enclosure in the yard of Mr Bates's house, up the road from the school. One day, Roger took a long piece of string, tied three bits of bread to it and left it in their pen. The ducks greedily swooped on it, and each gulped a piece of bread and string — and waddled around the enclosure, quacking pompously in a dreadful tandem, unable to escape from each other. Roger had timed this deed for lunchtime, and had told his friends; the word spread and soon the whole school was roaring with laughter at these unfortunate birds. 'Who *did* this?' demanded Mr Bates at rollcall the following morning, but Roger didn't own up, and nobody told tales either.

Mum, whose favourite Roger was (he never had to chop wood as Harry and John did: 'He's going to be a surgeon and it will ruin his hands,' said Mum), always took his part in any fights with the rest of us. And Roger did precisely as he liked, his wholesome choirboy looks apparently convincing Mum that he was innocent. She had an expression for some children: 'Street angel, home devil': it seemed extraordinary to me that she was unable to see how well this described my brother!

When his turn came to read the lesson after dinner, however, it *was* hard to believe that this angelic-looking boy was the demon I knew. Every evening, Mum brought out the huge family Bible that normally stayed in the front room, and we took turns to read a passage from it, chosen according to the Methodist study guide to which Mum subscribed. She was a very strong Methodist and a strict churchgoer, and made sure that we all were too. I never enjoyed reading aloud: for one thing, the book was huge and the three columns per page of tiny print were difficult to read. I tried to read as Mum had taught me, being very careful with commas, full stops and semi-colons, but sometimes I couldn't see them very well, and Mum corrected me. Then again, the Methodist reader always seemed to demand passages from the Old Testament when it was my turn, full of difficult names. To this day I cannot say 'Nebuchadnezzar' correctly at the first attempt!

After reading, Mum led prayers, usually about the necessity for being good. (Roger was particularly convincing at those.) I wanted God to love me, and so tried to be as good as possible, but sometimes the whole process puzzled me. If God loved everybody, why did he do such dreadful things to people? Even though the Egyptians had enslaved the Israelites, it seemed rather unfair to visit boils, floods and seven-year plagues on them. It hadn't been everybody's fault. I could never mention these doubts to Mum, who would have accused me of being a naughty girl, so I just kept feeling uneasy about God, a growling and vengeful person with a long, white beard.

I felt much happier about Jesus, because he talked to children and was kind to animals. But I never understood how he could be the son of such an unpleasant father.

I think I also liked Jesus because the picture of him in my Sunday school reader looked exactly like Len Gale, a travelling pedlar who came round door-to-door about once a month selling pegs and string. They both had long, sleek, dark hair, a brown, curly beard and large, brown eyes. Put Len Gale the pedlar into a white robe instead of his shabby shirt and elastic-sided boots and moleskins, and he'd look just like Jesus, I thought.

After Sunday school one day, I mentioned this to my best friend, Alma, who knew Len Gale too. Being wicked and a fearful giggler, Alma immediately christened him 'Jesus'; whenever we opened our Bible reader, showing Christ at the Sermon on the Mount, we nudged each other and got the giggles. Nobody else knew why, of course; I was a little worried about it, fearful that God the Father might decide that we were as bad as the Egyptians had been, and visit a plague of locusts upon us.

What made it even funnier was that we often saw Len Gale at church meetings; he was very devout. When this happened, Alma and I were practically purple in the face — and one morning we nearly expired. Mr Pearson, the minister, invited members of the congregation to pray in turn. Up got Jesus. He folded his hands across his best Sunday jacket, rolled his eyes to heaven — he was a great eye-roller — took a deep breath and was about to speak, when Mrs Luddenham next to us stood up and said very quickly, 'Oh merciful Lord . . .' and kept on praying. Jesus stopped rolling his eyes and looked most put out, but had to stop and sit down. When Mrs Luddenham had finished, Jesus stood up again, folded his arms as before, raised his eyes . . . and this time Mrs Davies, the grocer's wife, beat him. Jesus had to sit down again, stroking his beard and pretending he'd just jumped up to see what would happen.

Mrs Davies stopped calling upon the Lord and sat down, and Alma and I, trying desperately not to laugh, held our breaths to see if Jesus would make another attempt. Up he got again, slowly, glaring around the congregation to see if anybody else would *dare* to leap in. No, everybody sat silently, waiting. He took a deep breath, folded his arms, rolled his eyes and said, 'Oh, L. . .' He had forgotten Mr Pearson, who didn't happen to be looking his way. Barely had Jesus got the first 'L' out when the minister decided that the prayers had gone on long enough and hastily petitioned God to listen to his humble servants.

Steam was practically coming out of Jesus' ears. We could tell that he wanted nothing more than to strangle Mr Pearson, Mrs Davies and Mrs Luddenham — and it was all too much for Alma and me. Alma had a habit of spurting little giggles through her nose, like a soda siphon, and she set me off giggling so hard that I shook our pew. It was worse when Mum opened her eyes and frowned at us, then leaned over from the other side and nudged me, hard. I could only bury my scarlet face in my hands and pretend to be very devout myself.

At the end of the service, Jesus stalked from the church, his beard bristling with rage. Alma and I tottered home together, Alma making little hooting noises whenever she remembered Jesus. 'When your mother nudged you, I thought I was going to *die!*' she said.

Alma and I were best friends for years — I was bridesmaid at her wedding — but we usually had a fight about once a week. Mostly this was because of *Jester*. This was an English comic paper that came out on Tuesdays and cost twopence, a strip story with black and white illustrations (not balloons, as comics had later) about clever English children and their adventures in the country and at the seaside with donkey rides and pierrots. I got more pocket-money than Alma did — threepence a week, a fortune, where she only got twopence — and she argued that I should always buy *Jester* because I had more money, and she would borrow it from me when I had finished. No, I said; we should take it in turns. That way we'd always have threepence to spend on sweets, no matter who bought *Jester*. The problem was that the one who didn't buy *Jester* was allowed to choose what sweets we bought that week; Alma liked sherbet balls and I didn't, because they cost two a penny and didn't last long enough. (Even though toffee cakes cost a whole penny, they would last for hours if you didn't suck them too hard.)

Pocket-money was very important. We all felt sorry for Redvers Rowe, whose mother was very mean (as if it wasn't difficult enough being called 'Redvers' after a British general in the Boer War). Mrs Rowe would say, 'Redvers, would you like a caraway seed cake?' He always said, 'Yes, please,' and his mother said, 'Well, you'll have to buy the caraway seeds yourself.' We thought this was absolutely outrageous, but Redvers didn't seem to mind greatly.

Redvers, who had large, red, prominent ears, was very interested in science. We all knew that, hopeless though he was, he was going to be famous because he was brainy. He knew more than anybody about Halley's Comet when it appeared the year I turned ten. 'It's going to be huge, right across the sky at night, shining and everything,' he said, before it appeared. I knew that was probably true — like everybody else, I had seen the reports in the papers, though I had not read them in detail. Redvers was the only boy in the class with the patience to work right through the long columns of print and to absorb all the information about trails of vapour, size, speed at which the comet travelled, and its relationship to the earth and the sun.

As time went on, the comet appeared more and more clearly. But it didn't look like a comet; over the hills of the Great Dividing Range was a shining stone with a long white trail behind it, covering about a quarter of the sky, night after night. It was even brighter than the Milky Way. During the day it hung in the sky like a bright little extra sun or a star at the wrong time. I would stand out in the yard at night, thinking how silent it was. All I could hear was a dog barking, somewhere behind the hills. I imagined a very faint hum as the comet moved, too slowly for me to see, across the heavens. Or did it go 'swoosh' like a rocket on Empire Day? Even Redvers didn't know.

Miss Curtis, our teacher that year, drew a circle on the blackboard, and gave it a long tail, like a tadpole. 'You won't see Halley's Comet again until 1985,' she told us. I thought about that for a long time. I would be older than the oldest person I knew: eighty-five! On the flyleaf of Mum's big Bible at home was a series of neat columns, with all the names of Mum's family in spidery writing. I liked the last column on the right, because I was there. 'Mary Polglase m. James Albert Smythe 1890' it said, and four lines were meticulously ruled downwards under Mum and Dad's names. From the left we were John Frederick, b. 1895, Henry Albert Arthur, b. 1897, Roger Norman, b. 1898, and lastly me, Dorothy Enid, b. 1900. I was very proud to be the only person in the family born in the twentieth century...and I wondered whether John, Harry and Roger would see Halley's Comet too. I was determined *I* would. When it came around again, I'd be waiting for it.

WORLD WAR I:
1914–1918

At first I thought it was the most wonderful adventure

At first I thought it was the most wonderful adventure

David Gleason's scrapbook is a modest quarto-sized volume with a stiff blue paper cover. Most of its greyish pages are blank. Even so, it is obvious that David was the sort of child who liked to get things right, for on the first page he carefully printed 'SCRAPBOOK'. This is followed by his name, 'DAVID ANTHONY GLEASON', and his address, in a town on Queensland's Darling Downs. Under that, David wrote:

> *Australia,*
> *The British Empire,*
> *The World,*
> *Earth,*
> *Space.*

The first item in the book is a cutting from the local paper, dated 6 August 1914, when David was eight. 'WAR DECLARED: ARCHDUKE MURDERED IN BALKANS' is the headline, in smaller type than the results of a local racing carnival.

Maps from the newspaper are scattered throughout the book: Egypt, Palestine, the French front, Belgium and — of course — Gallipoli. All the cuttings have been raggedly scissored, and are not always stuck straight on the page; the amount of puckering around them shows that David had a heavy hand with the glue pot.

Postcards stud the pages, some in gaudy colours, others in sepia or black and white; David was more interested in the picture than the messages on the back. Pale camels march past unbelievably triangular pyramids; dispirited black-and-white lions flank Nelson's Column; a

*can-can girl kicks up saucy heels and a frilly petticoat under the words
'Bienvenu à Marseilles'.*

*There is also a snapshot faded to the colour of weak tea. A
young, fit-looking man in AIF uniform — standard issue boots,
puttees, rifle over the shoulder, slouch hat tilted carefully to the right —
stands very straight, gazing directly at the camera. His stance is
correct, his uniform obviously new and well pressed. On his right are
an older man and woman, his parents; the man in a dark cloth suit
and tie, with brightly polished boots; the woman in a long coat and
skirt, with wide-brimmed hat pulled down on her forehead. On the
soldier's left is a girl of his own age, twenty or twenty-one. She is
a couple of centimetres taller than he, and her shoulders droop as
though she is conscious of this difference in height. She, too, is wearing
what seem to be very good clothes: three-quarter-length coat, long skirt
and high-collared blouse. Her hair is pulled back from her rather
sharp-featured face. All four people look serious and proud. The
photograph has a sense of occasion about it: this may be their last
chance to be photographed together.*

That's Michael Rode with his parents and my sister Elaine; Elaine
and Michael were unofficially engaged. Dad took that photo in
our back garden the morning we all went down to the station to
see Michael off to the war. He was one of the first volunteers from
the Darling Downs district, and we were very proud of him.

It was a very cold day in August, with grey clouds and thin
rain. I had a bitter argument with Mum about wearing my
knickerbockers and long socks. They were normally kept for Sundays, and I hated them because they were dark brown wool and
scratchy and uncomfortable. But Mum insisted I look my best for
the sake of the family. I thought this was nonsense. Why should
anybody look at an eight-year-old boy when Michael and the
others were there in their splendid new uniforms? But Mum won,
and I grumbled down to the station with her, Dad and Elaine
in Dad's new Model T.

It seemed that everybody in town had come to see 'the boys'
off: the line of buggies and cars stretched right along Station
Street. Mr and Mrs Rode were with a large group of relatives in
front of the station building; Michael, with thirty other young
men in slouch hats, badges and buttons and stiff khaki, was lined

up about twenty yards away. We joined Michael's parents, and nobody said much. I felt very small and ached to go with the soldiers, to swing my kitbag onto the train as he was about to do, wave goodbye and march into battle.

Michael's group were lounging and chatting, waiting for the mayor to come and wave them off. Suddenly Michael turned and winked at me. I tried very hard to wink back, though I'm not sure he could have seen my eyes through my glasses. Then Michael left his group and came over.

'Would you like to come, mate?' he asked softly. I nodded. 'Yeah, I can understand that,' he said, 'but you won't ever be old enough. The war'll be over in six months and we'll be back before you know we've gone.' I think the last part was for Elaine's benefit; she was standing just beside me, looking at Michael, not saying anything.

Ernie Harris and his brass band were tootling cheerfully away too, playing 'Rule Britannia' and 'Tarara Boomdeay'. They played it over and over again.

'Better get back to the boys,' said Michael. I could see that he was tense and excited, and wanted the farewells to be over. He strolled back to his group and Elaine grasped my hand, very tightly. This was most unlike her; although she was twelve years older than I was, and was almost a second mother to me, she didn't show her feelings much, ever. I squeezed her hand back, but she wasn't even looking at me. Her eyes were following Michael.

The band stopped playing; Michael and the others formed lines and stood to attention in their immaculate, brand-new khakis. Mr Allnutt, the mayor, had arrived at last, accompanied by a few of the town councillors. I knew we would be there for a while yet, as Mr Allnutt never missed the opportunity to make a speech — and this was probably the most important occasion in the town's history. In fact, that was the first thing he said. 'This town has provided more soldiers than any other in the Darling Downs area,' he announced very importantly. He then went on to talk about departing warriors, duty to the Empire and the conflict between good and evil. The drizzle persisted; Elaine put up her umbrella, but Mr Allnutt kept reading from his little bit of paper, apparently not even realising that his coat collar was getting wet. He spoke for about ten minutes, while the soldiers stood silently in the rain. And at the end he urged the soldiers and their families to have faith in God, and quoted:

> *To every man upon this earth*
> *Death cometh soon or late.*

And how can man die better
Than facing fearful odds
For the ashes of his fathers
And the temples of his gods?

He finished and stepped back, but the applause was as thin as the rain. I was disappointed because I'd expected the whole speech to be as rousing as the beginning had been. Why did Mr Allnutt have to mention dying? Soldiers were killed in wars, I knew that — but *our* boys wouldn't be. They were going off to help the Mother Country fight the enemy and they would slaughter heaps of Huns and Turks.

Mr Allnutt finished his speech not a moment too soon. The train, which had been waiting by the goods yard, chugged into the station. Rain still kept falling but nobody moved away. The soldiers broke line and became ordinary blokes again: farm workers, shop-keepers' assistants, publicans, horsemen, drinkers at the pub. On his way over to us for his final goodbyes, Michael passed one of his mates who wasn't going, gave him a punch on the shoulder and they laughed. The rain splashed over his boots and puttees. 'Wanna polish me boots again, Mum?' he asked Mrs Rode, who didn't laugh.

Everybody suddenly realised that the time had come to say goodbye. Mr Rode grabbed Michael's hand and shook it hard, 'Goodbye, son,' and Dad politely shook hands with his future son-in-law when Mr Rode had finished. Michael kissed Mrs Rode, nodded at Mum, and grabbed Elaine by both arms. She hugged him more fiercely than I had ever seen her embrace anybody, but not for long because Mum and Dad and Mr and Mrs Rode were watching. Michael winked at me again, said, 'See yer, Specs,' and walked nonchalantly over to the carriage. He turned and waved, and climbed in. The train puffed slowly out of the station with everybody waving hats and handkerchiefs, and set off on its way to Brisbane.

Mrs Rode gasped. 'Oh. . . I forgot to give him his sandwiches,' she said.

Life settled back to normal, except that so many of the young men weren't around town any more. There wasn't much news about the war for a long time. But my Uncle Perce, Mum's brother, knew a lot about it anyway. 'I'd like to be in the stoush meself, but they don't want old blokes like me,' he said. 'You gotta be real fit.'

War was a very expensive business, he told me one day when we were rabbiting out in the paddocks near town. 'See,' he said, 'what with paying all those soldiers six bob a day, plus all the shells that are fired, which cost money, and uniforms and all the rest of it, I reckon this war is costing the Empire five million quid a day. That's thirty-five million quid a week, you know, because they fight on Sundays.' I asked Uncle Perce if he thought the fight was worth the money. He looked grim and nodded. 'Yeah, we have to beat the Krauts.'

Uncle Perce seemed much keener on beating the Krauts than were some of the young men who joined up after Michael and his lot left. More and more large boys sidled into church wearing brand-new uniforms; kids at school boasted that their brothers, cousins and even fathers had joined up. The only one I knew personally was Snow Harris, who had been a beau of Elaine's before she took up with Michael. Just after he got his new uniform, I saw him in the grocer's shop buying a bag of flour. 'G'day, Snow,' I said. 'You gonna kill thousands of Turks?' Snow was one of the strongest young men in town, with forearms like tree trunks, but he wasn't a quick thinker. He looked confused. 'I dunno,' he muttered. What sort of noble warrior are *you*? I wanted to ask.

I couldn't understand why we were on the side of the French, who were Catholics, and against the Germans, who were Protestants like us. Catholics were strange. They had a church in town, and a convent not far away, and we occasionally saw the nuns in the street. But they kept very much to themselves. Why were we fighting with them?

I looked forward to hearing from Michael what the war was really like but, when his first postcard came from Egypt towards the end of 1914, I was disappointed. It looked exotic enough — with palm trees, camels and pyramids, and it was the first letter I had ever seen from overseas, but Michael said very little. 'Dear Mr and Mrs Gleason and David,' he wrote. 'We've been here for months and we still don't know when we'll have a go at' (there was a scribble that looked like 'Jacko'). 'Will let you know. Love to everybody, M.'

Why couldn't Michael go and find the Turks or the Huns? I wondered. Why did they have to wait until the enemy found *them*? Nobody knew the answer except, of course, for Uncle Perce. 'They're studying *tactics*,' he said, nodding wisely. The Turks knew we were in Egypt; the trick was for the Australians to be somewhere the Turks didn't know about, he said. This made sense, but it didn't answer my questions. Elaine was often helpful in assisting me to understand things, but she had just received a letter from Michael herself, and I gathered it didn't have very much about the Army or the war in it.

Then came the episode of the Brewsters.

Joan and Shirley Brewster were in my class at school: they

were twins who looked exactly alike, with pale, rabbity faces and skinny hair in plaits. None of us liked them much; they stayed together all the time, didn't seem to have many friends, and didn't play any of the jokes that twins are supposed to play on other people. 'Which one are *you*?' the teacher would ask, laughing, and they always whispered, 'I'm Shirley,' or 'I'm Joan.' We all knew that their father had a bad heart and couldn't work much, and the girls sometimes stayed away when their mother had one of her 'turns'. I think now that Mrs Brewster had epilepsy, but we only knew then that she was often ill and that the twins were needed to look after her.

The twins had an elder brother, Cecil, one of the strongest-looking men around the district. He was a solid worker who never said much; we often saw him in his dray picking up the girls after school if he happened to be driving past collecting supplies from the station to take to the grocery shop or the pub. I had seen him lift a huge beer keg off the dray and carry it into the pub without sweating.

I first realised that Cecil wasn't popular when I heard Mum and her best friend, Mrs Holder, discussing him in Dad's chemist shop one day after school.

'Why *should* Cecil Brewster still be working around here when all the other boys have gone off to fight?' Mrs Holder asked crossly. 'It isn't right.' And a day or two later, Alan Holder, who was a class ahead of me, baled up Joan and Shirley Brewster in the playground. 'Your brother is a lily-livered coward,' he said. 'He's too scared to go and fight.' Joan and Shirley looked as though they were about to burst into tears. They huddled together as usual, and eventually Joan said, 'He's not,' but that was all.

The following week Mrs Holder told Mum that Horrie Davis, who was in charge of recruiting for the area, had gone to see Mrs Brewster to ask why Cecil was still working and not in the Army.

Then Joan and Shirley turned up for school, red-faced and sniffing. They hardly said a word to anybody, just hung their heads. And during the day the word spread around the school that somebody had sent Cecil Brewster a white feather.

That clinched it for me. When I went into Dad's chemist shop that afternoon, I said: 'Cecil Brewster is a *coward*!' Dad, who knew about the white feather, just glanced at me and went on making pills. Normally I loved watching him measure out the white powder on his tiny scales, shape it into pills, cover it with sweet icing and put it carefully in tiny moulds, but not that day. I knew Dad wasn't pleased with me, but what had I said?

After about a minute he straightened up and wiped his hands on his starched white coat. 'Have you ever thought what would happen to Cecil Brewster's family if he went to war and was killed?' he asked.

I shook my head.

'His father can't work, his mother is sick and he has two young sisters. If Cecil didn't work to support them, they would probably all starve.' He gave me one last level look and turned back to making pills. I had nothing more to say, so I slipped off my stool and walked home, very thoughtful, and ashamed.

I decided to do something to show Joan and Shirley Brewster that I understood Cecil hadn't deserved his white feather. In the playground the next day, at recess, I asked, 'Would you like some of my apple?' But they only looked frightened and giggled as usual. 'No thank you,' said Joan politely. I felt snubbed and annoyed, because I had only been trying to be nice. So I ate the whole apple myself. Blow them!

I started seeing Cecil coming out of the pub early in the afternoon, which was unusual, because he wasn't a drinker. And one day, when I was doing the shopping with Mum (Elaine was out somewhere), I saw the publican, Mr Turley, struggling into the pub with a huge keg of beer. It was far too large for him, and he was red-faced and staggering.

'Morning, Mrs Gleason,' he gasped.

Mum ignored his greeting. 'Why are you doing that?' she asked.

'Nobody else to do it,' he told her.

'What about Cecil Brewster?'

'Oh...he's too busy,' muttered Mr Turley. This was too much for Mum, who knew that Cecil was having more and more trouble finding work.

'You're like the rest of them...just because he can't join up, you're persecuting him,' she said. Mum could be pretty fierce when she wanted to. She glared up at Mr Turley; he wasn't a big man, but she was thin and seemed about half his size.

'Scuse me, Mrs Gleason, I've got work to do,' was all he said, but I could tell by the way he looked at Mum that he didn't like her for saying that. He disappeared with his keg, and we walked on, Mum's lips tight.

From then on, Cecil was at our place a lot, doing odd jobs like mending the fanlight over the front door, or painting our parlour. I couldn't see that a lot of these things needed doing, but Mum and Dad insisted. And Cecil never went into uniform.

I don't think my parents' attitude to Cecil Brewster made them popular with some of the people in town, but my parents were regarded as slightly cranky anyway. For instance, we didn't eat some of the food that other people did; Dad was very keen on fresh vegetables, and cereals, and brown sugar. He never let Mum cook meat twice, and fried food was forbidden. 'The frying pan and second cookings cause the most deaths, apart from pneumonia,' he said. So we never had shepherd's pie. Dad and Mum were afraid of meat going off in summer.

We also had iodine added to the drinking water at home, to purify it, and our water tanks were vacuumed out when they got low after a long, dry spell. We only drank rainwater from our own tanks.

Oddest of all in other people's eyes, we didn't have any medicines in the house at all. 'Pretty strange for a chemist,' people said. But we had only aspirins and bandages. 'If you're fed properly and you're healthy, you don't need drugs,' Dad said firmly. And Elaine and I were very healthy indeed. Even now I'm reluctant to take any medicines, even antibiotics! And I've never lost my love for brown bread, even though the kids at school wouldn't share my sandwiches.

When the war had been going for about eight months, as the sun grew sharper and the nights became cool enough for an eiderdown on my bed, we heard about a battle in a place called Gallipoli. Uncle Perce knew all about it, and described how our soldiers had stormed ashore from boats in the Dardanelles and attacked a huge force of Turks. He showed me what had happened by moving matches and pipe cleaners; the matches were Australians, rushing up the hill into fire from the Turkish guns, the pipe cleaners (twisty and untrustworthy) were the Turkish soldiers. I knew that one match was worth a dozen pipe cleaners.

But where was Michael? In defiance of Mum and Dad, Elaine wore a little enamel badge with his regimental colours on her summer and winter coats. This was instead of the engagement ring that Mum and Dad refused to let her have; they said she was too young to think about marrying and they would discuss it when Michael returned. Because Michael was in the 9th Battalion with other Queenslanders, we knew he had probably been among the first ashore at Gallipoli — but that was all we found out for some time. Elaine kept saying, 'I know he's all right,' and, as the landing was described in the papers in terms of maps, arrows and dotted lines, at first I felt inclined to believe her. It didn't seem real.

Then, as we heard more about it, the landing became first brave, then heroic. Our Anglican minister preached a sermon comparing the men at Gallipoli to the Spartans at Thermopylae, which didn't mean much to me. I understood Bill Rattray's words much better. Bill, the dour old clothes-prop man who travelled from door to door, said, 'Them blokes was sent in to do what wasn't possible. They didn't know the Turks were there, waiting for them, and when they did find out, they just kept comin'.'

We started playing Turks and Australians in the bush behind the pub after school. Two teams were chosen by lot (this was the only fair way to do this, because nobody wanted to be a Turk). The Australians were supposed to creep towards the Turks, who were at the top of the hill near Mrs Manson's place. I became very good at dodging between rocks and making sure no twigs cracked under my feet; some of the Turks had very sharp ears. If they heard you, they were allowed to turn and shoot you; if you managed to get to the top of the hill silently, you were allowed to shoot them. Time and time again I came home with my shirt dirty and my shoes and socks scuffed because of Gallipoli, and Mum was anything but pleased with me.

I remember writing school compositions. I hated doing them, since drawing was my strong point, not writing. My composition started: 'War was on. Our brave soldeirs were doing batel with the Turks. They stromed the cliffs at Gallipoli' (about the only word that wasn't misspelled) 'and got over. They are still there.' Miss Scott, our teacher, was annoyed. 'You are nine. You should be able to do better than that,' she said.

Nora Pennington, whose father ran the local paper, produced a composition that Miss Scott liked much better. She smugly read it out to the whole school at assembly, referring to the 'dastardly Turkish hordes' and 'the Australians, noble scions of the Empire'. Nora used to pinch phrases from her father's more flamboyant editorials.

I came home one day to find Elaine in floods of tears. 'What's the matter?' I asked uncomfortably. She sniffled, and waved a dirty piece of paper, scrawled over in pencil. 'Michael's all right,' was all she said. I couldn't see why that was anything to cry about, and asked if I could see the letter. But Elaine refused; she showed it to nobody. However, Mrs Rode called on Mum to tell her that Michael had landed on Gallipoli 'without a scratch', and had written that the landing had been 'pretty bad'. Was that all? 'Michael doesn't say much in letters,' said Mrs Rode apologetically.

Soon afterwards Mr Hopkins, the headmaster, came into our classroom, looking very serious indeed. Miss Scott interrupted our mental arithmetic lesson and we all stood up to say 'good morning', but he didn't say anything immediately. He had to clear his throat three times.

'Len McKinley won't be at school today,' he told us. Interesting news, but hardly worth a visit from the headmaster. Was Len terribly ill?

'His brother Harry has fallen at Gallipoli,' said Mr Hopkins. He gave us the rest of the day off as a mark of respect, and I walked home trying to feel solemn. The way Mr Hopkins had expressed it, Harry had fallen over and not got up. But he was, really, dead. I didn't know much about death. When I was very small, a woman had been knocked down by a car outside our house. Before anybody else had come, I'd seen her lying on the road, in a black coat, buttoned boots and a hat, which was still on her head. Her dress had ridden up and her bare legs had been scraped by the fall. I couldn't see her face, so I didn't know who she was. Later, Mum had told me that she didn't live in town, and her relatives had to be found from somewhere else. This stranger had looked as though she had fallen over and decided to go to sleep. Is that what Harry looked like?

In the playground just before we all went home, the girls in the class cried for Harry McKinley, and for Len. They seemed to do it so easily; all they needed was to think sad thoughts, and the tears came out, apparently. I couldn't cry, and nor could the rest of us boys. We scuffled on the way home, as usual. Harry McKinley was the town's first dead hero, and the Anglican minister held a memorial service for him. The church was packed, with people standing around the walls and spilling into the porch. Harry McKinley's mother's eyes were very red under her black veil, and her shoulders were shaking, but Len and his father stared sternly ahead through all the prayers and hymns. A month later, a scrolled brown varnished board was put up on the right of the pulpit. DULCE ET DECORUM EST PRO PATRIA MORI was at the top in large gold letters, and underneath appeared just one name: 'McKinley, Henry George'.

We began hearing a lot about 'the war effort' and people stopped saying the war would be over in six months, or even in a year. Whenever I came home from school, the house was full of women clicking knitting needles and manipulating dark wool, and making huge quantities of socks, vests, mittens and mufflers, as well as sewing pyjamas and shirts. Mum ran Red Cross classes with first aid and bandage rolling. I asked her when the wounded soldiers were coming home, so we could look after them, but she said that first aid was always useful, and that the rolled bandages were being sent overseas, to Gallipoli, and also to France.

In the months after the Gallipoli landing, a few red crosses appeared on gates around town. The local signwriter painted several gold names under Harry McKinley's on the church's honour board. Mrs Gates came to work in Dad's shop, to dust the glass shelves that held the bottles of medicines, and was very nice to me. 'I really appreciate what your dad's doing,' she said, and I didn't know what she meant for years. Dad supported her after her husband was killed, and Dad and Dr Cook paid her baby daughter's expenses for a long time.

Mum, who was a leading light in the CWA as well as the

Red Cross, spent more and more of her time on the war effort. I used to help her load the car with blankets, medicines and food. But she wasn't to be trusted with clothes. Once Elaine said to Nora, our maid: 'Nora, have you seen my blue jumper?'

'What blue jumper?' asked Mum quickly. Elaine knew immediately. 'Mum, you gave it away! How *could* you?'

'Don't be silly,' was all Mum said. 'You have another blue jumper.' She admitted that she'd unravelled the jumper and knitted it up into a muffler. 'They need it in France more than you do,' she said.

Elaine's main contribution to the war effort was to organise musical evenings in aid of the Red Cross, the Wounded Soldiers' Fund or the Belgian Relief Fund. I thought these were quite jolly, even though somebody was bound to make a speech about our brave lads suffering in the trenches. We all sang 'Tipperary' and 'The Rose of No Man's Land'. Elaine, who had a beautiful contralto voice, rather fancied herself as a soloist, and usually draped herself picturesquely by the piano. I knew that she would be wishing Michael could see her. I particularly enjoyed the evenings at the Holders': they had a pianola, which pushed out music if you pumped the pedals vigorously. A cylinder turned above the keyboard, and the keys moved all by themselves.

With all this activity going on around me, I felt it was clearly time for me to do my bit. We were supposed to do all in our power to help the little Belgian children who, Uncle Perce said, were continually being skewered on bayonets by the Kaiser. My whole life was dominated by these foreign children. When I didn't eat all my spinach at dinner, Mum would say reproachfully, 'The little Belgian children would be grateful for that.' As I held my breath and tried to chew noisily at the same time, ignoring the squashiness of the vegetable that I hated most of all, I grew more and more annoyed. If the little Belgian children wanted spinach, they could have mine. It would serve them right.

Still, I decided I'd better do the right thing. For sweeping out the grate, washing up and polishing the family shoes, I was paid threepence a week pocket-money, a penny of which I donated to the Belgian Relief Fund. My mate, Bill Powell, and I walked for miles around town, picking bits of wool off the fences of the sheep paddocks. When we had enough of the dirty brown fibre, we divided it and I took my share home, washing it carefully, trying to get rid of the dung and the burrs, and gave it to Mum: 'You can make socks with that, Mum,' I said. I don't know what she did with the wool; she couldn't possibly have knitted anything with it!

Poor Bill. His mother was the district Red Cross knitting

champion, and she insisted on teaching him how to knit. He protested bitterly that knitting was something that only *girls* did, but Mrs Powell was implacable. 'There's a war on,' she said. The result was that one day I came home to find Bill, red-faced, tongue hanging out of the corner of his mouth, sitting with his mother and the other women of the Red Cross circle, awkwardly winding khaki wool round a pair of knitting needles. This was the funniest thing I had ever seen — I could hardly *wait* to tease him about it. But he was bigger than I was, and I knew that if I said a single word, Bill would drop knitting needles and wool and fetch me a punch in the eye. Bill never became as good a knitter as his mother. I think he made the worst pairs of socks that ever warmed the feet of Australian soldiers on the Western Front.

Nora Pennington, the good little girl who had written the composition about Gallipoli, was the school's champion sock knitter. At lunchtime and recess, she sat with her ankles neatly crossed and her boots buttoned, turning the heels of the socks very prettily. She eventually won the district record for the numbers of socks, mufflers, mittens and balaclava helmets knitted by anybody under the age of thirteen; her father made sure that the news reached the front page of his paper, with the heading 'LITTLE NORA DOES HER BIT'. The rest of us longed to grab her knitting, rip the stitches out and snarl the wool up for her, especially Bill.

John Turley, the publican's son and the school bully, had a good racket going. With a couple of friends he collected bits of iron, kerosene tins, bottles — any bits of scrap they could find — and sold them to the grocer. John would pay the younger boys to find stuff for him: the going rate was a halfpenny a pound. Because I was interested in earning more money, I worked for him. It was hard, my first taste of sweated labour, but it paid quite well. John became a confirmed capitalist because of this first business venture. When he grew up he became an SP bookie in Brisbane.

I desperately needed money because, in a fit of patriotism, I had decided to donate *all* my pocket-money — twopence a week on top of the penny that had already gone to the Belgian Relief Fund — to the Red Cross. When I announced this to Mum, she looked dubious and said, 'Are you sure you want to do this?' 'Yes,' I said crossly. Sacrifice was in the air. But the smug glow I felt as I gave my pocket-money to Mrs Holder faded very quickly. Without money to buy sweets or my weekly comic paper, I soon regretted being so generous — particularly since my efforts didn't seem to be making the war any shorter. But I couldn't break the deal; I would have lost too much face with Mum. She must have realised how I felt, because a couple of months later she told me that the Red Cross could probably do without my twopence. I didn't protest at all.

Almost every week there was a button day. All the women I knew sold little Union Jacks or Australian flags or blue and white rosettes on wooden trays, as well as buttons. The buttons themselves were very attractive: about the size of a shilling, made of tin, and covered with transparent celluloid. Printed on the tin were pictures of Haig, King George V, Jellicoe and Kitchener (the last disappeared after he was killed in 1916). My favourite buttons were the flags of the Allies, all of which I collected and of which I was very proud.

Raffles were also an important part of the war effort. On one notable occasion, Fred Belcher, a carpenter, donated his pride and joy; a replica of the cruiser HMAS *Sydney* made entirely of matchsticks. The Red Cross put it on display at the school before raffling it, and I used to stay behind to gaze at it with longing. It was the most beautiful thing I had ever seen. Masts, rounded funnels, the long, sleek lines of the cruiser, all had been faithfully copied from photographs. Fred had inked in the portholes, and glued a tiny Australian flag made of painted paper on the bridge. It was complete, perfect in every detail.

I loved that model passionately, and wanted to win it more than anything in the world. For weeks I saved up my twopences to buy as many raffle tickets as possible; going without sweets for over a month was not too high a price to pay for the *Sydney*'s sake. On the day that the raffle was drawn, I was almost ill with the suspense. All for nothing: the loathsome Nora Pennington, who wouldn't have known a cruiser from an ocean liner, had the winning ticket. I didn't know whether to kill her or myself.

Early in 1916 Bill Powell had a birthday party. This was quite an event; we didn't go in for such things in our town, and besides, 'there's a war on'. We all turned up in our best clothes on the appointed Saturday afternoon, clutching small gifts. I brought a handkerchief and tie that Mum had made (feeling sorry for Bill because it was such a dull present). But that was nothing compared to some of the other presents poor Bill received. One of his aunts turned up with a lumpy parcel which had two spikes visible under the brown wrapping paper. Bill unwrapped it to find knitting needles and grey wool. Tim Kennedy brought a tin of bully beef: 'Mum made me,' he muttered by way of apology. And Nora Pennington presented Bill with a pea soup sausage, a lump of powdered dried peas wrapped in a bit of cotton material, tied at each end like a sausage. 'The soldiers dropped it into boiling water to make soup,' she explained. Judging by the look on Bill's face, he was not sorry that that particular present was destined for the Western Front.

As the war continued, I heard the names of places I couldn't pronounce: Ypres, Messines, Broodseinde, Passchendaele. The maps in the paper grew more complicated, with arrows everywhere. And we started to hear about the dreadfulness of the Flanders mud.

Michael didn't write often, only scribbled messages to Elaine and to his parents, and Elaine didn't tell us in any detail what he said. When I asked her, 'Is it true that there are rats as big as kittens in the trenches?' having overheard Uncle Perce, Elaine turned on me savagely and said, 'Be quiet! I don't want to hear you mention the trenches!' But she did tell me that Michael had written that the mud in the trenches was about four feet deep and that men had to be pulled out of it by ropes; he wrote, too, that he was suffering from trench feet because he had been in water up to his knees for almost three days without a break and his feet were so swollen that he couldn't get his boots on again. Of the horrors of being surrounded by grey and swollen corpses, contaminated water, and being shelled without mercy, Michael said nothing, then or later. He just kept asking for more socks and warm clothes.

More names were lettered on the church's honour board, more black armbands appeared in the school playground and in the streets. When we discussed the story of the plagues of Egypt at Sunday school, with the Angel of Death killing the firstborn sons in all houses without sacrificial blood sprinkled over the door, I thought of the red crosses on the gates of the houses around town that the Angel of Death *had* visited. Every day or two, it seemed, somebody's son died in the mud and barbed wire.

The most feared man in town was Mr Bagot, the Anglican minister.

He was a mild little man with a wife and a couple of children, an unassuming person who always said 'hello' if you met him in the street. Not like a minister at all, I always thought; he wasn't pompous, he didn't preach about hellfire; you got the impression that he and God were quite good friends really. Though Mr Bagot wouldn't go and have a drink with the blokes in the pub, he was quite happy to come and visit, yarning with Dad or other men around town while he puffed on his old black pipe. His sermons were slow, he made a few unsmiling jokes every Sunday and not many during the week: he was generally described as 'a good bloke for a parson'.

Mr Bagot was feared because it was he who received the

government telegrams that told families their sons had been killed at the front; it was from Mr Bagot that people first heard the news.

I came into Dad's chemist shop late one afternoon to find him talking to Mr Bagot.

'It's Wal Smith,' he said. 'I had to take the telegram to Margaret this morning. That's the second boy they've lost.' He looked grey and sombre. Dad was standing, listening, saying nothing.

Mr Bagot said, 'Daniel, they all look at me as if I'd killed their boys myself.' Dad clasped his shoulder for a few seconds. Then they both turned and saw me.

And at first I had thought the war was the most marvellous adventure.

Uncle Perce had more information than anybody else about the dreadful things the Germans were doing on the Western Front. 'It's a well-known fact that the British shells contain more copper than the German ones,' he told me. 'The British fuses have twenty-four ounces of gunmetal, and the French and German ones only have three and a half ounces. The Huns know this, of course — they're clever enough for that — and they offer rewards for all British fuses collected.

'Now, if we assumed that our artillery fired forty thousand rounds into the German trenches during one day and only half the fuses were collected, our guns would actually supply the enemy with enough copper to make a quarter of a million shells. Think about that, nipper! Those bastards will do anything to win.'

When the Australian losses in France and Flanders were at their greatest, all the windows of Mr Haenke's bakery were smashed. Nobody knew who did it.

The Haenkes' were a German family who had lived in town for many years. Mr Haenke, who spoke polite, efficient English, was pleasant and harmless, and he and his wife ran their bakery business very well. Most people seemed to like them.

I overhead Mrs Holder telling Mum at a Red Cross sewing circle meeting that, though she was sorry Mr Haenke's windows had been broken, she wasn't surprised. 'When all's said and done, he's a German,' she said. 'He's probably been laughing at us since the war started. You can't trust him.' I'd seen Mrs Holder buying bread at Mr Haenke's bakery a dozen times.

Rudi, the Haenkes' only son, was about thirteen. He was rather flash-looking, with blond hair and blue eyes and a beautiful complexion, and was a self-contained and quiet boy. I'd never had a conversation with him, as he was a year ahead of me at school; he seemed to have quite a few friends. But after the smashing of his father's windows, I noticed that he often ate his lunch alone in the playground. And then a new name for him went round the school: Rudi the Hun.

One lunchtime John Larsen and a group of the biggest boys in the school came up to Rudi, who was quietly eating his sandwiches as usual. They surrounded him. Rudi stood up, wiping his mouth nervously with the white handkerchief he always carried.

'Hello, Hun,' said John Larsen. Rudi didn't answer.

'Well, you are a Hun, aren't you?' There were about half-a-dozen boys with John Larsen, and they moved closer to Rudi until they encircled him completely. They started chanting, 'Rudi the Hu-un, Rudi the Hu-un.'

Rudi went red, and was obviously considering the wisest thing to do. Normally a dignified boy, he didn't fight back at once; then John punched him in the chest.

Instantly, Rudi turned and butted John fair in the stomach. '*Ooh*,' we gasped, thrilled; from all over the playground boys and girls came running to see the fight. 'Come on!' shouted John Larsen, and Rudi disappeared under a tangle of thrashing arms and legs. Larsen and his mates threw him to the ground. 'Leave me alone!' yelled Rudi. The rest of the school — including me — stood around, just cheering and egging the Larsen gang on. Nobody helped Rudi Haenke.

After a few minutes, Larsen grabbed Rudi, who was still wrestling, scarlet-faced, furious. 'Help me take off his shirt,' he said to his mates, who obeyed happily. I was fascinated to see that Rudi's chest, under his shirt, was bare; he didn't wear a short-sleeved woollen vest as the rest of us did.

'You're gonna march around the playground wavin' your shirt like a flag and singin' "Rule Britannia" for bein' a Hun,' said John Larsen.

'Yeah!' chorused his mates. 'Yeah!' agreed the rest of us.

Rudi cried, 'I won't,' and struggled like a maniac, but there were too many people holding him. He had absolutely no choice.

'Go on,' ordered Larsen. And so, shivering and bruised and scratched, Rudi Haenke marched around the school playground three times, waving his shirt like a flag of surrender, and feebly singing 'Rule Britannia', followed by the rest of the school laughing and calling out, 'Rudi the Hun! Rudi the Hun!'

Soon afterwards, a FOR SALE sign appeared on the Haenke bakery with its boarded up windows. The whole family had left the town. Mrs Holder told Mum that they had gone to live in the internment camp about a hundred miles away, and her tone implied that really it served them all right. I never saw Rudi Haenke again.

The Huns were not the only enemy to be feared; the Yanks were suspect too, even though they had just come into the war on our side. I learned that you couldn't trust the Yanks because of Les Darcy. Like everybody else, I was convinced that he was the greatest boxer in the world. Pictures of him appeared everywhere, left foot forward, fists bunched, a look of intense concentration on his face. He'd fought well-known American boxers in Sydney and defeated every one of them. Then he went to America after enlisting in the Army (his mother had him discharged, finally, as a minor) and we were sure he was going to win every single fight there was.

Then we heard he was dead, before he'd had a single bout in America.

I discussed this with Uncle Perce who, as usual, had a theory. 'You know why Les Darcy never had a fight in Yankeeland?' he asked, his eyes narrowing. 'You know how bloody good he was, don't you? He never had a chance to show what he was made of because the Yanks lured him over there and killed him. Killed by the Yanks! I don't know that I wouldn't rather have the Huns. At least they fight fairer.'

On a hot day at the end of the following school year, 1918, we were all chanting our tables: 'Seven sevens are forty-nine, seven eights are fifty-six, seven nines are sixty-three...' while the flies buzzed and droned around our heads. Then we heard a crowd yelling in the road outside. The tables stopped in a ragged chorus.

'Just a minute,' said our teacher, Mr Horricks, and he stepped outside the classroom. A few moments later he returned, beaming, and accompanied by the headmaster.

'Good morning, children,' said Mr Clark, who had one of those faces that always look serious. We wondered what was happening.

'Children,' he said, 'the Armistice has been signed. The war is over. You can have a holiday for the rest of the day.'

Wonderful news! We dashed out of the school before Mr Clark changed his mind, racing each other down the street, bumping, punching, hitting each other with our schoolbags. No more war!

The place had gone mad. Total strangers shook hands with each other, laughed and hugged; Mr Bagot, the minister, kissed my mother on both cheeks, to their mutual astonishment. Elaine was laughing and crying at once as she linked arms with Mr and Mrs Rode and marched down the street past the bank. Ernie Harris got members of his brass band together before they disappeared into the pub, and they were all tootling 'Tarara Boomdeay', just as they had four years before.

It was a wonderful day. The word got around that Mr Turley, the publican, had offered free drinks all round, so everybody flocked down to the pub. Uncle Perce, breathless and red-faced, told me, 'Kids are allowed too...come on, nipper!' and we rushed over, too. The place was crammed with roaring, singing men in their shirt sleeves, and I was unsure about going in. Even Uncle Perce paused. 'Just a minute,' he said, and disappeared into the shouting crowd. He emerged carrying a glass of beer and a green-stoppered bottle for me.

'There you are, nipper,' he said. 'Bottoms up!' So I drank to the end of the war in lemonade.

In May of 1919, we heard a knock at the front door. Elaine, who had been waiting for it, rushed and flung it open. Standing on the step was a stooped man wearing a faded, battered uniform. He had a tired face and old, frightened eyes. He was Michael Rode.

THE 1920s

The war didn't go away

❧ *The war didn't go away*

'I was a kid who thought a lot,' says Norman Lowe. His level blue gaze is still that of a serious boy, a child who spent hours building things with his Meccano set, or reading magazines to find out how radios are made. A good, quiet boy, whom adults approvingly called 'young man' from an early age.

But there is nothing priggish about him: he has always taken pleasure in getting things right, doing them properly. And while he was growing up in a South Australian country town immediately after World War I, he noticed a great deal.

We always called it the War, or the Great War. My cousin Bill, who had been too young to go, referred to it as the Big Dustup. Its shadow lay across my childhood.

In the middle of the main street, between the bank and Murphy's General Emporium — where you could buy almost anything you wanted — was the new, shiny war memorial, which was erected in 1924. It was a granite obelisk about five feet high, on which was carved the figure of a soldier standing to attention with his rifle. Fourteen black-etched names were on the pediment and when I was very small and learning to make sense of letters, I spelled them aloud to myself. HALL was easy, O'HAGEN slightly more difficult, and I couldn't understand why there were two HORLEYs. Had somebody made a mistake? Mum told me that the Horley twins, Bob and Jack, whose father ran the local stock and station agency, had been killed in the same week at Pozières.

I knew that the war memorial was a sad thing, bringing back memories to many people, but I couldn't feel solemn about it. It was too useful as a base. 'Race you to the soldier!' we used to say when we played chasings.

Like most of the other kids at school, I paid a penny a week to join the League of Nations. 'You're helping make sure that the war doesn't happen again,' said Miss O'Connor, my third class teacher. This seemed the most important thing I could possibly do, but I was a little sorry. I had been born a year after the war ended, and I wouldn't have minded grabbing a rifle or bayonet and having a go at the enemies of the Empire myself.

Every year, 25 April was a quiet and solemn day in our town. I knew that Anzac Day was special, and turned out to watch the march that took place, rain or shine. The fathers of my friends at school marched, the men who had brought back swords, belts and postcards from the Middle East or England or France. Sometimes the kids brought these mementos to school. 'If my dad knows I've taken this, he'll wallop me!' said Dave Pearson, showing me some French francs and a couple of British pennies. Mr Short, the Methodist minister, who had been a padre during the war, marched in his captain's uniform. On ordinary days he wore a dark suit and dog collar and looked as though he was on serious business. On Anzac Day he looked serious, too, as he marched with a brave and swinging stride, but the buttons of his uniform jacket strained across his chest, the riding breeches he wore were a darker khaki than the jacket, and his Sam Browne belt was pitted. On Anzac Day, Mr Short looked uncomfortable and slightly foolish, as though he had been caught out wearing fancy dress.

One year, we had a new teacher who had come all the way from a small town in Western Australia. He was a thin, terribly shy man whose voice hardly rose above a whisper and who couldn't make us keep quiet in class. We used to give him hell. But on Anzac Day he led the procession. Pinned to his dark blue and shiny suit jacket was a reddish-purple ribbon. We gasped. 'Gosh! he's a VC!' After that we were very polite and respectful to him. We asked him what he had done to get the VC, but he would never tell us.

There were returned soldiers around town who showed me what war could mean for some men. On my way to school in the mornings, I had to walk past the Spencers' house. Dave Spencer, who had been shot in the head at Villers-Bretonneux, sat hunched on the verandah all day, wrapped in a grey blanket, an old man of thirty who stared at nothing. I used to smile and wave at Dave Spencer, who frightened me, because I told myself that if I was nice to Dave, none of the others would attack me. Especially not Bill Summerville who, we thought, had strangled forty Germans with his bare hands.

Bill was mad. Every afternoon at four o'clock he marched up and down the main street, from the fire station to the war memorial and back, wearing a disgusting khaki Army coat and a pair of tattered trousers and holding his left arm stiffly at waist level as though he had a rifle sloping over his shoulder. He moved his right arm back and forth, back and forth, as though he were marking time, and he growled to himself, without words. Adults smiled pityingly as he marched past them, and sometimes kids followed him, snickering and calling out, 'Mad Bill!' But I did not. I was terrified of him. When I was very small I used to imagine him marching up to our house one night, bursting open the door and strangling me.

I think what frightened me most about Bill Summerville was his eyes. When I went to a museum in Adelaide, I had seen a photograph of a group of soldiers clustered around a dressing station behind the lines in France. One had been looking straight at the camera. His eyes were white and dead and there was no expression in them, no life. Bill Summerville's eyes were exactly the same.

Then there was Lift-Ya-Feet, a local drunk who stepped high all the time, as though he was clearing landmines or wire. If he went past the school at lunchtime or recess, we were lined up at the fence, ready for him. 'Here he comes, ole Lift-Ya-Feet!' we chanted. We heard that the poor man eventually went to the police station to complain to the sergeant. Old Lift-Ya-Feet was a bit of a bore, and he went on and on about how the nickname showed no respect for a man who had almost died for his country, and how the police should do something. Finally, the sergeant, who was getting irritated, managed to get rid of him. As he showed him to the door, old Lift-Ya-Feet tripped over the mat. Without thinking, the sergeant snapped. 'Look, why the devil don't you lift your feet?'

Another former soldier lived in a tent just out of town; I never knew his name. He was camped by a stock gate next to the road that crossed a local property, and whenever anybody went past he would spring out and open the gate. He wore an Army greatcoat at all times of the year, always looked itchy and stank like a stable. Whenever Dad saw him, he always gave him six-pence, which was accepted with a nod, no words. 'Poor devil,' said Dad. That man would have been about Dad's own age.

Dad himself had never gone to the war: something I learned when I was very young, though I don't think he told me. He enlisted in the AIF at the age of eighteen, in 1914, but his parents hauled him out because they said he was below the age of consent, twenty-one. Every year he tried, only to have his parents refuse permission, and finally he made it. He was on the wharf, ready to embark, but as he waited, the news came through that the Armistice had been signed. I know that not going was a source of shame to him, and he never mentioned it. In a way, that was typical of

Dad's pattern: he was always about to achieve great things, do what he had always wished to do, but he never made it. When I was seven, there was a lot of talk that we were about to sell up and go to live in Adelaide. I was excited about that, but something went wrong at the last minute. He wanted to run his own business, but could only become the local agent for Ford. Mum often said, 'Just Dad's luck,' in a joking tone, and for years I never knew how badly he had disappointed her.

So, when the other boys brought badges or money or photographs of Egypt to school, I had nothing to show. 'What have *you* got?' asked George Benson, whose father's AIF badge I had dutifully admired. I shrugged. 'Couldn't be bothered bringing anything,' I said in what I hoped was a bored voice. 'My dad doesn't *need* to show off. He's got a lotta stuff at home he doesn't show anybody.' Boasting about one's father's achievements, I implied, was in poor taste. Fortunately, George, who wasn't too bright, let the subject drop, and I was safe.

When I was ten, there was a tea and cakes afternoon at the local RSL hall. We were all looking forward to it; 'FOR CHILDREN ONLY' the notice in the paper had said. With no grown-ups, we could eat as many cream buns as we liked!

We all had to line up in twos, outside the hall, about thirty children, our faces washed and ears clean. I was paired with George Benson, and we pushed and shoved our way towards the door with the other kids. Standing behind a desk at the entrance was Miss Mortimer, the local librarian, who was asking every child something before allowing them inside. She didn't seem to be demanding money; the party was free.

Then, to my horror, I heard her say: 'Is your father a returned soldier?'

I went cold. The party was only for the children of ex-servicemen. Nobody had told me. What would I say? How could I disgrace Dad? What would George Benson do to me?

Our turn. George and I stepped up to Miss Mortimer. She smiled at us sweetly and asked the fatal question. 'Yes,' said George casually...and 'YES!' I almost yelled.

I didn't enjoy the cakes much, even the ones with pink icing. I hadn't let Dad down, but I had told my very first lie.

$\mathscr{I}$ *was taught to mind my own business*

Ruth Mottram runs her fingers ruefully through her flossy hair. 'It was the bane of my life when I was a kid,' she says. 'Wouldn't stay tidy. I was never allowed to grow it long because it never did what it was supposed to, so I always had it in a very short curly bob, like I have now.' Her mother and grandmother, she said, had long, straight, shiny hair which they always wore in a bun. 'It always needed about one hairpin to stay in place and never fell down,' she says. 'My hair was fine and flyaway like my father's. It was the only thing I inherited from him, and it was bad!'

I was born in Melbourne in 1916, so I don't remember the war at all. My younger sister was born at eleven minutes past eleven on 11 November 1918: Grandma used to say that the two minutes' silence on Armistice Day every year was in memory of her!

My sister was christened Margaret after Mum's sister, who died shortly after my sister was born. Once I asked Grandma what Auntie Margaret had died of. 'A broken heart,' snapped Grandma, and I knew I wasn't to ask any more questions. Mum told me years later that Margaret's fiance had been killed at Passchendaele and Margaret was never the same again. She died in the flu epidemic when I was three. Auntie Margaret had been 'the pretty one', Mum said, with dark, curly hair and brown eyes and a dazzling smile. 'She was the favourite,' Mum said. But Grandma wouldn't have her picture in the house. When my aunt died, before my sister was a year old, Grandma said to Mum, 'Please change the baby's name.' She couldn't bear to hear the name Margaret, Mum said. So my sister became known as Kath, and has remained Kath ever since.

Kath and I never really got to know each other until we were teenagers. We weren't brought up together because Mum and Dad separated when I was only four, and they eventually divorced.

I was taught to mind my own business

I went to live with Grandma and Grandpa in their big, dark house at Malvern; Kath went to Grandma's sister, Great-aunt Wilma, at Beaumaris. We met at Christmases and birthdays, but didn't have a lot to say to each other because we went to different schools and had different friends and interests. I always found Kath a bit silly when she was little; she giggled all the time and loved playing jokes like asking me about my stamp collection and then, when I showed it to her, saying: 'Well, there's another stamp for you!' stamping on my foot and running away. I cut out pictures and enjoyed colouring in and doing complicated jigsaw puzzles; Kath was bored if she had to sit still for more than three minutes at a time. 'Come and play chasings!' she'd say.

Grandma didn't altogether approve of Kath; she thought, as I did, that she wasn't serious enough. Great-aunt Wilma, who had never married, was a little, fluffy woman who wore fashionable clothes and who didn't seem to have the remotest idea about managing Kath; she let her do more or less what she liked. Grandma and her sister were chalk and cheese, like Kath and me. Grandma, only eighteen months the elder, looked at least ten years older than Great-aunt Wilma. She wore brown skirts and long woollen jumpers and lisle stockings, and at home you hardly ever saw her without her apron. Her hair was parted in the middle and secured by bobby pins on either side, with a bun at the back. Great-aunt Wilma, on the other hand, had probably never donned an apron in her life: her dresses were almost knee-length, she wore sheer stockings and high-heeled shoes, and was talking about having her curly hair shingled. 'That's all right, if you want to look like mutton dressed up as lamb,' sniffed Grandma.

Kath and I didn't live with Mum because she worked as a live-in housekeeper and couldn't take us. She came to visit me on Wednesdays after school, her afternoon off, unless she was having a quarrel with Grandma about my upbringing. 'How *dare* you tell my child there's no Santa Claus!' I overheard her say hotly when I was five. Grandma explained reasonably, 'I want her to know about what's real and what isn't...you can't expect her to believe in Father Christmas all her life.'

'And I suppose you've told her there aren't any fairies, either?' said Mum.

'Of course.'

'But,' said Mum, 'she's so little.'

'Never too early,' said Grandma.

I couldn't understand why Mum was making such a fuss. Grandma had told me about Santa Claus the first Christmas I was with her, and I accepted that; I thought the man who dressed up in a cotton wool beard and red coat and trousers at Myer's every year was foolish. I could never understand why grown-ups had to dress up.

When she came to visit, Mum always took me out somewhere, to have a milkshake or an ice-cream. We caught a tram into Collins Street and went to the same little coffee shop, with wooden booths and lace doilies. Mum got me a chocolate nut sundae in a tall glass; she always had tea. I loved the chocolate and the ice-cream, even though I knew they were bad for my teeth. Mum, who was blonde like Great-aunt Wilma, and had red cheeks and blue eyes, laughed a lot at nothing. 'You don't mind if I smoke?' she always asked me politely; when I said 'no', she brought a long black holder out of her bag, fitted a Capstan into it and lit up, inhaling as if she was eating the smoke. When she had finished, she said, 'Don't tell your grandmother,' which always made me feel bad, because I didn't like to have secrets from Grandma.

Mum and I didn't have very much to say to each other. 'Are you enjoying school?' she asked.

'Yes, thank you,' I said; Grandma and Grandpa had sent me to a good school and I was very proud of wearing the uniform.

'What are you studying?' I tried to tell her, but it sounded very dull, and I knew she was bored before I had completed my second sentence.

When we had finished our tea and nut sundae, Mum paid the bill and we went back to Malvern in the tram.

'Thank you, Mum,' I said, always. 'That was very nice.'

Wednesday afternoons were like this, more or less, for years.

Mum didn't talk to me about Dad at all, and I never had the courage to ask her about him. I don't even know what he looked like; there were no photographs. Somehow, though, I learned that he had been shot in the head during the war and had a plate in it (What sort of plate? China?), and that had made him peculiar, so he drank too much. Occasionally I heard Grandpa say 'drunkard' and 'won't ever change', so I knew that Dad was still alive and around, somewhere. But I never saw him. I know he must have come to see Mum and Grandma to discuss divorce; Mum told me years later that she saw him then for the first time in many years, but she wouldn't tell me what he looked like. Whether he paid maintenance to Mum, or helped Grandma support me, I do not know.

I felt odd not having a father and not knowing what had become of him, but I knew better than to ask Mum or Grandma or Grandpa about him. I was taught to mind my own business.

Nobody spoke to me about the war, either. I knew that war was a dreadful thing; it had made my aunt die of a broken heart and turned my father into somebody who wasn't mentioned.

Strange men came knocking at the door sometimes. They were usually dirty and unshaven and smelly. They often carried little trays slung round their necks by a leather strap. 'I'm a returned soldier. Would you like to buy some matches, dear? Need any shoelaces?' I always said 'No, thank you' and shut the door quickly. If Grandma was in the house, as she usually was, I never went to the front door when these men knocked. I was frightened of them, and I knew they were not all right because Grandma had a special note in her voice for them, letting them know that they were not quite as good as we were. Very occasionally she let one dig the garden or chop wood for the copper. If I came home from school and saw a man in dirty clothes pulling up weeds, I always bolted past him, too scared to reply to his, 'Afternoon, young lady.'

Not far from us was a vacant block which suddenly started to sprout potatoes, beans and carrots. It had been bought by a Mr Dowd under the soldier settlement scheme. 'He's trying to grow vegies to support his family, and maybe sell some too, but I don't think he's making a go of it,' Mrs Moulds at the corner shop told Grandma when she went to buy some flour. For some reason, I was terrified of Mr Dowd, and never went past his block if I could avoid it. Once I saw Mr Dowd lurching up the street. He passed me and I caught a dreadful smell, sour and sweet at the same time. I knew that he had been drinking, having come from the pub near the station. Mr Dowd obviously had 'no moral fibre', as Grandpa was fond of saying about people who drank.

I knew that the war was bound up in men's drinking, somehow. But it seemed to me that if you had no moral fibre in the first place, the war brought this out and you were forced to drink. This meant war was a dreadful evil. But people who *did* have moral fibre managed very well and became heroes through the war. As Grandpa said, you only had to look at General Monash: he had moral fibre and was a hero, even though he was Jewish.

Life at Grandma's was very settled and peaceful. I had my own room, my own dolls, and was very well cared for and protected. I told Grandma and Grandpa everything: like the time that Mr Hill, our teacher, accused me of talking to the girl who shared the desk with me — I was innocent — and whacked me around the legs. Grandpa went to see the headmaster, and the girl and I were made slate monitors. That was a great honour, because it meant making sure that everybody in the class had a duster for her slate. Everybody's slate had a hole in the corner, through which was threaded a piece of string with a slate pencil on the end. These slate pencils were about six inches long and a quarter of an inch thick; everybody had a stack of them, because they were very cheap and broke easily. You rubbed out what you had written with a rag or a duster: my job was to hand these out. It was a very responsible job, but it wasn't pleasant because the slate rags smelled dreadful when you opened the tins they were kept in.

Grandpa and Grandma were very proud of me the day I came home and told them that I was using pen and ink, with real nibs and ink in inkwells. And later, when I learned how to multiply and divide fractions, work out simple and compound interest, convert chains to acres, or calculate tax at the rate of a shilling in the pound. I came top of the class in English because I was the only one who could fill in the missing words in sentences such as 'as...as a beaver' and 'as...as a lark'.

Grandpa and Grandma always encouraged me to do well at school, and I told them only about my successes, never about my failures, because I didn't want to disappoint them. I wanted to let them know that I was bright and would 'get on': I wouldn't have to work as a live-in housekeeper, like Mum. I knew that Mum had disappointed Grandma and Grandpa, and I was determined not to do the same.

Grandpa, who was tall and thin and smiled a great deal, usually wore a starched collar with his shirt, except on weekends when he was doing the garden. He had a steady job as a piano tuner at Allans in town, earning over six pounds a week: very good money. He could get sheet music cheap, so I was the first person in my class to learn the words of 'Horsie Keep Your Tail Up' and 'Yes, We Have No Bananas'.

One afternoon, when I was nine, Grandpa came home followed by two men who were carrying a wooden cabinet the size of a small modern refrigerator. It had an elaborate criss-cross pattern on the front and seemed to weigh a ton. 'Over here,' said Grandma, directing them to the corner of the lounge room. Our first real gramophone! It had a turntable and a large, heavy arm and you fitted a needle at the end of the arm and turned the handle to make the turntable revolve. I soon became quite expert at this and never used the needles more than once. We kept the needles in an old Shinoleum tin. Soon we gathered a huge collection of 78s in paper sleeves, and Grandpa and I listened to Peter Dawson singing 'Boots,' or Harry Lauder (whom my grandfather thought was hilarious), Gladys Moncrieff or Galli-Curci singing 'Meditation' from *Thais* or 'Softly Awakes my Heart' from *Samson and Delilah*.

That wasn't the only music in the house. Sometimes Grandpa and Grandma would invite friends for supper on Saturday nights, and they would gather for a singsong around the piano...'Roll Out the Barrel', 'Tarara Boomdeay', even some of the sad songs from the war.

Grandma and Grandpa didn't have a particularly large social circle: some of their friends were colleagues of Grandpa's at Allans, and others were women with whom Grandma played euchre on Wednesdays. But still we saw or heard a number of people during the course of a normal day.

First was the iceman, who came very early in the morning. I never heard him because he delivered his ice while I was still asleep. Grandma left the front door unlocked and money on the table for him; he left change if necessary. A block of ice was always safely in its compartment at the top of the ice chest when we came down for breakfast.

Not long after the iceman came the milkman, whom I sometimes heard as he slid a full billy of milk into the hatch off the kitchen. Then there was the greengrocer, who delivered vegetables two or three times a week. He had a small market garden near us and delivered carrots, potatoes and pumpkin to all the women in the neighbourhood. He was a thin, stringy Chinaman who drove a horse and cart. I wondered whether he would say, 'Ching chong Chinaman velly velly good,' the way we did in games at school, but he never spoke. Grandpa called him Ah Fat because he was so skinny, which I thought was a great joke. Though she didn't generally like foreigners, Grandma tolerated Ah Fat. 'He may not speak English, but he doesn't try to cheat you,' she said.

I liked going with Grandma to the grocer's shop to buy flour from the big barrels and sugar which was scooped out of a deep vat; it never seemed to crust on the top, like our sugar in the bowl at home. The shop also sold treacle, stove polish, knife powder, oatmeal and kerosene, which I had to pump from the large tin in which we bought it into the lamps in the living room. I liked the shelf with all the cleaning products on it: Bon Ami with the chicken on the tin and the motto 'it hasn't scratched yet', and Old Dutch Cleanser, which had a scuttling woman with no face on the label. The grocer also sold cod liver oil and castor oil — which I loathed, but dutifully took every morning to keep me regular — Heenzo for coughs and colds, Dr Morse's Indian Root Pills and Woods' Peppermint Compound.

I remember the first time I tasted some new black stuff Grandma had bought for breakfast. It was called Vegemite and was supposed to be good for you because the label said it contained yeast and vegetable extract. Grandma said it was too salty, but Grandpa and I adored it, preferring it to the Gentleman's Relish that Grandpa had always used. Sometimes Grandma let me make the toast to spread it on; her new gas stove had a grilling plate, which was a great novelty.

Grandma always did the housework, though I was sometimes

allowed to help her dust the ornaments and the holland blinds. She had the first vacuum cleaner I ever saw, a roaring monster that was twice as good as her carpet-sweeper. But Grandma had help. On Mondays, Mrs Pollock came to help her do the washing, and stayed all day. One of my favourite occupations was going down the backyard to the washhouse, a small wooden building adjoining the toilet, and helping her boil and wring and rinse all the clothes in the copper. The place always smelled of clean sheets, hot water, steam and Reckitt's Blue when Mrs Pollock was there. I wasn't allowed to do the heavy work — moving the sheets and towels and other heavy things around in the copper with the stick or adding the water that Mrs Pollock boiled in the huge kettle on the kitchen stove — because 'little girls can get themselves burned', Mrs Pollock said. My particular job was to shave up the big yellow block of Sunlight soap into small slivers to go into the copper.

Mrs Pollock also did the ironing, if she had time after the week's wash, and I used to watch her. Mrs Pollock had arms like a wharfie, and her figure fascinated me. Her bust was only slightly more prominent than her huge stomach, and she wore pastel-coloured jumpers with the underarms dragging and skirts done up with safety pins. She was a very delicate ironer. She used two flatirons, which she heated in turn on the kitchen stove, running them carefully over the clothes on the wooden ironing board. My job was to sprinkle the clothes with water before she ironed them, using an old tomato sauce bottle with holes punched in the cap.

As I helped her, Mrs Pollock confided her troubles to me. They all concerned her daughter, Thelma, who was a worry. She was only twenty and had a good job as a secretary: not exciting work, but a steady wage. But Thelma never saved a thing. All she wanted to do was go out drinking and dancing the turkey trot or the gypsy tap at the Palais de Danse in St Kilda. 'What's she going to put in her glory box?' demanded Mrs Pollock. 'She's almost twenty-one; high time she thought of getting married.'

Thelma fascinated me. She seemed to lead such a wicked, sophisticated life. Grandma said she was 'a fast flibbertigibbet'. All the same I was curious to meet her.

One afternoon I opened the door to the most elegant women I had ever seen in my life. Her dark hair was cut nearly as short as Grandpa's, fluffed out at the back and sides and cropped fiercely at the neck. Her dress reached only to her knees, she was flat from shoulder to hip, and wore high-heeled shoes with straps. Her lips were red, her eyes rimmed with black stuff like that worn by Theda Bara in the films, and her nails were ruby talons. It was Thelma! At last!

'Hello, chickie. Is my mother in?' she asked. Her jaws moved in a strange, mumbling rhythm, and I realised that she was chewing gum. I gaped at her for a second or two; she must have thought I was an idiot. So that's what a fast flibbertigibbet looked like! I was thrilled.

I saw Thelma quite often after that — at the pictures. Grandpa and Grandma used to give me a shilling a week to go. Thelma was always in the back stalls, even at the matinees, usually draped around the neck of a young man of the sort Grandpa called a lounge lizard.

Going to the pictures became my great passion in life. There were many cinemas to choose from: the Bijou, the Regal, the State, the Rex, the Imperial, the Palais, the Criterion. Sometimes the mighty Wurlitzer was playing when I came in. Picture palaces were just that, palaces; my favourite, the Imperial, had elaborate columns on both sides of the stage, crowned by the gilded statues of women wearing Greek costumes, holding red beacons lit with electric light. The ceiling was a blue-painted dome with little electric lights dotted all over it to represent stars. (When I was a teenager a friend of mine who worked as an usherette told me that backstage was a notice for the last usherette to go home after the show: 'Please switch off the sky before leaving.')

All the kids at school adored the pictures. We used to gather at the 'picture tree' at school and act out the parts of the films we'd seen on the weekends. The picture tree was a spindly gum in the playground with one low branch sticking out at right angles to the trunk, a branch that came in very handy if we'd seen a Douglas Fairbanks film because the boys would swing from it in the correct swashbuckling manner. We always remembered everything we had seen; somebody was chosen to do the subtitles, and woe betide that boy or girl if they got them wrong! The rest of us were very quick to correct the offender.

My ambition was to see *Ben Hur*, the great silent movie. I'd read all about it, and knew that a man had driven a chariot from Melbourne to Sydney to promote the film. I pleaded with Grandma to go; everybody else was going, I argued, and it was religious. But Grandma said no. 'You'll only get upset at the chariot race,' she said. This was one of the few times when I was furious with Grandma; I was disgusted. 'Read the book,' she said. As there was no way I would be allowed to see the film, I consented with a very bad grace. I spent ages ploughing through Lew Wallace's book from the local library, but found it pretty heavy going. I would much rather have seen the movie.

On the other hand, I had no ambition to see Rudolph Valentino in *The Sheik*. All that eye-rolling didn't appeal to me; I thought it was soppy. Mrs Pollock told me, however, that Thelma had been to see it five times and was going back again. She was desperately in love with Rudi. Because she spent so much on adoring him, it seemed obvious that Thelma's glory box was in even greater danger than usual.

But I loved *Uncle Tom's Cabin*. Like many of the other silent films, it was preceded by a stage show. Before the screen was lowered for the film, out trooped a whole lot of gaily dressed actors with boot polish on their faces, and a girl wearing wonderful golden ringlets, a long white dress and a blue sash. She was Little Eva, and the group busily set about re-enacting her death. When Little Eva fell back on the bed and all the sorrowing party said, 'She am dead! Lordy, she am gone tuh heaven!' I felt tears running down my face. Edna, the school friend I was with, hissed, 'Put your hanky in your mouth.' Edna had never been known to cry at anything. I obeyed her quickly, but it was no use. I gave a most heart-rending sob, and almost swallowed the handkerchief.

When I saw my first film with sound, I was amazed. Speech sounded tinny and slow, not like normal words at all. The film was *The Jazz Singer* with Al Jolson: did Americans really talk like that? For some reason I had thought they sounded posh, like the British, only with strange words like 'gee' and 'honey' and 'golly'. But everybody spoke so badly, leaving the final 'g's off words — worse than some of the kids at school. Why? Grandma knew, 'They're all gangsters,' she said. 'They haven't been properly brought up.'

The British were much better. I remember going to see *Rookery Nook* starring Ralph Lynn and Tom Walls and laughing at it very much. Unfortunately, I was taken by Miss Carrington, my high school teacher, who irritated me intensely because she always got a joke about two seconds after everybody else had finished laughing. In the middle of a quiet passage, the whole theatre would hear a hearty 'Ha ha ha!' from her.

But change was coming to Malvern. The paddock where Mr Dowd the soldier-settler had tried to grow vegetables was suddenly a mulberry-brick home; more cars were appearing in the street and a garage sprang up on our corner. I suppose that was progress. For me, life changed when Mum suddenly remarried: a pleasant widower called Fred Tolhurst, who worked in the Patents Office in town. I was sixteen and getting difficult to manage for Grandpa and Grandma; Kath and I left our homes and moved in with Mum and her new husband. It worked quite well for a while, and I left school and got a job as a secretary in an accountant's office. I lost the job later, in the Depression, but it was wonderful while I had it.

❧ You had to be fast and tough to survive in our family

Daniel Herbert still eats faster than most people. 'When you're a member of a large family, you have to eat quickly or you don't get seconds,' he says in slightly shamefaced justification. His elbows stick out as he eats his peas with the fork turned the wrong way. 'But I've always eaten everything on my plate,' he says.

Here we all are together, one of the few family photos I have. I was eleven when it was taken, on Mum and Dad's fourteenth wedding anniversary. We never looked as clean and tidy as this normally! See how well grouped we are, and how we go down in steps? That's Mum and Dad on the left, of course; Dad has his best brown preaching suit on, and his gold watch-chain. Mum looks severe with her hair in a bun like that, but she wasn't really. In fact, Mum was a saint. Now, here we are in order. That's Andrew, he looks a bit starchy, very much the eldest son. The boy who looks like a square tower with a frown is me. I'm almost as tall as Dad, always could give Andrew an inch or two. The girls are Sarah and Eleanor. They both had white-blonde hair, from Mum's family, the Holman Beaumonts. Sarah and Eleanor had a life we boys knew almost nothing about; they didn't have much to do with Andrew and me. They helped Mum in the kitchen, of course, as girls do. The long-jawed, serious one is Harry. He was the most handsome of us; had a good profile, not with the Herbert snout the rest of us have! Harry was always like Kipling's cat who walked by himself. Never said much. The two little boys are Edward and Robin. Edward was all right, but Robin was a bit of a whinger. He seemed to spend his life shouting, 'Wait for me!'

The little girl sitting cross-legged at the front is Lucy. She looks like that because she's Mongoloid. They call it Down's syndrome now. Lucy was born when I was seven. She couldn't ever do much, not even talk, and she never went to school, let alone read or write. The rest of us didn't play with her; she was

You had to be fast and tough to survive in our family

sort of around the place while we were growing up. Lucy was Mum's special pet. I think Mum believed she was a judgement from God for her own wickedness. Lucy always took part in family worship, of course, and she came with us to church on Saturdays.

I say on Saturdays because we were a Seventh Day Adventist family. Dad, actually, was one of the great men of the church; he'd brought hundreds of people into the faith. You should have heard him preaching! He was really something, standing up in a pulpit or in tent meetings calling on God to smite the ungodly and reward the faithful! Real fire and brimstone. I think Dad would have made a great actor; he knew exactly when to lower his voice and plead to sinners to repent and when to sound like the Last Trump on the Day of Judgement.

We were a godly household. If we did anything naughty, Dad would thump us (except the girls) but Mum would pray over us, which was *much* worse! We never referred to ourselves as Adventists or Seventh Day Adventists except to outsiders; our religion was 'the truth' to us, and people who were converted were 'brought into the truth'. We regarded ourselves as normal people within a special gathering — a small whirlpool in a big dam. We believed that every word in the Bible was literally true, and followed its teachings absolutely. The Bible said not to eat meat, so we were vegetarians; we called that sort of eating 'health reform'. For many years it was considered very odd not to eat any meat at all. Nowadays, of course, a lot of people are vegetarians. We were fashionable and doing the right things before anybody else!

From sunset on Friday until sunset on Saturday was the Sabbath, the Lord's Day, during which we prayed, went to Sabbath school or Bible class, and read devotional texts. We didn't do any work that wasn't necessary; we would feed the fowls but not gather the eggs, do the milking but not separate the milk. As we lived on a small farm on the north-west outskirts of Sydney (which was all farms, market gardens and bush then) there was plenty of work we didn't do on the Sabbath!

When I started showing promise as a front-row forward at high school, the Sabbath made my life a bit difficult: all our matches with other schools took place on Saturdays. But that was too bad. God had to come first.

We weren't allowed to dance; dancing could inflame sinful passions. But music was all right, provided it was consecrated to the Lord. Consequently, we played and sang a great deal: we were a pretty musical family. Sarah could play anything on the piano just by sight reading, she still can, and Eleanor had a very sweet soprano voice. Andrew played the violin and I was a dab hand on the trombone. We four eldest got together with friends and formed a musical group called the Hebron Club, and gave concerts every now and again. We had a whale of a time!

On the whole, we were self-sufficient. We grew all our own food ourselves, except for the Sanitarium health foods which we got in bulk wholesale. We kept bees, baked our own bread and cakes, grew tomatoes, peas, beans, lettuce, cabbage, corn, potatoes and almost any fruit you care to mention: Jonathan apples, Watts early peaches, Coxes at Christmas, Alberta peaches in February, nectarines, apricots, Granny Smiths.

We preserved plums, apricots, peaches and nectarines. Men's work, usually done by Andrew and me, was to pick the peaches and bring them in. Women's work (Sarah's and Eleanor's) was to peel, cut and stone them and put them into kerosene tins to be cooked.

Both sides reserved the right to criticise what the other did. Sarah and Eleanor often condemned the standard of the fruit we had chosen; we would come in and say to them, 'The tin's only half full,' and prove we were right by shaking it. Andrew and I had to solder the tin down before the fruit was cooked, and we wouldn't do that if the syrup for the fruit hadn't been made to our satisfaction.

It was a man's job to cut wood for the fuel stove, as well as wood for the fires. The stove wood was cut into short bits, the firewood in longer pieces. The stove had to be kept going all day for cooking and baking (women's work, of course). It had cast-iron rings in it, which were removed or not, depending on the size of the saucepans. For the biggest saucepan — used for making porridge in the morning, for instance — all the rings were taken out and the pan sat over the fire.

We were a great family for 'turns'. Everything was done according to a sort of roster. For instance, on Friday night, which was bath night, we boys took it in turns to cut the wood for the chip heater, light the fire and turn the water on. The girls went first, then the boys in turn, all taking care to keep the fire going so the water didn't go cold. Then Mum had her bath, followed by Dad. Any female guests we had were first of all, and then any male guests, before we all had our turn.

The problem with the chip heater was that, if you didn't control the flow of water, it could go red-hot; we had to force air through the bottom and then it choofed like a train. On Sunday mornings, we took it in turns to empty the ashes at the bottom of the chip heater.

For lighting we used kerosene lamps, which had to be turned

down fairly low for fear of cracking the glass. For outside, we used a hurricane lamp. Trimming the wicks and adjusting the light were women's work. When we got electricity, we thought that was the greatest thing that ever was!

We all had our jobs to do. Andrew kept fowls, I had cows, kept down the back called 'the paddock', which I suppose was forty to fifty acres. My daily routine was this. At a quarter to six, summer and winter, I got up to milk the cows, having cut the chaff the night before. (Though I ended up with forty cows, only ten were being milked at any one time.) Then I mixed the chaff with bran, water and lucerne, put it all in a trough, baled up the cows and milked them. They took about ten minutes each. We had an Alfa-Laval separator for the milk; I fed the skim milk to the calves and kept the rest. The calves I always found a pain in the neck. When they're suckling their mothers, they butt the udder impatiently to get at the milk, to shake it loose. If you give a calf a bucket full of skim milk and it decides to do that, the whole lot goes head over tip. It is no fun on cold, dark winter mornings trying to find a bucket and skidding on milk in wet grass.

I kept the whole milk for the house and the cream for the butter the girls made (butter was women's work). If there was more milk than we needed, I put it aside to be sold. Then I scalded the separator, which the women of the house washed. All that took me until about half past seven, when I had a wash and dressed for school. (None of the men wore underpants in our house, only trousers, and we had two shirts a week.) Breakfast was one of those bran breakfast cereals (which I've always liked), stewed peaches and cream, which I supplied, and two eggs, not one. Ever since I was a child I was convinced that real men ate two eggs.

Mum made the bran we ate for breakfast; Dad used to go to a flour mill in the city and buy three bushels of wholemeal flour at a time. We had wholemeal bread sandwiches to take to school. I was a bit ashamed of this because, unlike the other kids, we never had white bread. Nobody would ever swap their sandwiches with ours. Well, I thought, if they wanted to eat white muck, that was their lookout. (I have to confess that the most popular person in the class was Jeannie Marlow, who always had white bread sandwiches filled with cold mashed potato.)

After breakfast Andrew and I had to go to school. We usually went by bike, about seven miles it was. In all the years we went to school, I cannot remember that we ever had a tail wind!

We returned from school about four o'clock and before I did anything else I had to cut the hay or chaff for the cows. We also grew sacchaline, cattle fodder rich in sugar. It was about six feet high when it was growing, with seed tassels like millet. I always cut enough for the night and morning feeds, using a chaffcutter.

In the summer, when it was lighter for longer, I might dig the garden — or else Uncle Dave and I ploughed around the fruit trees when we had to. People occasionally turned up to have their cows serviced by Belshazzar, my bull. I was terribly proud of Belshazzar. He was really fierce. None of that red rag nonsense; Belshazzar would charge at everything that moved — except me, for some reason. I remember once a smart-alec colleague of Dad's came to dinner and boasted that he could subdue any animal, didn't matter what. 'Let's see you with Belshazzar,' I said, and led the way out to the paddock. Belshazzar took one look at the man and charged him; the poor bloke ran for his life and only just got out of the paddock in time. Well, laugh! Mum told me off about that. She said it wasn't right for a boy my age to laugh at a grown man.

I was also very proud of my Jersey heifer, Mandy. She was a house cow, who produced ten quarts a day, enough for scalded cream, milk and butter. When she calved and we left the calf to suckle her for three days, her milk was stringy stuff called beestings which the calf could not drink. We took the calf away and fed it with a finger dipped in milk that the calf sucked. Eventually we induced the calf to follow us to milk we had warmed; then, after about a fortnight, it drank milk by itself.

When we took the calf away on the third day, we put Mandy on a thirty-foot chain, then tethered her to the apricot tree with a collar and a leather strap. The calf was tethered in a corner where the mother could see it, and Mandy went berserk, the way all cows do. But she was more energetic than most; as long as the calf was in view, she carried on a treat. The local dairyman decided to show what a good fellow he was and grabbed her chain and cracked it like a stockwhip. He just made it up the apricot tree in time.

We had Mandy for six years and every time she calved it was the same performance. The number of times I had to scramble under the barbed-wire fence! Once my uncle menaced her on a horse; she reared up and attacked him and he had to punch her on the nose.

Eventually we sold her, and we warned the buyer about her. He led her away. After she had calved, we saw him again. 'How was she?' we asked. He just shrugged, 'Good. I just patted and milked her, even with the calf there.' We never believed him.

Mealtimes were chaos; sometimes fourteen of us sat down to table. I am afraid our table manners left a lot to be desired; they always do when you're in direct competition with so many other people for the food you want! But we always ate what was on our plates, whether we liked it or not. I still do, though I jib at chokoes, which I think are the most boring vegetable God ever made. (If we wanted to describe somebody as colourless, we used to say that he or she had the personality of a choko.)

As well as the ten of us, visitors often dropped in: Dad's fellow pastors and their families, for example. Then there would be great discussions on obscure points of Adventist doctrine. 'Brother Herbert, you don't know what you're talking about! There's no health in you!' Dad's colleagues would say as they shovelled in the peas and potatoes and nutmeat or rice casserole.

There were always at least two relatives staying with us. For most of my childhood, for instance, Uncle Dave was there. He really irritated me. 'Uncle Dave, would you please pass the bread?' I would say, but often Mum's delicious wholemeal bread would be gone before I managed to have some, because it was no use asking Uncle Dave anything. He was deaf.

Uncle Dave was a huge, sandy man with a habit of blinking slowly. Because he had had scarlet fever when he was a child, his hearing was permanently damaged. If anybody shouted at him, he got huffy: 'I can hear you; I'm not deaf!' Pride prevented Uncle Dave from getting a hearing aid, even when Andrew became a doctor and tried to persuade him to do so. He didn't like those newfangled things, and his wishes had to be treated with proper respect.

He was almost illiterate; when he was a child there had been no special schools for deaf children, and so reading and writing remained foreign to him all his life. He was brought up as a sort of family pet. I'm afraid I was a little embarrassed that here he was, a grown man and a relative, who couldn't read and write as well as young Edward. It was shameful! But you could always understand Uncle Dave. He spoke a kind of basic English: 'You bad boy, Danny, go get cows.' But he had other attributes. For instance, he was strong as a mallee bull. He had massive shoulders and arms, and it was wonderful to see him working around the fruit trees on our block across the road with two horses and a single-furrow plough. His furrows were always straight and even. One of my jobs was to hoe around the fruit trees with Uncle Dave and, though he seemed to move very slowly, he got through the work much faster and more thoroughly than I could.

Though I admired him for his strength and persistence, Uncle Dave often exasperated me — but not as much as he irritated Sarah. When she was embarking on young ladyhood at about the age of ten and said, 'Mum, I *wish* Uncle Dave wouldn't drink tea out of his saucer. He slurps!' Mum gave her one of the sorrowful looks she specialised in and told her — and us — that we had to be nice to Uncle Dave because he had had a sad and difficult life. She never went into details, but years later we learned that Uncle Dave had married and adopted a son. His wife left him (we never met her) and took the child with her, so he came to live with us for the rest of his life and never saw either of them again, as far as I know. I don't think that Sarah considered this gave him the right not to use a cup and saucer in the normal way, though!

The other relative whom we saw most was Auntie Vere. She was Dad's eldest sister. Dad's parents had died when he was very young, and Vere had been faced with the job of bringing up Dad and the other brothers and sisters, eight in all. Vere had married long before Dad grew up, but she and her husband didn't get along too well, and so she was often with us. There was tension in the kitchen when Vere came to stay. She knew how to do everything better than Mum did, or thought she knew, and Mum and Auntie Vere only tolerated each other, being polite and stiff-faced when they were working together in the kitchen. Auntie Vere was not attractive. She looked like the wowser spinster in a Norman Lindsay drawing: tall and angular with a long and disapproving nose, and she always wore black, even in the height of summer. We weren't particularly fashion-conscious in our house, but even then I realised that a long, black dress to the ankles, black stockings and black lace-up shoes were not what most women in Australia wore during the 1920s.

Auntie Vere had a thin, harsh voice and a habit of sniffing when anything offended her. When it was her turn to ask the blessing before meals, we knew we were in for at least ten minutes of exhortation to the Lord and that the soup would probably be cold at the end of it. She took great trouble to quote from the most obscure Old Testament texts, too: from books such as Habbakuk and Hosea. This was very much to Dad's taste; he loved a good argument, and the more arcane the better! The rest of us escaped as soon as possible. Andrew scandalised her one day when he crossly looked out of the window into the pouring rain and said, 'Heaven help the Irish on a day like this!' which was a family expression. Auntie Vere sniffed and said, 'Heaven will, my dear.' A real female Calvin.

The girls found her particularly difficult to put up with. She smelled. Not like somebody who didn't wash, because she was very fastidious about matters of personal cleanliness. No, Vere suffered badly from rheumatism, and used some liniment that smelled of formic acid, like crushed ants. Poor Sarah, Eleanor and Lucy had to share a room with her when she came to stay. They did not enjoy it.

On the other hand, she certainly regarded us as one of the

crosses she had to bear, particularly because of our 'animal spirits'. One morning at breakfast, Sarah was more than usually pert to Uncle Dave, who lost his temper and punched her on the arm. Without even looking at each other, Andrew and I rose as one: *nobody* was going to hit *our* sister, even a relative. We pulled Uncle Dave out of his chair and wrestled him to the floor. Well, it was quite a scene. There was Mum, frenziedly scolding us (Dad was away preaching in Cowra at the time), poor old Dave was grunting furiously and trying to shove me off his chest while he broke Andrew's grip on his arms, and poor Auntie Vere was calling upon God to bear witness to the wickedness of her nephews!

Dad's work as an evangelist meant running missions in many parts of Sydney, and in towns of New South Wales: Parramatta, Granville, Drummoyne, Bathurst, Cowra. As I've said, he could call forth fire and brimstone like nobody else I've ever heard. He became so popular that when he preached in the largest auditorium in Melbourne, hundreds and hundreds of people came. He was even written up in the *Bulletin*: 'Satan scurried out of the hall with his forked tail between his legs when Mr Herbert arrived.' Evangelism was good business for the church, because every family converted had to pay tithe (one-tenth of their income) every year; the descendants of some of those families are still doing so.

In the 1920s and 1930s, revival or tent meetings were very popular. Lots of religious groups ran missions, including of course the Salvation Army: hundreds of people came along to sing, pray and perhaps be converted. Some were looking for the truth; to others, of course, it was cheap entertainment, just as interesting as the pictures and better than the radio before radio really took off.

A fundamental belief of Adventism is that the world will shortly come to an end, and that this has been predicted in the Bible, most notably in the books of Daniel and Revelations. Dad's job was to show people that this was so and to urge them to repent before it was too late.

We all had our part to play in Dad's missions, particularly Andrew and me, as the two eldest sons. Very early on the morning before the mission took place, we distributed handbills and stickers all over the area, in as many different places as possible (telegraph poles were particularly good). They showed Atlas holding up the world but teetering on the edge of a cliff. The caption read: WILL CIVILISATION HOLD IT? HERBERT MISSION... with the date, the place and the time.

We were always looking for ways to make Dad's missions as vivid as possible, and one year Andrew and I hit on a little bobby-dazzler. We must have been about fourteen and twelve respectively at the time. Our idea was based on the Biblical description of the

idol with feet of clay in the Book of Daniel, revealed to Nebuchadnezzar in a dream. The idol's head was of fine gold, its breast and
arms of silver, its belly and thighs of brass, its legs of iron, its feet
part of iron and part of clay. God sent a stone that struck the idol
upon its feet, and broke it to pieces.

Andrew and I decided to make this statue. We bought two
six by three sheets of thin, not corrugated, iron. Using a magic
lantern, we projected a picture of the statue from a devotional text
so that it filled both sheets, which were standing on top of each
other; together they were about twelve feet high. We marked the
depth of the head, body, legs and feet on the sheet iron, and cut
the iron into four sections with tinsnips: one each for the head,
chest, loins and feet. We traced the sections in turn using the
lantern image. We got gold paint for the head, painted the back-
ground in dark blue, and drew the features in black. The chest
was done in silver paint, the loins we did in a mixture of black
and gold to represent bronze, and the legs were done in a com-
bination of Silvafros and black.

The feet of clay were a bit of a problem; brown paint didn't
go too well on sheet iron. But we consoled ourselves that they
were meant to look crook, which believe me, they did!

When we had finished, we had a colourful sheet-iron replica
of the picture in four sections, and we then cut it out carefully
with tinsnips and screwed the sections together with hinges so
that the whole folded flat. We made a hinged base for the statue,
and bored a hole in the top, near the head, through which we ran
a cord.

Dad delivered his sermon in front of about three hundred
people, and he was really getting stirred up. The image was folded
flat, concertinaed, beside him.

Dad said: 'And, lo, the head of the image was of gold — the
Empire of Babylon!' Standing at the side of the stage, Andrew and
I hauled on the stout cord over a pulley, and the head section rose
from the stage.

'The breast and arms were of silver!' Up came the next
section, silver painted; this represented the Persian empire that
conquered Babylon.

'His belly and thighs of brass'; we pulled the next section,
panting a bit by this time. This represented the Greek empire.

'His legs of iron, his feet part of iron and part of clay.' By the
time Andrew and I had hauled the fourth section, symbolising the
Roman Empire, into place, Dad was standing next to a twelve-
foot-high image, while Andrew and I, red-faced, were hanging
onto the cord and praying that the pulley, attached to the proscenium, wouldn't break.

Dad said, 'And, lo, thus were the four great empires of the world shown to Nebuchadnezzar!' His voice was loud and ringing, and he stepped aside, gesturing dramatically. 'These represent the four great empires of the world! But the Lord said that all these empires, and all worldly empires, will decay.'

This was our masterstroke: representing the stone that destroyed the idol. A fine wire with two pulleys ran from the top right-hand side of the statue to the wings, on to which we threaded a cushion.

'And a stone descended!' cried Dad thunderously. We let the cushion go; it whizzed down the wire on its way to the wings. When it came close to the statue, we let go the cord that held the statue erect. The statue collapsed with a mighty clatter, the cushion went into the wings. All that was left on the stage was Dad and a small heap of concertinaed metal.

'Thus all worldly empires collapse and fall!' roared Dad. He had to stop there; the audience rose to its feet and applauded fervently, and he couldn't be heard for at least two minutes.

When the clapping and shouting died down, Dad stepped forward and delivered the message: 'The Lord our God shall set up a kingdom which shall never be destroyed, and it shall stand forever!'

The statue was the hit of the mission, and we took it to many of Dad's meetings after that. He was very pleased with us both, and we were pretty proud of ourselves.

Because I was taller than Andrew and sounded commanding and authoritative, Dad decided I was destined to succeed him in the ministry. It was accepted, from the time I was very young, that 'Andrew will be a doctor and Daniel a minister'. I knew this was my lot, and smiled when people praised me for being a worthy successor, but the whole thing disturbed me.

See, from the time I was about ten, I didn't like being different from the other kids. I tried as hard as possible to do the same things they did; every week I'd secretly take some of the money I made by selling our surplus milk and go to the local newsagent to buy boys' weeklies, the *Gem* and the *Magnet*, and, later, the *Triumph* and the *Champion*. They spelled the great world outside to me, the world in which bold English schoolboys confronted the menace of the enemies of the Empire. They meant Greyfriars School, with Harry Wharton and Bob Cherry and Hurree Jamset Ram Singh from India, the black nabob who made the others laugh when he said things like, 'The joyfulness is terrific,' and midnight feasts and Billy Bunter, the fat, greedy boy. The magazines spelled England, the world of Sexton Blake and Nelson Lee, the cleverest detectives in the world, whose jobs were to discover criminals who stole diamonds from English lords and ladies.

I used to buy these things secretly because they were regarded as frivolous and wicked and I should have been reading improving literature and devotional texts. As minister's children, we had to set a standard of behaviour: we were the Herberts and therefore better than other people. Dad was very strong on this, his children all had to be brighter, stronger, more upright than anyone else. So, if they'd known that I crouched under the bedclothes every night with a torch, avidly consuming the adventures of British schoolboys and detectives, I would have had a sermon and possibly the strap from Dad, and a sorrowful prayer from Mum. The guilt I felt was considerable, and of course that added to the fun of reading!

But Dad did have his human moments. When I was about thirteen, Andrew and I built a crystal set. We bought a kit at the electrician's shop; it consisted of a bit of mica, the crystal (about one-third the size of a fingernail), a cat's whisker, which was a very fine piece of short wire, and wires. We built the set in a wooden cigar box (I can't remember where we found that, because nobody we knew smoked), and other bits of wire connected a set of headphones to the cigar box too. The crystal acted as a resonator. Andrew and I strung an aerial outside the verandah; it was about sixty feet of wire, which we fed into the room. The whole system was connected to the electricity supply.

Mum and Dad were a bit dubious about this, but they thought it was all right as long as we listened to the proper things. Dance music was out, of course, but we weren't interested in that anyway. We spent hours bent over the contraption with headphones on, arguing fiercely about whose turn it was to wear them. When you put the headphones on, you were cut off from the world, and there would be a lot of maddening humming and crackling as we moved the cat's whisker across the crystal or around it, trying to pick up a signal. It was very tedious, because as soon as you found a burst of music or a voice, you almost instantly lost the signal and you'd have to start again.

But we persevered for years, mainly for the sports results, especially the cricket. We listened to the ABC's Test series in the early 1930s, too. As soon as the rest of the boys were asleep, we would creep out of our beds, huddle next to the window, where the reception was better than anywhere else in the room, and listen to the thin voices coming in from Lord's, or from the ABC studios in Sydney, where the announcer would hit a rubber pad with a pencil to simulate the sound of bat hitting ball. It was riveting to hear the progress of the match, ball by ball, and utterly maddening when, in your excitement, you moved the cat's whisker too far and lost the signal again. But it was much better than reading the Test scores in the paper, because they were always a day or two out of date.

At about four one morning I got carried away. 'Stan McCabe is out! Oh, *no!*' I must have shouted more loudly than I thought because next thing Dad was at the door, striped pyjamas, rumpled hair, furious. 'What are you boys doing out of bed at this hour?' I was so shocked I could only stare at him but Andrew, who was faster with his tongue than I was, explained what we were doing. Listening to the cricket. I thought Dad was going to explode. He started to say what a waste of time it was, how we needed our sleep, how deceitful we were being, and so on. Then, when he had reduced us both to a state of red-faced shame and defiance, he turned to go.

'Er,' he said, and I was astonished to see that he appeared slightly embarrassed, 'what's the score, boys?'

Above all else I longed to be a pilot. The names of Parer and McIntosh, Goble, MacIntyre, Ross and Keith Smith and Harry Hawker were pure magic. But my hero was Kingsford Smith. I believed, and still do, that he was the greatest aviator the world has ever seen and I'll never forget how proud and excited I was the day he landed in Fiji after his non-stop flight from Honolulu in 1928. Imagine: in the air for thirty-five hours, climbing above the clouds to fix his position, with storms battering him from all sides — and doing all that in a tiny second-hand Fokker triplane with a body like a bootbox!

I read everything I could get my hands on about Smithy and Hinkler (who was pretty good, too, but not quite tops). I spent hours sitting on my camp bed in the glassed-in verandah I shared with my three brothers, surrounded by magazines and books about flying, and hoping Mum wouldn't notice I hadn't cut the chaff for the cows yet. Every time a plane went over the house, Andrew and I dropped whatever we were doing and ran like mad to the vegetable patch out the back where you got the best view, and looked up. 'It's a Tiger Moth!' 'It's an Avro!' We always had flaming rows about the names of planes, and I was right more often than Andrew was.

I had no idea how you went about becoming a pilot, and I couldn't think whom to ask. My future was apparently so well laid out that any suggestion that I might want to change it would have been greeted with anger and sorrow. Me, be a pilot? Nonsense! Andrew would have told me I was 'talking like a Yank'. That was the worst possible insult; it meant you were loud and boastful and big-noted yourself. Whenever anybody skited, we said, 'Oh yeah, and the Yanks won the war, too.' Everybody knew that we'd fought the Germans for years in the war and the Yanks waltzed in at the very end and took all the credit. Besides, Yanks were sneaky; you couldn't trust them. They murdered Les Darcy because he was too good a fighter for them, didn't they?

I thought that, if things grew too intolerable, I might flee the country, go to England to live. I was certain to be allowed to be a pilot there. But I was a bit suspicious of the English, too; I knew they had a weak, soft side to them. I had known all that from the time I was three, when I went with Dad and Andrew to see the Prince of Wales. Thousands of people lined the road, and Dad put me on his shoulder, which meant I had a wonderful view. Over the blur of grey felt hats I saw six glossy horses and their riders, wearing red and blue uniforms and white gloves. Any minute the Prince of Wales would sweep past on a huge, coal-black charger, snorting fire from its nostrils. I was firmly convinced that the Prince would be twenty feet tall and would wear a golden helmet just like the picture of Goliath in my Bible book.

Presently an open touring car glided past, carrying a very short man in a nondescript uniform, who was waving as if he didn't mean it. I thought he was probably an old man the kind Prince allowed to be in his procession. But everybody went mad and started waving handkerchiefs and Union Jacks. Dad said to me, 'Come on, son, wave! It's the Prince of Wales!'

That little pipsqueak was *royalty*! I had never been so disgusted in my life!

That convinced me that any Australian was worth two of an Englishman; I didn't really want to go to a country of such little men.

But it didn't solve my problem. I didn't like being different, I wanted to be able to go to the pictures and play football on Saturdays like everybody else did. Loyalty to the family (and fear of what God would do if I expressed these treacherous thoughts) kept me silent and dutiful for a long time. But when I was eighteen or nineteen and enrolled in the first year of a ministry training course at Avondale College, I couldn't stand the conflict any longer. So I left, and took my chances with everybody else in the Depression.

THE DEPRESSION

We did all right . . . we were privileged, I suppose

*W*e did all right . . . we were privileged, I suppose

In Margaret O'Connor you can still see traces of the country town larrikin, the 'wild girl'. She has the unruly, flyaway hair, mischievous eyes and button nose of someone who used to lead the other kids in her class on fruit-stealing expeditions or fights in the playground. 'I had a pretty strong right arm,' she says. 'I needed it, too.'

I grew up in a tiny railway town in northern New South Wales. Its name is Willow Tree, but we called it the Willa.

When I was a kid during the 1930s, there was no proper sealed road leading through town: the bitumen led only through the central street, and dwindled to dirt a few miles out on either side. When the road gangs started work during the worst of the Depression in the early 1930s, they spent a lot of time filling in potholes and smoothing over the dirt road. One particular pothole was done about once a week. They used to say it kept the road gangs in work for years!

There were quite a few sheep properties around the district, many of which used horses for hauling or work around the place. Cars weren't very common until after the war. Every winter, after the harvest, Fred Bates came around the area in a covered wagon to repair horse collars, winkers, anything that needed it.

All the horses had to be shod, of course. I loved going to the blacksmith's shop, especially if one of the draught horses was being 'done'. The blacksmith, Mr Schofield, was a wizened little man with the strongest arms I had ever seen. He had two sons who worked with him. 'Mind if I watch, Mr Schofield?' 'No, Margaret, but keep out of the way.' The place smelled of metal and sweat and horse, and I loved watching Mr Schofield take a red-hot shoe from the forge, put it on the anvil with pincers and hammer it carefully into shape. Mr Schofield explained that it cost about six shillings to have a hack shod, if the hot shoe were fitted to the hoof. But sometimes people bought cold shoes, shaped to fit the horse: 'Don't fit the hoof exactly, they don't,' said Mr Schofield crossly. 'Ruin a good horse that way.' Mr Schofield and his sons fixed wheels on cars and carts too.

By the end of the 1930s, the Schofields were open only three days a week. Not only had the Depression affected business badly, but there were many more cars in the Willa. 'Not the same,' said Mr Schofield. 'I suppose you have to have cars, but there's nothing as good as a horse.'

It was an interesting place, the Willa, mainly because there were so many different social groups. Top of the scale were the graziers who had properties in the country around the town, near Quirindi, or as far over as Inverell. The station owners we saw most of were the Cunninghams, whose place was about forty miles out of the Willa. Because Dad was the bank manager, they often invited us — Dad, Mum, my sister, my brother and me — over to Sunday tennis parties or gymkhanas. The house was a typical homestead, with green-painted French doors leading on to the verandah all around. It had a tennis court out the back, main-tained by the Cunninghams' full-time gardener, and a beautiful rose garden, too. 'How does Mrs Cunningham manage to grow roses in *this* climate?' wondered Mum enviously.

My brother and I sometimes went over there, without our parents. Visiting the Cunninghams was regarded as a great honour, but I loathed going there — mainly because I disliked the two children, Roger and Alison. Alison was small, with one of those porcelain complexions that doesn't tan, and curly blonde hair; she was about my age. Because she was pretty and dainty, she always made me feel as though I was the size of an elephant and just as clumsy. My brother and I were required to make up a four for tennis, and playing as Alison's partner was hell. 'I'll get it!' she would cry, swooping gracefully up to the net and hitting a deft crosscourt shot while I stood flat-footedly by the baseline. Alison's conversation was all about her visits to Sydney, the parties she had been to, what she wore. I could never compete, and usually subsided into red-faced silence.

If I disliked Alison, I detested her brother, Roger. He was a few years older than Alison and I, with a red, pimply skin and a very superior expression. He called his parents 'mater' and 'pater' and seemed to find it necessary to mention that he boarded in a very good boys' school down in Sydney. Moreover, he would take over the property when his father died. He seemed very keen on this.

I particularly disliked him because of the way he treated Dixie.

Dixie was a young Aboriginal maid whom the Cunninghams had brought down from the Northern Territory. She was very

black, and fat, and had pretty curly hair. You never got a word
out of Dixie; she just stood and giggled behind her hands if you
spoke to her, and wouldn't look at you directly, just tucked her
chin in and looked up at you through a tangle of fringe.

After the Cunninghams had stylishly beaten my brother and
me at tennis, we always trooped into the dining room for afternoon
tea. This was terribly formal, with china plates of sandwiches,
cake plates and forks and linen napkins, thin and delicate cups of
tea and a silver teapot. I never understood why: there were only
four sweating kids to appreciate all this! Roger, who must have
been about twelve, pressed a bell at the side of the table. In
trotted Dixie. He said, in a very superior voice, 'Dixie, we don't
have any fruit cake.' Not, 'Dixie, would you mind bringing us
some fruit cake, please?' Dixie giggled, went to the kitchen and
returned with a plate of cake. Roger didn't bother to thank her, of
course, just took it, and she went back to the kitchen. A minute
later, Roger pressed the bell again. 'Dixie, we don't have any
jam.' She went out and brought it in. And again, after that,
'Dixie, we don't have any cream.'

All this to show what a big man he was. I flew into a boiling
rage and to this day I cannot understand why I didn't empty the
cream jug all over Roger's dark, oily head. Too well brought up, I
suppose.

Anyway, one time I was so angry after he had treated Dixie
to his little performance that I rushed out to the kitchen to find
her as soon as tea was over. Dixie was washing up, looking just
the same as usual. I suppose I was slightly taken aback: I'd
expected her to be crying and in need of me to hug her for
comfort. 'Dixie,' I burst out, 'you don't have to put up with him.
Why don't you just leave? Go back to your people?' Dixie turned
and looked at me, giggling through her hair as usual. I couldn't
understand her reaction, and didn't until I went out to a black
settlement later and saw how her people lived.

We weren't nearly as high up the social scale as the Cunninghams and some of the other graziers, but we lived well enough to
have maids too. Many well-to-do people did then. We always had
them, one at a time; they did the general cleaning around the
house (Mum had a bone disease and was sometimes in bed for
weeks). When we had dinner parties, which we did from time to
time, the maid had to dress up in a black dress and a little white
lawn apron with a white lace frill around it. Maids also had to
wear caps, rectangular pieces of voile frilled with lace and threaded
through with black ribbons, just like those in the movies. That
was when the bigwigs came to visit. On ordinary days, our maids
wore old clothes and aprons.

Most of the maids we had were young country kids who

stayed a few months and left. (It now occurs to me — what on earth did Mum and Dad do with all the different uniforms? Because our maids came in all shapes and sizes. Maybe they took their uniforms with them when they went.) I didn't really have much to do with them — even then I thought it was wrong to employ people to do your housework — but I became friendly with one or two.

When I was about twelve, we had Edna Tully, who came from over Quirindi way. Edna could, it seemed, recite the plot of every movie that had ever been made. I don't think she saw too many — but she was an avid reader of movie magazines. She was mournful-looking and thin and stringy, the last person you'd expect to have dreams of love and romance. Yet she would grab a mop and pretend to be Rudolph Valentino making mad passionate love to Vilma Banky, or spend ages telling you the plot of *Lives of a Bengal Lancer* which she didn't like too much, she said, because there wasn't enough 'PASH-shun' in it.

Edna was also a *True Romance* addict. Under the stairs in our house was a cupboard about four feet long and three feet high, where old newspapers and odds and ends were dumped. Edna and I had a pact. I would climb inside the cupboard and wait, my knees jammed up to my chin, sitting on old piles of *Chronicles* and waiting for Edna to appear. When the coast was clear, the door opened cautiously and Edna would thrust a pile of *True Romance* magazines into my eager arms. She must have spent her entire wage on them. Torch in hand, I pored, bug-eyed, over stories about beautiful young girls who had been kidnapped at birth and who were really princesses, not waitresses, and gorgeous young men with flashing, though cynical, blue eyes who laughed through their teeth. 'Their love was a living thing...it tore and writhed at their souls.' Wonderful stuff!

Edna was also addicted to *True Crime* magazines, and that's how I first heard about Squizzy Taylor, the leader of Melbourne's underworld, as well as the Shark Arm murder mystery. The juicier the better for Edna. I brooded about the poor Pyjama Girl whose body had been found near Albury wearing only silk pyjamas with a yellow dragon on the back. What had happened to her?

A few months later Edna left, to be replaced by Joy. Joy was really something. For a start, she was a dead loss as a maid. When we had guests she would slouch up to the table, chewing gum, and say, 'Are youse ready to eat?' But after all, she had been a circus performer, and she was the most wonderfully exotic human being I had ever seen. She was drenched in lily-of-the-valley perfume, her hair was redder than Ginger Rogers' could ever be, and she *smoked*. For some reason, she had decided that dancing on the backs of horses under the big top wasn't for her. I asked her about that, but she never wanted to discuss it.

All Joy wanted to talk about was what she called 'life'. This generally meant giving me a lot of fascinating information about how not to have babies. I hung on her every syllable one day as, dusting the front room, she told me how she had given herself an abortion. 'Me mate Sandra told me,' she said, 'two bottles of gin and hot baths. She was right. Worked like a charm.' Another way not to have a baby if you were in a fix was to get on a bicycle and pedal around strenuously, preferably up all the steep hills in the district.

I was about nine or ten, I suppose, and all this left a great impression on me. Joy's facts of life left Edna's *True Romances* for dead. I used to worry if I saw Mum or any other woman having a gin and tonic before dinner in case a baby fell out, plop, on the carpet in front of the fireplace. And I didn't ride my bike up hills for a long time. God only knew what could happen.

Joy was with us for only a few weeks: it seemed much longer to me. Then one day she disappeared. I later found out that she had been sacked when Dad came home one night and found her reclining on the lounge with her legs up, holding a half-empty bottle of brandy and smoking a cigarette. When she saw Dad, she said, 'Hi, darl. At the circus I charge 'em five pounds, but you can have it for three!'

Yes, we were well off, on the whole. Mum dinned into me at a very early age that I was very lucky to have a father with a steady job at a time when so many people who were just as good as we were couldn't find work at all. (She did this so effectively that when I accidentally knocked a chip out of the kitchen wall by pushing a chair back too hard, I was terrified that the bank would find out and turn us out of their house. That small piece of chipped plaster looked like a crater to me.)

Mum had a social conscience: just because a man had no job, he wasn't necessarily an evil person, just an unlucky one. There was a large group of unemployed in town; some lived in a colony of corrugated-iron shacks down by the railway tracks, near the fettlers' camp. The kids who came from there were unmistakable: they came to school with dirty knees and crusted lips and lice in their hair, clothes that never fitted and noses that didn't stop running. And they always looked tired.

One woman, Mrs Hewitt, whose son Alf was in my class, always wore the same blue cotton dress and high-heeled tan shoes without stockings, summer and winter. On the coldest days she had a grey cardigan. I wondered why she always wore the same things and why her hair so rarely looked clean, and then I realised she didn't have any other clothes. That was a real eye-opener to me.

Alf Hewitt and his mates were anything but downtrodden: they were really fierce, aggressive little kids. It was as much as your life was worth to cross them: about the matter of shoes, for instance.

I dug up an old school photo the other day — the Willa Primary School in 1934 — and it shows a scowling group of boys and girls of all shapes and sizes standing in front of the weatherboard school. The girls are wearing old skirts and blouses or dresses with jumpers, and the skinny-legged boys are in shorts and shirts and raggy jumpers. Only three children in the photograph are wearing shoes: my brother, my sister and me. We only wore shoes that day because Mum would see the photograph and give us hell if we were barefoot like all the other kids.

The boys really got into us about our shoes. They were mostly fettlers' kids or the sons of unemployed men, and they thought that we were pretty stuck-up, not nearly as tough as they were. Ken Aspinall boasted that he could walk barefoot across the railway tracks in summer without getting the soles of his feet burned, and Andy Kelly used to go round in winter breaking the ice in puddles by striking it with his bare heels.

They'd follow us all the way to school, jeering: 'Softies! Softies! Think you're smart, don't you?' And so the three of us used to hide our shoes in a culvert on the way to school. We would leave home with our shoes brightly polished and our socks clean, and whip them off and hide them as soon as we possibly could. On the way home we'd put them on again, so Mum wouldn't know. We became quite expert at this, even stomping through puddles on the way home on rainy days so our shoes would be wet enough. Mum couldn't understand why we never wore our shoes out, but always grew out of them!

The kids disliked us for other reasons. Somehow they found out we had a bath every day: nobody, but nobody did *that*. 'You must be filthy if you need to wash every day,' said Andy Kelly and his gang, and at recess they would follow us around the playground chanting: 'Stinky, stinky!'

One summer we had a school picnic in a local paddock, which had become a dustbowl. We left our lunches in a cool spot and went off exploring with the teacher, who was explaining about birds and their habits. We had salad sandwiches and fruit and raisins and cheese neatly done up in little packets; the others had bread and dripping or lard. When we came back, the ants had got into everyone's lunches. This didn't bother Andy and Ken and the others, but I kicked up a hell of a fuss. I wasn't accustomed to eating spoiled food. I wasn't going to touch something the ants had been at, thank you very much. Ugh! I must have been a real pain in the neck, but funnily enough I wasn't teased too much about that. 'The trouble with you is you're too well fed,' said Alf Hewitt. I've never forgotten that.

I was often in the firing line for port fights on Fridays. The rule was that, after school, we settled any grudges built up during the week by donging each other with school cases (we called them ports) filled with rocks. These were pretty rough fights, I can tell you.

There was a lot of ritual associated with port fights. Everybody would gather under a particularly straggly gum tree not far from the railway. (It's not there any more, the main road has destroyed it.) There was only one major port fight per week, not a whole programme, and somehow all the kids knew who was fighting whom, and why. Boys and girls often fought each other. By the time everybody got to the port-fight tree, there were shrieks of 'I bet her' and 'I bet him' and everybody waited.

The first step, if you were involved, was finding the right rocks. They had to be big and heavy enough to cause as much damage as possible to your opponent, but not so heavy that they prevented you lifting your school case. Gathering the rocks was something you did yourself; your friends wouldn't help you.

You lined up facing your opponent, both of you holding your school cases that were practically breaking your wrists. When the person who had won the week before cried, 'Go!' you both swung your cases back and tried to hit each other. It was very important to try and hit your opponent's head, but this rarely happened: a case full of rocks is not the most difficult thing to dodge. If the handle of your case broke and your opponent's didn't, that was tough luck: there was no such thing as fair play and your opponent would move in. If both handles broke, you moved in and started punching and slapping each other. While all this went on, the rest of the kids stood around and cheered and yelled, 'C'mon!'

I seemed to get into port fights about once a month, and often came home on Friday afternoons with a bloody nose or a bruised mouth. 'What happened to *you*?' cried Mum. I shrugged and told her I got into a fight at school. She always said, 'Don't you let those rough kids beat you up any more!' but nobody could do anything about it. I wasn't sure I wanted to; I rather enjoyed port fights, which I often won. Mum had enough sense not to carry on too much about them. All she did was ask me when I was going to stop being such a tomboy. I didn't know!

Only one thing united the kids at the Willa; love for the movies. Going to the pictures was a real treat, even more enticing because the Willa had no theatre of its own and used to depend on the travelling picture-show man.

This was Vic Sauros, a man of about thirty-five with black, patent-leather hair and mournful, brown eyes. Vic looked hand-some enough to be a film star, perhaps in the Ramon Navarro tradition. Posters were plastered up all around town announcing his arrival.

He swept into town in an open tourer with his projector and the cans of film in the back, and he drove purposefully to the huge tin shed with a board floor that did duty in the Willa as a hall. It looked as though it had been a shearing shed in a former life. Vic set up a rolled-up screen at the end of the hall (a screen that had sinister blotches on it from many years of duty), with the projector at the other. We all sat in canvas-backed chairs or on benches dragged from all sorts of places.

Projector, screen and cans of film formed Vic's basic equip-ment, plus a roll of tickets which he sold before the show. I think he was typical of picture-show men in country towns; these travel-ling flicks were much cheaper than the pictures in city cinemas.

Vic was only around for one, two or, at the most, three nights a month, and during his visit he was the most popular man in the Willa. We all adored the movies. From the moment somebody turned out the lights in the hall, the projector whirred and the card flashed up 'ABSOLUTE QUIETNESS MUST BE MAINTAINED WHILE TALKING PICTURES ARE BEING SCREENED', I was spellbound.

The first movie I ever saw was *The Silence of Dean Maitland*. not in fact a talkie. I was very young, and I can't imagine what I made of its story about sundered hearts and passion. But just seeing those huge, flat, black-and-white people making faces and passionately acting their story on the flickering screen captivated me. For no reason that I can remember, I cried when it was over. Mind you, I seemed to make a habit of doing that. When I heard William Holt sing 'Goodbye' from *The White Horse Inn* a little later, I sniffed my way out of the hall, too.

Thanks to Vic, I saw dozens of movies in those years: *The Island of Dr Moreau, King Kong, Dracula.* I hated Shirley Temple because she was disgustingly cute, and liked the George Wallace comedies. But the film I remember best is *Lives of a Bengal Lancer*, which I didn't see.

Days before Vic's arrival, posters were all over town. Every-body in the Willa was a Gary Cooper fan and when Vic flung open the doors of the hall, the entire place was lined up ready to buy a ticket. All five of us went: Mum and Dad, my sister and brother and me. We waited. Vic switched off the lights, up came the numbers, which we always read from the screen in a sort of countdown; four, three, two, one... then the titles and the wonderful stirring music. I sat back and sighed in ecstasy. Two minutes later... WHOORP. Everything stopped. This wasn't unknown, of course, and the polite thing to do was to sit for a few minutes while Vic struggled with the film and the projector and got it going again. (He wasn't always perfect at this; sometimes he couldn't start at the same point, so you missed little bits of the film.) But twenty minutes elapsed this time, and the Willa's roughnecks were doing a lot of slow handclapping and catcalling. A rattled Vic yelled, 'I'm sorry! You have passes, I give you, you come back tomorrow!'

We all trooped out, very disappointed. But you can't keep the Willa down; the following night we all reappeared. Vic's second full house. Four, three, two, one, titles, music... WHOORP. Exactly the same as the previous night! And Vic couldn't get it started again either. At this point Mum and Dad jacked up. Vic had said everybody could return for a third try the following evening, but they decided it was a waste of time. If Vic hadn't been able to get it started on two previous occasions, there was no guarantee he would succeed on the third, and they didn't want to bother going for another fiasco and couldn't see why we did. I begged and pleaded, pledged undying love for Gary Cooper ('and you know you love him too, Mum') but no good.

The third night, of course, the whole thing went off without a hitch. The school was talking about *Lives of a Bengal Lancer* the following day. I sulked and brooded, and didn't forgive Mum and Dad for a long time. Suddenly Vic Sauros looked a lot less like Ramon Navarro and more like Boris Karloff.

Whether rich or poor, all the kids were fervent supporters of royalty. There was great excitement in the Willa in 1934, the year the Duke of Gloucester came to visit Australia. He was coming through to see us on his way from Brisbane to Sydney. We prepared for him for weeks. The royal train would cruise majestically into the station, the Duke would alight, make a speech and accept a bouquet, and continue his regal progress to the south.

The council decided that the fettlers' shacks and the tents of the unemployed down by the railway needed fixing up. 'I suppose they're gonna give us runnin' water and plant some of them quick-growin' trees in front of our place, so the Dook won't see us,' commented Stan Crossley, who worked on the railways. 'Might ask for a new verandah and a coupla statues for the front garden, too!' In fact, all the council did was remove the worst bits of corrugated iron and replace them with new sheets. Stan Crossley commented that they should give everybody great big Union Jacks to cover everything. 'Real patriotic, that'd be!'

All the kids were taught how to bow and curtsy in case the

Duke should stop and speak to us. We found out from Mary, who wrote the social page in the local paper, that you always called a Duke 'Your Grace'. (Grace Lindsay in my class came in for a lot of teasing because of that.)

I was furious because I hadn't been chosen to present the bouquet, even though I was the best reciter in the school. That honour had gone to June Parker, the daughter of the local stock and station agent. She was a real sook and I brooded bitterly. Couldn't string together two words to save her life, and look at her! Didn't *she* think she was something!

The day of the Duke's arrival was hot and clear. We were out in force for hours before the train was expected, in our best clothes, hair combed, Union Jacks and Australian flags in our sweaty hands, ready to wave loyally. There he was! The train was coming! We waited tensely as it chuffed closer and closer — and it went straight through the station. The Duke and Duchess of Gloucester disappeared from view in a regal blur; we didn't even see them. We were stunned. June Parker hurled her bouquet after the train and stomped off, sobbing.

The Willa's loyalty to the Crown survived even this blow. Two years later, anywhere from the pub to the playground, you could buy an argument about the rights and wrongs of Edward VIII's abdication. Some of the girls in my class thought it was *so* romantic that the King of England would give up his throne for Love. I couldn't agree. What? Give up the chance of bossing a whole Empire around, wearing those beaut crowns and robes, just for the sake of a woman? And a Yank, too, who came from a country of racehorse poisoners? What sort of lounge lizard was this Edward?

A lot of poor people came through the Willa during the Depression. Often I came home from school to see Mum standing on the back step talking to a young man in his twenties or thirties who had a blanket roll slung across his back and who wore a filthy coat and trousers. 'Got any work you want done, missus? Any food to spare?' Mum always had a large pot on the stove full of stew or soup, and she would say, 'Wait,' and disappear inside, reappearing with a tin dish full of stew and a spoon. This was what she gave them even on the hottest days; I suppose she thought they needed at least one nourishing meal, whatever the time of year. They used to eat their soup or stew by the woodheap; Mum never invited them inside. She always found something for them to do too, usually chopping the wood. Mum didn't believe in giving them money because she thought they would only spend it on grog.

Once, while I was skipping in the backyard, a very young,

thin man came through, looking dead tired, and I knew that he couldn't possibly chop any wood because he looked so weak. (I think he probably had TB.) His blanket roll was tied up with a really heavy piece of rope, as thick as a hawser. He could hardly stand. 'Here,' I said, slapping my skipping-rope into his surprised palm, before running away.

Sometimes these men talked a bit to Mum about what they were doing. I learned that quite a lot were travelling north to Queensland, because they thought work would be easier to find there. 'And at least it'll be warmer,' they added, stamping their feet in their cardboard-soled shoes. Many had come from Sydney or Melbourne in search of whatever employment they could get; some had never done physical work of any kind. 'I've never bagged wheat or dug roads, but I'm sure I could learn,' said one stocky, dark man who told Mum he used to be an accountant in Geelong.

Mum often sent me down to Sparkes's grocery shop in town, the big one near the police station. About once a fortnight I would see a group of men in there, dirty, unshaven, lined up humbly at the counter. They had been to collect their fortnightly ration coupons — the susso — from the police station and were at Sparkes's to cash them in for groceries. (A single man could earn a pound a fortnight doing odd jobs and still qualify for five and sixpence worth of food in town, or ten and six in the country, as food relief.) I always felt ashamed of our lavish grocery order — flour, sugar, butter, breakfast cereal, tinned camp pie — when the men on the susso were in the shop. It seemed so unfair that we could order whatever we wanted, however much it cost, when a skinny, half-starved man old enough to be my father was standing next to me, near the sacks of sugar and flour and hanging coils of rope, looking like a dog that had just been kicked and receiving tiny amounts of the same things as I was. As soon as Mr Sparkes had given me my 'poke' — a twist of paper with a few boiled sweets inside — I got out of the store.

I later learned that Mr Sparkes, like a lot of other shopkeepers in country towns, didn't like the susso system much — but his reasons were quite different from mine. The food coupons had to be redeemed by the government, which took a very long time to pay. Sometimes the Sparkeses were in debt for three or four hundred pounds because the government was so slow in honouring the food relief tickets. So I knew why Mr Sparkes would mutter, 'These blokes can't afford food, but they can always come at a beer,' though I still thought that was a terribly unfair thing to say.

Sergeant McKendry, whose job it was to distribute the ration coupons, was my hero. He was so nice and smiley that I was

determined to marry him and become a policewoman one day.
(This was after I had been a famous film star and an actress and a
writer.) He let me and my brother use the Willa's only cell as a
cubbyhouse. We played Ned Kelly and cowboys and Indians in
the lockup with great enthusiasm. Occasionally, though, Sergeant
McKendry would have to haul a drunk in, often somebody who
was on the susso, and we lost our cubbyhouse for a day or two.

Sergeant McKendry often had to deal with some of the Willa's
'characters'. There were a few loonies. Harry Kirk, for instance,
never moved out of the public bar of the hotel, or so Dad said. I
suppose he wasn't really very old, and he looked harmless enough
with his unshaven chin and stained moleskins .and filthy shirt-
tails, but all us kids knew that 'Harry Kirk' was another name for
'evil'.

We had heard a lot of stories about him. One was that he had
spent years in gaol for murdering his wife very slowly with an axe;
the other was that his son was connected with the Shark Arm
murder case. (Well, that stood to reason — the Willa was miles
from the ocean, and anyone who chose to go all the way down the
coast near Sydney Harbour for the fishing, as Jeff Kirk did, was
bound to be a suspicious character.) When Harry got really
drunk, he would lurch out of the public bar and stand outside to
watch all us kids when we came home from school. He gave the
boys lollies and sprinkled the girls with cheap scent. I came home
stinking of carnations about once a week. Ugh, I hated it!

Another person to watch was the Chinaman who ran the
market garden just outside town. We never spoke to him, didn't
even know his name, and didn't give him one either. He was fat
and yellow and dumpy, and when I saw him waddling down the
street I decided he was about a hundred and forty years old. He
never spoke to anyone. If he spoke to you, he could attract evil
spirits, and the way to get around that was to throw your hat on
the ground, spit on it and run around it three times backwards.
Then, if he chased you, you had to escape, or else you would be in
his power forever. As far as I know, nobody ever tried to engage
him in conversation.

Clem Shirley lived by himself in a tiny wooden hut near the
fettlers' shacks. He had a hunched back and a withered arm, and
was quite pleasant — except that once he told me that his hunch-
back was full of lead and he could pull it off his back and kill
people with it. I believed him, too.

I made a bit of a name for myself around the Willa because
of my artistic achievements. As I've already said, I was the
champion reciter of the school, and the biggest ham of all time.
Whenever the inspector called, I was always brought forth to

deliver my party piece. 'What are you going to recite for us today, Margaret?'

'Adieuadieubylordbyronsir,' and off I went, with heartrending gestures.

> *Adieu, adieu, my native shore*
> *Fades o'er the waters blue.*
> *The night winds sigh, the breakers roar*
> *And shrieks the wild sea mew....*

'Thank you, Margaret, that was very nice.' But I wasn't going to be cheated, because the best bit came next.

> *The sun that sets upon the sea*
> *We follow in his flight.*
> *Farewell awhile to him and theeeeeeeee...*
> *My native land* (long pause for effect) *goodnight!*

Oh, there wasn't a dry eye in the house, I can tell you!

But the occasional recitation on state occasions wasn't enough for me: I craved fame and fortune. So it was that I conceived the brilliant idea of delivering recitations in the back bar of the local pub. Afternoons after school I would drop in. 'Hello, dear,' said Mr Furness, the publican, beaming. 'Come and recite for us!' This was wonderful. Up I'd jump on the bar and get stuck into ballads like 'Flo's Letter' or 'Come Home, Father Dear' or even 'Clancy of the Overflow' and 'The Man from Snowy River'. Hand-wringings, lavish gestures, even sobs! I cannot imagine to this day how the squatters who'd dropped in for a beer and a yarn managed to hear me out, right through, without laughing, but they did.

When I had finished, they all applauded madly and bought me a lemonade. In my short school skirt and shoes and socks (I always fished them out of the culvert for this, my public), I would toast them by raising my glass on high and shouting, 'Here's to 'ee!' like the words on the glass-mirror picture on the wall behind me.

I was having a great time, until Mum found out somehow. She hit the roof and refused to let me go any more. Even though Mr Furness tried to convince her that 'these men have the utmost respect for Margaret', she wouldn't give in. I was furious with her. What had I done that was so wrong? And I was *good*!

When I wasn't being completely full of myself reciting, I sometimes eavesdropped on pub conversations. They all seemed to concern a man named Jack Lang. I was dying to ask the men about him, but I knew they wouldn't tell me anything, so I kept listening. Jack Lang, it appeared, single-handed, was responsible for the entire Depression. He had forced men to lose their jobs. He had refused to honour overseas interest payments, and barricaded the treasury. Lang was a Bad Man. Once he got going, I understood, even the banks couldn't do anything.

This didn't square with what I learned from the kids at school. The fettlers' children turned up one week wearing badges with LANG IS RIGHT on them. Billy Miller told me that his dad had said that Lang was greater than Lenin. I had never heard of Lenin, but I was impressed. So, according to the kids, Lang was God Almighty. I knew which way my own allegiances went. I yearned for my own LANG IS RIGHT badge and nagged Mum to get me one. She refused, indignantly: didn't I know how awful That Man was? I argued and argued but couldn't budge her, so I had to bribe one of the kids to let me wear his badge to school instead. Better than nothing.

I didn't know that, like so many people, Mum and Dad hated Jack Lang with a loathing beyond comprehension. Mum thought he was a traitor to the working class; Dad thought he had betrayed the ALP.

One day in 1932 I listened to the opening of the Harbour Bridge on our big radio. Mrs Davis, who lived next door, was visiting. 'And now Mr Lang is starting to make his speech...' (the speech was not actually broadcast — they didn't give you all that then) '...and a terrible thing has happened. An Army officer has ridden up and slashed the ribbon with a sword! He is being dragged off his horse by detectives!' So Lang had been pipped at the post by somebody in uniform!

'Hooray!' cried the woman from next door, who liked Lang about as much as Mum and Dad did. 'You beauty!'

'Pity they didn't put the sword through Lang,' Mum muttered.

Not long afterwards we went to Sydney; my first visit there. I can't remember why we went now, but it had something to do with Dad's work at the bank. For me and my brother, the highlight was going to be a trip across that marvel of modern science, the Sydney Harbour Bridge. Like everybody else, I knew it was the largest bridge in the world and the longest in the southern hemisphere.

We plunged into the underground at Wynyard, and boarded a train ready for the trip across to Milsons Point. What would it feel like going over the harbour? I'd never done it before; the only body of water near the Willa was a rather sluggish creek. The train sounded like the machines of hell to me, a country kid who wasn't used to city or mechanical noises. I waited for a life-changing experience, waited and waited while the train ka-dunged, ka-dunged on its way. There was a flat bit, then the train stopped at a station. 'When are we going over the bridge?' I asked Mum. 'We've just been açross it,' she said. I was outraged. The Harbour Bridge was a great big nothing, just another dirty adult lie. I would have nothing to tell the kids at school, nothing to boast about. I was so disgusted I couldn't even be bothered making anything up!

But from the age of ten I was beginning to realise that nothing was what it was cracked up to be and that there was great injustice in the world. I started to do what I could; my way of changing the world was to argue with everybody, which considerably irritated most of the adults I knew. But the world disturbed me.

I'd always been a great reader, thought not a particularly 'intellectual' one. The Willa's library didn't really cater for kids with social consciences or intellectual pretensions. We had a few books at home; historical novels, mostly, which I found dull. I enjoyed English school stories about midnight feasts and jolly japes, and the Anne books by L. M. Montgomery, which I borrowed from my city cousins. The school library didn't have much, just dusty, green-covered tomes about missionaries bearing witness and singing hymns (and occasionally being eaten) in the field. As far as magazines went, Mrs Furness from the pub took the *Saturday Evening Post* and *McCalls*; I had *True Romances* courtesy of Edna and I loved *Cole's Funny Book* too.

So many questions had no answers. Why were there poor people who couldn't get work? It wasn't their own fault. I'd stopped hearing that war couldn't happen again; it might. How could I stop it? I joined the League of Nations, hoping my weekly threepence would do something. And if war was so terrible, why did teachers say that the Great War had been glorious? And why, on the other hand, did my aunt, who had been a nurse in France, tell me such gruesome stories about wounded men?

Hoping to find ways of preventing war, I started reading the newspapers when I was about twelve, and that's how I learned that a civil war was going on in Spain. Nobody in the Willa seemed to know anything about this, or to care a great deal. When Mussolini invaded Ethiopia in 1936, I knew there was trouble. I worried about everything; the men who came through town looking for work, Dixie the Aboriginal maid and her family and other Aborigines, the poor Spanish whose homes in Guernica had been bombed. What could I do about that, growing up in the Willa? I'd fix things when I grew up, I vowed. I'd even join the Labor Party.

I wanted to grow up more than anything. In those days you had to stay at school until you were fourteen, an eternity. I was torn between leaving and getting stuck into the world's problems immediately, or staying on for a year or two and perhaps going to university eventually (if I was bright enough; nobody from the Willa had ever been to university). What made the decision harder was seeing what happened to the kids who left school the moment they could. This was still in the middle of the Depression, and they had to try and get whatever work they could around the place. There was very little going around the Willa, and I kept bumping into kids I knew hanging around the pub, cadging drinks and smokes from anyone they could find. Some of them drifted away, on the wallaby, or fled to Sydney or Queensland in search of something to do. There wasn't much going there either.

I stayed on at school for another year, as it happened, though I didn't go to university until much later.

When I left school I left the Willa and went down to Sydney. I travelled around for years, got married, had kids, got divorced, all that, and didn't return to the Willa for about forty years. Then in 1982, I went back because the school was celebrating its centenary; I was suddenly interested in finding out what had happened to everybody.

They'd come from all over Australia. I couldn't believe what I saw; Andy Kelly and Ken Aspinall, my former tormentors, were white-haired businessmen wearing suits. They told me they'd been unable to find jobs until they went into the Army in 1939. Alf Hewitt drove up in a Merc. A lot of the others wore flash suits and drove expensive cars too. It was wonderful. You'd never have known their families couldn't afford shoes when they were young. Most of the kids I'd been to school with could buy and sell me now, I'm telling you!

❦ *I grew up hating charity*

Tom Doherty is small and slight with fierce blue eyes. He speaks quickly and bitterly, dealing out facts about himself. Occasionally he cannot think of the right word, and when this happens his eyes narrow in frustration. 'I never had much of an education,' he says defiantly. 'I had to leave school when I was twelve to earn a livin'.' His eyes dare you to sympathise.

I was born in 1925 in Wilcannia. Then Dad lost his job as a station hand, and we had to move around to find work. Mum did a bit of washing and general cleaning where she could find it, but when there were six of us, it was a bit tough. She had to spend all her time looking after us, specially Dennis, the baby, who had croup a lot of the time.

We all eventually moved near Moree. We lived with a dozen other families down by the river, and Dad worked as a rabbit trapper. It wasn't much of a place, where we were. We all slept in a tent, using chaff bags sewn together as mattresses, which we stuffed with rags. (When I got into the Army later on, I couldn't sleep on the bunk beds in camp because they were far too soft for me.) Mum cooked on an old fuel stove somebody had found on a tip somewhere, which Dad had fixed up. We didn't have proper toilets, of course, and a lot of the time we got water from the creek for washing. Someone had rigged up a rainwater tank nearby, and all the families used it for drinking water. We lived there for about two years. Dad said, 'We'll find somewhere better soon,' but we didn't, because it was the worst of the Depression. I would have been about eight when we arrived there.

Poor Mum. She did what she could to keep us decently fed and clothed, and it was very hard. She didn't eat properly; none of us did. Often dinner was a slice of bread with beef dripping, which was cheap. Mum had dark circles under her eyes all the time; she was always tired.

113

I grew up hating charity

The nice people in Moree never talked to us. We were the wild Irish down by the creek. But, as I said, Mum insisted on trying to make us respectable. We went to school when we could, and always to Mass on Sunday. I had one pair of grey shorts and a shirt and a jumper which I wore to church — no shoes, we couldn't afford them — and that was the best we could do. But whatever we looked like, we went to church. Mum was a very devout Catholic; she'd been given a small statue of the Virgin Mary that we took with us wherever we went.

We didn't have an easy time, but we did a lot better than some. At least we were together as a family. We knew several people who'd been split up because of the hard times.

Near us lived Mrs Henderson and her three kids; she was a friend of Mum's. Her bloke had gone up north to try and get work — a lot of them did then, because it was supposed to be easier in Queensland and at least the weather was warm. He went off with his swag one morning, and she never saw him again. Never heard from him either. So there she was, trying to manage on handouts and doing a bit of ironing for the rich ladies in town. She had a hell of a life. Always sick she was too, with colds or a cough, or a bad back. The three kids were real whingers. They were scrawny and lousy, and they never washed. Whined all around the place, had fights, never went to school, threw stones at the other kids and all the dogs around the place. I didn't like them much; none of us did. When we complained, Mum always said, 'Marge Henderson has had a hard life,' and told us to feel sorry for her and the kids because they were even worse off than we were. But I never liked the Hendersons. Felt sorry for them, yes, but never liked them.

There were some great old characters around then. Like Harry, an old swaggie and metho drinker who lived in a bark humpy a couple of miles the other side of town. He was always wandering around, wearing one of those Army coats, dyed black, winter and summer, and Army boots that he got from somewhere that were bursting apart at the seams. He stank to high heaven, and we tried to keep out of his way. Every couple of weeks he staggered into town to collect his susso from the police station, but I bet he didn't get much food. Swapped the coupons for grog. When he was drunk you'd see him staggering around, quoting the Bible. Someone told me he'd been a minister of some sort before the grog got him and he was kicked out. On still nights you could hear him roaring: 'The Lord God Almighty in his infinite justice and mercy will punish the enemies of Israel!'

A lot of blokes camped under the bridge up the creek a bit.

They were mostly single men, passing through, looking for work on road gangs or anything else they could find. You saw that a lot, then. Almost every bridge in the country had a couple of men living underneath, cooking on campfires when they could trap rabbits, washing in the creek sometimes. In winter it was really hard for them.

Men often drifted through our camp, men on the wallaby. Not just country blokes, either; city blokes too. You could tell which were which. When you saw a man wearing moleskins, a shirt, no hat and shoes — not boots — you could bet your bottom dollar he came from the city. One day a young chap came hobbling into our camp — you could tell by the way he walked that he had terrible blisters on his feet. I must have been about ten, I suppose. I went over to tell him that he shouldn't be there, he was trespassing. 'G'day,' I said. He blinked down at me; he'd obviously been walking for days and nights on end, and was dog-tired.

'Where do I go to get my rations, please?' he said. Very posh accent. You could tell by his voice that he was educated, could have swallowed the dictionary. I told him where the police station in town was, and he thanked me and limped off. I reckon he'd have had a bit of trouble finding work. He didn't look like a bloke who was used to living rough.

There were quite a lot of blokes like him. When Dad got some work digging roads, he told me that some of the city blokes coming through wanted the work. Nobody asked them what they were used to doing normally, the foreman just asked them, 'Do you want a job?' Yes, they said, always, and they'd grab a pick or a shovel to show how keen they were to get going.

According to Dad, they'd last an hour or two, then their soft hands would start to blister and they told the boss they couldn't stand the work any more. Was there something else they could do? The boss always said no, and told them, 'If you can't do the work, get out and let somebody else have a go.' God knew there were dozens of men who would take that kind of work. If they refused to leave, or got drunk and abusive, the cops were called in to move them on. The sergeant in Moree, who was a big, powerful man called Kennedy, told Dad once, 'Ah, some of them fought me all the way to the lockup. They were mighty men!' But they weren't road workers.

We were always glad if Dad could get road work, or digging, or any kind of labouring job. He was little, but he was tough, and it meant we wouldn't have to draw the susso ourselves. See, we hated it, especially Mum, who thought it was admitting defeat to get a handout from the government. Lots of people didn't; Mrs Henderson thought Mum was mad to hate the susso. '*They* gotta do something for us,' she said. 'It's not our fault we can't get work.'

'Yeah,' said Mum, 'but it's *charity*!' And she never changed her mind about that.

Charity. I grew up hating it. I knew how broke we were, but I didn't want anyone pitying us, or giving us handouts, thanks very much. That might have been all right for some people, but not for the Dohertys.

I still remember walking home from school one day and being stopped by Mrs Rice, one of the rich ladies around town. I hardly knew her, we had nothing to do with people like her. Couldn't imagine why she wanted to talk to me. I hadn't done anything wrong.

'Would you like to come home with me for a few minutes?' she asked. I was about ten, I suppose.

'Yeah,' I said. She'd never bothered about me, or us, in the past, but I suppose I was curious. I followed her up to the posh part of town, and I went into her house, which had a real carpet on the floor, curtains, a piano, everything. I'd never seen a house like that before. The walls were even painted the same colour.

It turned out that Mrs Rice was the secretary of the unemployed relief committee in Moree. 'I'm sure your family needs clothes, now winter is coming,' she said. She was a nice lady, really. She was right; we didn't have any warm jumpers, or none that fitted us, and I knew Mum was a bit worried about that.

Mrs Rice led me into one of the bedrooms — and I couldn't believe my eyes. Piled over the bed, on the chest of drawers, on the floor, even underneath the window, was the largest number of clothes I had seen in my life. There were trousers, jumpers, coats, singlets, pants, of all sizes and shapes. And shoes! Mrs Rice opened the wardrobe, and there were dozens and dozens of pairs. High-heeled smart shoes, boots, sandals, almost any kind of shoes you can think of. I must have gaped, because Mrs Rice said, 'Somebody in the district bought up the stock of a shoe factory that went out of business. Then he kept the shoes in his house, and always let — er — men coming through choose a pair for themselves. We took over the lot.'

Well, that finished me. I started to get a bit hot under the collar. Was she saying that she thought we were no better than swaggies, down and outs on the wallaby? If so, I wasn't going to take any charity from *her*. I didn't think these things consciously; they were just instinctive. No, thanks. On the other hand, we really did need warm clothes...

In the end, I stammered and stuttered and grabbed a pile of things; I can't remember what they were. Mrs Rice was a bit surprised that I just picked them up from the piles, didn't look at sizes or styles or types of clothing or anything. 'Is that all you want?' she asked.

'Yeah,' I said. 'Thanks very much.' And I practically ran out of there.

When I handed the stuff to Mum, I told her that Mrs Rice had found these clothes and thought they might be useful. I didn't tell her how many Mrs Rice had.

I'm still a bit like that; proud, not wanting to have people feel sorry for me. I'll do anything rather than have people do that.

It was the same at school. Where I went, at Moree, until we left town when I was ten, was a pretty mixed school. There were the rich kids whose fathers had jobs, and then there was us. All the rich kids were good at lessons and sport, and you could tell them from us, too, because they wore shoes.

I wasn't any good at school, so I never got much of an education. I didn't think it was because I was dumb, either; I can learn things fast enough if I really want to. See, I went rabbit trapping with Dad at nights so we could earn some money, and we never got home till about three in the morning. I had to go to school every day, so I got about four hours' sleep a night. That meant I was tired in class next day, and the other kids called me 'Dopey Doherty' because I was too sleepy to do mental arithmetic and spelling.

Some of them picked on me, too, because I didn't have the right clothes for school. I remember at the end of one year going to school wearing a singlet that had been cut down from one of Dad's. I didn't give it a thought until recess; then some of the kids gathered round and told me they could see my ribs sticking through my skin because the armholes were so big. And it was the same with lunches. Poor Mum; she couldn't give us sandwiches with proper fillings, only dripping or lard. So all the kids who had meat or tomatoes or lettuce in their sandwiches used to line up at lunchtime and call me 'lardy, lardy'. I hated them.

Sometimes we had to have special equipment for school — coloured pencils or a woodworking ruler or something like that. If I knew we were having woodworking class, I'd stay away from school that day. I wouldn't stand up in front of the other kids and say we didn't have the money for it. If I got caught out, and the teacher said, 'Doherty, where's your ruler?' I'd shrug and say, 'Couldn't be bothered bringing it.' Sometimes I got told off or caned, but that was a lot better than saying we were so poor. Same with shoes. 'Where's your shoes, Doherty?' 'Shoes? I don't wear shoes. Don't like wearing shoes.'

I got to be very tough pretty quickly. I needed to make money, not a lot, just enough to survive and to help Mum and Dad and the other kids. And there's a lot you can do if you're a tough Irish bush kid.

What did I do? Almost anything. See, glass bottles were returnable. You got a penny each for bringing some back to the shop and twopence for others. I got to be the best bottle collector in town: lemonade, soft drink, beer, you name it. The moment the pubs or the grocery shop closed, I was there with a chaff bag. And I went around all the paddocks in town, looking for bottles people had thrown away. A lot of the kids did that then, and I had a few fights with some of the boys who thought that a particular paddock was their territory. But they didn't need the money as much as I did. Pretty soon, I combined with two other boys, and we collected empty bottles together. We had our own areas, and God help any kids who poached! We made sure their pencils disappeared from their school desks, or cut the handles off their school cases, or something like that. And if they complained to anybody, we fought them in the playground after school. They soon learned.

I'd knock on doors round town. 'Any bottles or paper, missus?' Newspaper was the best because the butcher bought it for wrapping meat in. The butcher and I were good friends; he sometimes gave me scrag ends or bones for stew.

The bottles I sold to Jack Morris, the bottle-oh, who had a yard on the edge of town. He'd accept jam jars, beer bottles, anything. Only a young bloke, I suppose, but he seemed very old to me. Jack wasn't married but he had a girlfriend, Mary, who was really fat. Talk about Jack Sprat and his wife! Mary looked after him and when I came to see them she'd always make me a cup of tea. Then she talked about the movies. We couldn't afford to go, of course — every threepence counted in our house — but she'd remember all the stories and act out the parts. Funny as a circus, she was; one week she'd be Shirley Temple, the next she'd be the bloke in *Frankenstein*.

I grew vegetables too. Beans and potatoes mostly; there was quite good land not far from the creek. Even when I was a kid I had green fingers, and could make almost anything grow. Still can, and we didn't do too badly with the vegetables.

I used to trap birds. Jack the bottle-oh got me that job; said that Mr Barrett, one of the silvertails in town, had an aviary and was always looking for birds to fill it. I thought he was mad; you could get finches, or budgerigars, or galahs or cockatoos anywhere, and they could be a pest, particularly the cockies. Why bother to collect them? I thought Jack was having me on. But no, Mr

Barrett was serious. So I made myself a box with wire-netting sides, got a stick and tied a bit of string to it, scattered some seed in front of and inside the box and hid behind a bush or something, clutching the string. I didn't have to wait too long. Some stupid finch or budgie or whatever came swooping down and gobbled up the seed. Soon as it was in the box I pulled the string, the stick gave way and there it was, trapped! Then I'd rush in and turn the box over quickly and put hessian on top. That wasn't too bad if the bird was little, but I had hell's delight getting the cockatoos out!

But, like I said, I spent a lot of time trapping rabbits with Dad. We went looking for burrows most nights with two really beaut dogs we trained, Scruffy and Tiger. They got to be the best rabbiters in the district. Selling rabbit skins brought big money: between two and five bob each. I spent my whole winters digging out rabbits, and bloody cold it was too. Today I can't eat a rabbit, not even look at one.

Yeah, it was a hard life, but not nearly as bad as it could have been. See, in the country you never really starved. There was always something you could do, some way to make a few pennies or a bob or two. It was much harder for city kids, I think.

❧ Cutting down, making do...we had to then

Marie Butler learned not to waste anything when she was a child. 'You never threw away soap until you'd used every last skerrick,' she says. 'And you had butter or jam on your bread, but not both. We couldn't afford it.' Now she uses butter and cream lavishly in cooking, will toss out half a pan of gravy, and paper bags and plastic bags are thrown into the garbage bin as a matter of course when she has finished shopping, instead of being carefully smoothed and folded in a drawer. There is an almost gleeful look in her eye as she does these things.

One day in 1932, when I was ten, I came home from school as usual to find Mum and Dad sitting at the kitchen table, talking. I was surprised and a bit worried; why was Dad home from work so early?

'Go outside and play, Marie,' said Mum in a no-nonsense voice. I started to argue, but she got up and practically pushed me out of the kitchen. As I walked slowly up the passage to our tiny bricked-in yard, I heard Dad say, 'Well, whatever happens, I'm not going on the susso.'

I froze in my tracks. The worst had happened; I knew immediately. Dad had lost his job with the Water Board.

That's the day the Depression really started for me.

I was the youngest of four, with three elder brothers. We lived in Flemington, in Sydney's inner west, close to the railway line that stretched right out to Parramatta and the mountains. Our place wasn't much, just one in a long row of terraces that were all exactly the same. Downstairs was a tiny living room with a window facing the street, Mum and Dad's bedroom behind it, then the kitchen; a passage, in which the gas stove stood, led to the backyard and dunny outside. Upstairs were the two bedrooms for my brothers, and my own little room, a glassed-in balcony at the

Cutting down, making do . . .we had to then

front, separated from the other bedrooms by a curtain. So we didn't live lavishly by any means.

My brothers were all bright. Fred wanted to be an architect, Clarrie a doctor: they were the two eldest, and they'd done well at school. They were fifteen and seventeen years old, and were clever enough to have gone on to university. But they didn't have a chance. They had to leave school, Fred and Clarrie, and so did Dave, the next one down. He was fourteen then.

I didn't think it was too bad at first. Every morning I watched Dad, Clarrie, Fred and Dave getting ready to go into town. They'd been up since four, seeing if there were any jobs in the *Herald,* and always said something like, 'There's a few jobs going at the IXL jam factory.' They were bright and cheerful at first, in their clean shirts and trousers and polished shoes. 'See you later!' They walked to the station, to take the train into Central and then a tram or two to wherever they'd heard the work was.

Not for a long time did I realise that they went to town every day when they knew there wasn't any work. Just for something to do. Clarrie told me later that he'd team up with a few of his mates and they'd walk the streets of Sydney all day, knocking on the doors of offices or factories and asking, 'Any work for a boy here?' Clarrie told me they used to worry about what they'd do if somebody said, 'Yes, we've got a messenger's job for one of you.' How would they decide who should have it? They'd be very fair, and draw lots. But they needn't have worried. They never had to make that decision because there wasn't a thing.

Anybody aged from ten to a hundred and ten could apply for any job, the younger the better. When Fred finally found a job in a factory, after nearly a year, he told me that he saw thirteen men sacked from the floor in half an hour; he never knew why. And the next day, two hundred men stood in line for those thirteen jobs. That wasn't uncommon.

Dad finally found a job as a labourer on the Putty Road near Singleton. Because the job was about a hundred miles from Sydney he couldn't come home during the week, but only on weekends. For the first few weekends, I remember he wore rags around the palms of his hands to protect the blisters he got in handling a pick and shovel. Mum had to prepare a week's sandwiches for him to take with him. But things could have been worse. At least he wasn't on the dole.

Anne Mason, three doors up, was the only person in her family who had a job. She was about Clarrie's age, and he sometimes took her to the pictures if he had any money. Anne I didn't like much. She was thin and rather bossy, a bit hard-faced. She worked in an office in town, and I saw her every morning, clopping past our house in her high-heeled shoes at about the time

I was ready to leave for school. On hot summer mornings I saw steam rising from her dress. This puzzled me until I realised that she had one black work dress which she had to wash out every night; often it hadn't dried by the following morning, so she had to put it on, wet.

One Tuesday morning I saw her stumbling home, crying, not even trying to wipe the tears from her face. All the starch and bossiness had gone out of her. I was amazed, and later heard from Clarrie that she had been sacked from her job. Because the weather was so hot, she and the other four girls who worked in the same office rolled their stockings down so they could be more comfortable when they typed. The boss came in, hit the roof, and sacked the four of them on the spot. They were replaced the following day; it was no trouble to him. I still can't believe how anybody could have been so unfair. But lots of things like that happened then.

While Dad was away, Mum decided she had to get a job. She was a good dressmaker and had made many of our clothes. At night I'd lie awake, listening to the click of the sewing machine. Up and down it went, up and down, as Mum worked the treadle with her foot. It was rather soothing to go to sleep to. No matter how bad things were, we never sold the machine; it brought us in a few bob from time to time.

Mum put a card up in the front window 'SKILLED DRESSMAKER, REASONABLE RATES, APPLY WITHIN'. Sometimes she got three or four orders a week. Women would buy, say, half a yard of coloured linen for sixpence and bring in a dress they'd worn for four years, which Mum would remodel. She'd cut off a collar and sleeves, perhaps, and transform a winter dress into a sleeveless one for summer. If the dress had been pleated she would carefully regather the skirt on the waistband. A lot of her business came from altering skirts or dresses or trousers that children had outgrown; she added false hems or even, in the case of dresses, a strip of material in a contrasting colour at the bottom. I always thought that looked rather pretty. Mum charged five shillings for altering a top and the same for a skirt or trousers. More than once Mum's job saved us from absolute poverty.

Somehow we had enough to eat, even if it was nothing more than bread and dripping. We rarely went to bed absolutely hungry.

I used to go down to Mr Ritano's, the corner greengrocer, and buy specks; fruit and vegetables that were spoiled and would otherwise have been thrown out. All you had to do was cut off the spoiled, or specked, parts and use the rest. And the butcher sold scraps of meat or soupbones for a penny or two a pound. We didn't starve.

At Christmas 1933, however, things were especially grim.

There was no money in the house, Dad's labouring job had come to an end, and only Clarrie had a job. All the same, Mum was determined that we would have a proper Christmas pudding. She made it with raisins and sultanas and lemon peel, and even put in a tiny bit of brandy. It looked wonderful, wrapped up in its white cloth, and we were all ready to boil it — when our gas was cut off because we were unable to pay the bill. There was no way of having it reconnected before Christmas, so there we were; with a splendid pudding and no way of eating it.

We sat around in gloom for a few minutes; then Clarrie had a brainwave.

'Have the Thompsons gone?' he asked. The Thompsons were our immediate neighbours; Mrs Thompson had told Mum that they would have to move from their terrace because they had heard that the rent for a house in the next street was sixpence a week less.

'I think so,' said Mum.

'Well, why don't we look and see if the council's disconnected their gas yet? We can cook the pudding on their stove.'

This was a brilliant idea, but there was still a problem; the Thompsons' front door was locked. Dave, who was small, worked out a plan. He climbed onto our kitchen table and prised loose the manhole cover in the ceiling. Then Dad helped him up, and he wriggled through the hole; as the Thompsons' house had exactly the same layout as ours did, there should have been a corresponding manhole cover in their kitchen. For what seemed like hours we sat there, Dad and Mum, Clarrie and Fred and me, waiting for something to happen. We couldn't hear Dave at all.

Then Dave was back, his clothes filthy and cobwebbed, his face dust-streaked, but he was grinning. 'Yeah, it's on! Give us the pudding!' We handed it up to him through the manhole, in its saucepan of water. He took it, boiled it on the Thompsons' stove and we had our pudding that year.

No matter how poor people were in our street, we were pretty good to each other. The local grocer let everybody run up credit, or 'tick'; so did Mr Ritano. But tick was only for food; we never asked for credit on other things. Mum sometimes did dressmaking jobs for neighbours and said, 'You can pay me when you have some money.' And the Burns family, who took over the Thompsons' house, were better off than most. I remember Mrs Burns coming over with a loaf of bread or some cakes for Mum. 'We couldn't eat this,' she always said. 'You'd better have it, or it'll go to waste.'

All the kids in the street played together; the road and foot-path were our playground. Nobody had a car, of course, because we couldn't have afforded one, and so playing hopscotch or cricket on the road was perfectly safe. We drew hopscotch grids all over the street with the edges of stones we had taken from the railway line. (We all promised our parents we would never, never go near the railway line because it was dangerous, but we always did.) And we girls played skipping, too. 'Old Mother Moore, she lived by the shore, she had children three and four, the eldest one was twenty-four and she got married to a tinker, tailor, soldier, sailor...' We played for hours, using ropes that somebody's brother had taken from a factory where he had found a temporary job as a packer. 'Up the Murrumbidgee, if you miss the boat you swim...'

We girls never played cricket. That was strictly for boys only. They played with a weathered old cricket ball and a piece of planking for a bat. The wickets were orange boxes. All the boys took cricket very seriously, especially after the Bodyline Test. Larwood was their hero, and everybody knew that the Poms were the lowest of the low, especially Jardine. If I really wanted to get a rise out of Paul Finlay, or Vic Davis up the road, all I had to do was wait until they bowled and call out, 'Cheat! Bodyline! Cheat!' It never failed; Paul would turn and threaten to thump me, pale with fury under his orange freckles. I learned to run very fast.

There was only one real rule in the street; keep away from Coral McCluskey. She was a large, red-headed Irish girl who came from the next street, but for some reason she thought she had the right to take part in our games. She'd stand, hands on hips, and say, 'You're all sooks, you're all babies, you can't even skip properly,' to us girls. We detested her because she was *so* holier-than-thou. She didn't have any right to be, either, because everybody knew her elder sister went with men, and her brothers were all on the susso, and her father could be seen, any day, lurching out of the Railway Hotel breathing cheap sherry. Coral was a liar, and she also knew exactly how to give Chinese burns so they really hurt. We tried to keep out of her way.

One day she came up to us after school and said. 'I saw the opening of the Harbour Bridge.'

'Yeah?' I said, in the sort of voice I hoped would tell her that I knew she was lying through her teeth, but that I didn't want my arm grabbed and twisted.

'Yeah,' said Coral, and went on to tell us what we'd already heard, about Jack Lang going to open the Bridge and De Groot galloping up and slashing the ribbon first. I was not impressed; everything she said had been in the paper that morning.

'What do you think of that?' Coral finished.

Elsie Forrest, who was much braver than I was (and further away from Coral's Chinese-burn-dealing hands), said, 'You're a liar, Coral McCluskey. How did you get to the Bridge? Somebody drive you in a car?'

We giggled nervously.

Coral didn't hesitate. 'I walked,' she said. 'It's not far.' This was a bit much to swallow, and Elsie wasn't giving up. 'That's why I saw you at the shop yesterday, I suppose. You must have walked back real quick.'

'I did,' said Coral simply. Elsie's courage failed her, and she gave up at that point.'

'Serves Jack Lang right anyway,' said Coral, tossing her head. '*Everybody* thinks so.'

'You don't know what you're talking about, Coral McCluskey,' I cried, bolder than I'd ever been in my life. Jack Lang was God in our house. Dad had told me that if it hadn't been for him, widows wouldn't have pensions, and people who were renting houses would have had all their belongings taken away by the police.

'I'll show you, Marie Dymock!' cried Coral. Before I could run away her hand shot out like a snake, she dragged me over and gave me one of the most painful Chinese burns I'd ever had. Tears came to my eyes, but I didn't cry. I felt proud that I'd stood up for Lang, and went around with my red arm for the rest of the day, taking comfort from having been a martyr.

We played in the street all the time, as I said, but there were some places where girls knew they were not allowed to go. Jubilee Park, about two blocks down the street, was definitely off limits. It wasn't a particularly inviting place anyway, being a dismal stretch of burned yellow grass with a couple of benches and a broken swing. It was an evil place, because men had been seen there. 'What sorts of men?' I asked Mum curiously. I knew she didn't mean drunks; they were everywhere, part of daily life, and all right if you kept out of their way and didn't talk to them. 'Men who expose themselves to little girls,' said Mum. I had no idea what she meant; the way she said it, it sounded dreadful.

Not long afterwards, I was walking past the park on my way home from a friend's place after school when I saw a man gazing hard at me through slitted eyes. I noticed that his trousers weren't done up properly and he was holding part of his body towards me. We were a modest family. I'd never seen my brothers or my father naked, and I ran away, feeling hot and rather sick. I never told anybody what I'd seen.

There wasn't much crime around the streets when I was growing up, but there was a great deal of drunkenness. We knew how to keep clear of the pubs on summer evenings at six o'clock, when the men were coming out, lurching down the street and vomiting in the gutters. But I started on a very brief life of crime when I was twelve. My best friend, Val, and I went to Coles and pinched things for a dare. We wandered nonchalantly up to the glassed-in counter, waited until the salesgirl had turned away, and I reached over and grabbed a fistful of hairgrips. Val, in a different section, took a handful of pencil sharpeners. Hairgrips were easy; you could put them in the pocket of your cardigan and they didn't show, but I was appalled to see that Val's pencil sharpeners made a rough lump in her pocket. She was certain to be caught.

Together Val and I walked down the aisle towards the front door, our feet sounding awfully loud on the wooden floors. I must have looked as guilty as sin. It was the longest walk of my life. The moment we hit the street we ran, bursting with giggles, bumping into shoppers, and we didn't look behind us until we'd gone a couple of blocks. Then we ducked into the doorway of a radio shop and examined our loot.

What would our mothers have said if they knew? In the end I buried the hairgrips in the backyard near the toilet. I thought of trying to flush them away, but what if they wouldn't go down and stayed floating in the bowl?

'There's always somebody worse off than yourself,' said Mum when I complained about something. And there was. We knew a lot of people who were having a harder time than we were.

I had been told that around Sydney were tent cities, on golf courses, waste bits of land, and in the Domain; on any vacant land available. People who couldn't afford to rent houses because they had lost their jobs lived in hessian tents. People even lived in caves.

More and more men and women trudged the streets, selling things: camphor, mothballs, pins, holy pictures, pens, collar studs, artificial flowers, pegs, second-hand clothes, gum tips. The mother of Thelma Barnes at school used to go door to door asking people to try margarine that she spread on little bits of bread: Thelma's mother had asthma, and I often saw her walking back from the tram with Thelma, who carried her case of samples. Thelma's father had just disappeared, and the family was having a really bad time. Even though there was no money and we knew that they lived on speck potatoes and bacon bits, Thelma and her mother were very fat, and they had whitish, unhealthy skin. They wore hand-me-down clothes that they couldn't afford to make over. I still remember Thelma coming to school in a tartan skirt made for a child about two sizes smaller. When they did get a bit of money, they spent it on fish and chips, not good food. It all went to prove what my brother Clarrie said, years later; poor people always get worse value for their money than rich people.

We used to visit Mum's sister, Auntie Clare, and Uncle Kevin and our cousins in Parramatta. Their three boys were about the same age as Dave and me. Uncle Kevin was a fitter and turner by trade, but he had lost his job, so he tried to make a living by training and running greyhounds. The dogs were penned up in the tiny backyard.

I never liked greyhounds — skinny, grotesque things — and I was shocked one day when we called in for dinner. Auntie Clare gave us all bread and dripping and thin vegetable soup, which was fine — it's what we would have had at home — but I couldn't believe my eyes when I saw her breaking three eggs into a bowl and taking them to the greyhounds out the back.

Mum or Dad said something, and Uncle Kevin's reaction was fierce. 'What's the matter with you? We gotta look after the dogs, see, because that's where the real money comes from.'

Our one luxury was going to the movies on Saturday afternoon. There were a lot of picture palaces near us. We all worked hard during the week to earn our sixpence for the flicks, gathering bottles and bones, or whatever we could find, and selling them to the bottle-oh. The best at this was Dave. If we got more than sixpence, we could buy a penny iceblock at interval.

The Rialto, which was the grandest picture palace near us, was run by two brothers, one of whom wore what I was convinced was a genuine diamond stickpin. I had never imagined such luxury. On Christmas in 1935 he opened the Rialto for a free show. The queue of parents and kids stretched for four blocks, and he had to turn some of them away, but not before cramming every available space with as many bodies as the theatre could hold. We all managed to get in. He ran a feature movie followed by a newsreel and a serial and then, at the end of the show, every child in the audience was given a paper bag that contained an orange, some nuts and boiled lollies. Luxury!

The Criterion, which was painted blue and silver and was a little further away from us than the Rialto, was very swish. (It became a supermarket years later, and has been pulled down now.) The owners ran competitions for the kids; I remember that once a prize was given to the child who brought the biggest potato. I can't remember what the prize actually was — obviously I didn't win — but the potatoes were given to a local hospital. The Cri was next door to an empty allotment, and sometimes the owners ran coin hunts for the kids after matinees. These were terribly popular. In no time, we were swarming all over the allotment like ants.

I had very definite tastes in movies; we all did. Mum and Dad loved Jackie Cooper and thought Shirley Temple was sweet. I loathed her because she was American and had naturally curly hair. Dave, Fred and Clarrie loved anything to do with war or the Foreign Legion. Clarrie read *Beau Geste* and saw the film with Gary Cooper about three times. Fred, on the other hand, was an aviation fan. He went all quiet when Pethybridge and Smithy disappeared, and announced that he was going to join the Air Force if he could. (He did when the war came; piloted Lancasters over the English Channel during the Battle of Britain and was shot down and killed over Germany in 1944.)

I thought Laurel and Hardy were wonderfully funny, and George Wallace was my favourite Australian comedian. I thought *Let George Do It* was one of the most hilarious films I had ever seen. I also loved the horror movies, *Dracula, Frankenstein, Dr Jekyll and Mr Hyde.*

Once my friend, Val, and I went to the pictures without any money at all. We thought we'd take advantage of the fact that the Criterion didn't issue passes at interval, so we could sneak in for the second half without paying. We normally didn't do this, but we were desperate to see Greta Garbo in *Susan Lennox*. We timed it beautifully, and were sauntering nonchalantly through the door when the manager caught us.

'Have you paid?'

We nodded vigorously.

'All right...what's the movie you've just seen?'

We looked at each other. 'Aah...*Susan Lennox*,' said Val at last.

The manager said, 'All right, you can go in.'

With sighs of relief we scuttled to the back stalls. The lights dimmed and on to the screen flashed: SUSAN LENNOX STARRING GRETA GARBO. The manager knew damned well we were lying, but he let us in all the same!

Not everybody was so nice to poor people who went to the movies. In one Sydney theatre, I heard, the police asked the manager to flash a notice on his screen during the intermission: 'Would any unemployed men please go to the front of the theatre where they will hear something to their advantage.' Naturally the manager, thinking he was doing the unemployed a favour, agreed. A large group of men filed eagerly into the foyer. They were met by the cops, who took all their names and threatened to stop their dole money, saying that if they could afford to go to the pictures, they certainly didn't need to be on the dole!

That story, which probably wasn't true, made Mum and Dad hopping mad... but it was the only time I ever heard of the police being bloody-minded in that way. Normally, I think, they were pretty good to the unemployed.

I was a pretty good student, especially of English and history, and my teachers told me more than once that I should sit for the Intermediate Certificate: 'You're bright, you should stay on and get a good job after you pass,' the headmaster said. 'Things will improve.'

I wanted to believe him. The Intermediate was the gateway to real life and independence, then. Only real brains did the Leaving, and went on to university. I knew that was out of my class, but I did think I could do the Inter.

I didn't even mention this to Mum and Dad, because I knew it was out of the question. Dad still didn't have a job for more than a few weeks at a time; my three brothers, too, were only in work for short periods, and the money Mum made from dress-making, though regular, just wasn't enough. Maybe, I thought, I could go and get a job as soon as I turned fourteen — the school leaving age — and read for the Inter at night. I was a great reader, devoured everything I could get my hands on. We weren't a great family for literature; most of the books around the place were thrillers, *True Detective* or Sexton Blake. I was beginning to enjoy Dickens and learned huge chunks of Shakespeare by heart from my schoolbooks, because I loved the words so much.

But we badly needed the money I could earn. I told the headmaster that, sorry, we couldn't afford for me to stay on for that extra year. He looked at me sadly and said, 'Try to study at night. We don't want to lose you, you know.'

But in the end I never went back to school, and took a job at a haberdasher's in Strathfield. It was a big shop, very posh, and I got twelve and six a week for serving behind the counter Monday to Friday and on Saturday mornings. My particular job was to look after the silk stockings. They were terribly expensive, five and eleven a pair, and women came in to have them mended; they were far too valuable to throw away. About once a week a man came in to collect the stockings and to mend them with a special crochet hook at a cost of something like threepence an inch.

The job wasn't too bad, really, except for the owner of the shop. The other girls, who were older than I, used to giggle about him and call him 'Monsieur Mobilgas' behind his back, because his hair was black and oily and slicked down with gallons of brilliantine. He had a nasty habit of coming up behind you at the counter and putting his hand up your skirt. Nobody complained; it was as much as your job was worth. Fortunately he left me alone, because I was so young — and also, I suspect, because I had a chest as flat as an ironing board. Still have!

I worked in that shop for almost three years, and was dismissed when I turned sixteen and he had to pay me more money. I was out of work for a while after that, but finally managed to get a clerical job in the city. Then the war came, and life changed again.

It's different now, of course. I tell my daughters about the Depression, and they can't understand what it was like. But they've both gone to university and have Arts degrees, so I'm thankful life has been so much easier for them.

&*I* can't remember wanting for anything at any time in my life

Leslie Woodruffe, who dislikes being called Les, is a large, pale man who does things as he has always done them, after due consideration. He peels an orange carefully, the little silver fruit knife moving precisely through the peel which comes off in a long curling strip. 'I've always peeled oranges like this,' he says, smiling gently. 'My mother taught me how to do it when I was a child.'

Leslie is a private person who describes himself, a little apologetically, as 'overly fastidious'. Though he says he likes people, he is not gregarious. He is not a man who gives away his secrets — a trait that was reinforced during his childhood, when he was a serious small boy in a house full of adults.

We were very lucky, I suppose. All through the Depression Dad had a steady job as an engineer with the South Australian public service. We had our own house, a two-bedroom bungalow in the Adelaide suburb of Walkerville, where I lived with my parents and Nan, Mum's mother.

One hot summer afternoon in 1933, just after my fifth birthday, there was a knock at the door. Nan opened it, to find Dad's brother, Uncle Harold, with his very pregnant wife, Auntie Margaret, and their daughter, Jean, who was about my own age. All three looked desperately tired, dusty and hot.

Uncle Harold was a balding, round-shouldered man who wore filthy moleskins and a shirt and boots that were bursting at the seams. In one hand he carried a cardboard suitcase. Auntie Margaret, who was thin and scrawny, wore a print dress and a grey cardigan (in such heat!) with a red felt hat clamped onto her straight, brown hair. Clutching her hand was Jean, pudgy and silent.

'We thought we'd come and stay with you for a while,' said Uncle Harold, 'if that's all right. Just until we get settled.'

I can't remember wanting for anything at any time in my life

Mum had joined Nan at the door and said, 'Of course,' rather coldly. They came in, dumped their suitcase on the kitchen table — the case contained everything they owned — and stayed for three years.

I had never met them before, thought I'd overheard Mum and Dad discussing them. Harold was a plumber by trade, who had somehow met and fallen passionately in love with a Tongan princess. He threw up his job, pursued her to the islands and begged her to marry him. Alas, the romance did not prosper and she threw him over. He returned to Adelaide, only to find that the Depression had really begun and there was no work for him. This did not prevent him from falling in love again, this time with a girl from Keith, a town in the south-east of the state, and he married her. Mum, who didn't approve of Harold or Margaret, hinted that he caught her on the rebound, and that no good could come of the marriage. However, they had a daughter, the rather pudding-faced Jean — and about two months after they came to live with us, a son, Cecil, was born.

Though Mum knew that it was her duty to take them in and look after them all, her patience was strained. She and Nan had sharp words about the housekeeping for the first time, and Auntie Margaret, who wasn't well, couldn't do a great deal. To do him justice, Uncle Harold tried to find work, reading the *Advertiser* every day for the pitifully meagre 'Situation Vacant' section, which took up about one-tenth the space of the 'Work Wanted' columns. Day after day he returned with nothing, but he remained cheerful. 'Something will turn up tomorrow,' he always said.

Now I admire him for his courage, but then I couldn't understand why he didn't seem to care. He made friends with me, or tried to, playing 'fly away Peter, fly away Paul' with bits of paper which he made disappear by some mysterious means. I enjoyed that, but couldn't quite forgive him or the others for disturbing my life.

It seemed to me that every time I got up to go to the outside toilet during the night I stumbled over bodies. Mum and Dad and Nan slept in one bedroom, Nan on what was known as the 'comfortable stretcher'; Auntie Margaret and Uncle Harold spread blankets on the living-room floor, and the very new baby howled its lungs out in a bassinet nearby. Jean and I slept in my room.

I swear that in the first two years of his life, Cecil was the noisiest and most croup-ridden child in Adelaide. He yelled incessantly, and nobody got a good night's sleep. Cecil drove poor Auntie Margaret to distraction. She had to get up about a dozen times a night to pick him up, soothe him and make him comfortable. I used to dread going to the lavatory and tiptoeing past him, because the slightest sound set him off. Auntie Margaret didn't have a good night's sleep for about two years, what with worrying so much about Cecil and Uncle Harold's failure to find work.

Though Cecil was irritating, I could tolerate him; after all, he was just a baby who whinged and snuffled and didn't know any better. My cousin Jean was a different story.

I had been given a set of Lakeland coloured pencils, of which I was extremely proud. Jean used to borrow them without my permission — even the boring black and white ones — and return them to the box, blunted. Furthermore, she made inroads into my stamp collection, which I'd started when I was only four. Things came to a head one day when we were about seven; she lost my pride and joy, a beautiful South American stamp with green and yellow butterflies on it.

I was usually a quiet child who like playing, or drawing, or reading by himself, but this was more than flesh and blood could stand. 'I hate you!' I yelled.

Jean gave me one of her infuriatingly smug looks and said, 'You touch me and I'll tell Auntie May' (my mother).

I grabbed hold of her plaits and pulled as hard as I could. She promptly burst into tears and yelled for Mum. When Mum appeared, Jean started sobbing very dramatically and told her that I'd been mean, horrible and beastly to her. Mum rounded on me straight away. 'Leslie, how can you be so selfish when Jean has so much less than you do? Share your things and let's have no more nonsense.'

It was so unfair! I don't think I ever forgave Jean for that episode, particularly for her look of sheer, smug superiority. Though we were in the same class at school, I took enormous trouble not to go anywhere near her. We had to walk to school together, but once in the playground I decided Jean did not exist.

The only way I could cope with the situation was to try and keep to myself as much as possible, drawing or painting in a corner of my room, or reading. I was passionate about jigsaw puzzles at one time, and spent hours trying to assemble a free one we had been given at the premiere of the picture, *Mutiny on the Bounty*, at the local theatre. It was a picture of the *Bounty* in black and white, made of very cheap cardboard, and I nearly went crazy trying to make the pieces fit together. It was badly made, and the pieces curled up and the layers of cardboard separated almost as soon as I touched them, so I had to give up. I made model aeroplanes of balsawood and glue, and fiddled with crystal sets for hours, trying to get comprehensible sounds through the static. (Another strike against Jean was her habit of using the earphones and not telling me where she had put them.)

About a year after Uncle Harold and his family came to stay with us, Dad's other brother, Uncle Clem, turned up. I had never met him before, as he had been on the wallaby around Australia for years. He arrived looking, I thought, glamorous and magnificent: I'd never seen a man with a swag on his back before, and his grey flannel trousers, filthy shirt and elastic-sided boots and wide-brimmed felt hat looked exactly like what a brave, swashbuckling uncle should wear.

Uncle Clem was very handsome in the Douglas Fairbanks manner, with wavy brown hair and a small moustache. He was also charming, and took for granted that he would be welcome. None of this, 'Do you mind if I stay with you?' nonsense about him: he assumed that his elder brother and family would enjoy having him to stay.

I adored Uncle Clem; he told such good stories about his adventures. He knew where there was a vast reef of gold stretching from central Australia down to the Gulf of St Vincent. 'Only a matter of time till I find it,' he said, winking confidently as he carefully lit a roll-your-own. 'I know exactly where it is; me and me mate, Snow, are going to get it. You want to come and help us when you're a bit older, Les?' I was dazzled by this idea, and instantly gave up my ambition to be a fireman.

But as time went on, Uncle Clem disappointed me. During the four years he lived with us, he talked incessantly about setting out to seek his fortune, taking to the road and seeing the world. He was just about to do so, he said, soon as the word came from Snow. But he stayed living in our house. Eventually I knew that he would always talk, always tell you what he was going to do — but never do it. Mum had a word for him, for all Dad's family except Dad himself. 'Shiftless,' she grumbled as she pounded dough on the bread board. I could tell that she wouldn't have minded Uncle Clem's head under her hands, either.

So, from the time I was five until I was almost eleven, there were ten people living in our tiny house; six adults and three children, including a small baby.

I noticed an increasing number of signs on fences, on gates, in front windows on the same theme: 'WORK WANTED'. They sprang up all over our suburb, all over the city. Reliable plumber. Reasonable rates. Dressmaker, cook, motor mechanic. Will work anywhere. No good offer refused. Some of these signs stayed on gates or fences for a long time, being replaced when it rained and the ink ran, fading in the summer sun, becoming flyspecked and growing steadily browner and curled up at the edges.

I must have been at school with very poor kids, but I don't remember singling them out. We played the same games at recess and lunchtime; cricket, marbles, swapping cigarette cards. I think the only time I recognised poverty at school was when I fell in love with Jessie McLaren, who had glossy, black hair in plaits and who shared a desk with me in grade four. Her father was a fitter by trade, and he didn't have any work for a long time. I knew that Jessie's family were entitled to get food coupons, like so many other people were then, and that they could have a certain amount of meat every week. Jessie told me that they ate tripe at least three times a week, and I was appalled. Tripe! The most horrible meat known to anybody! Nothing could be worse. When I grew up and married Jessie, I vowed she could have chicken and ice-cream every day if she wanted it, not just at Christmas and birthdays.

I used to hate going into town on the tram with Mum to buy clothes or shoes. At the corner of King William and Rundle Streets we always saw several old ladies, singing hymns in quavery voices, holding out their hands for money. No matter what the weather, they were there, and I used to rush past them. One woman in particular gave me the horrors. She was very thin, with brown skin and lank, greyish hair, and she always wore the same green dress, winter and summer. She must have been much fatter at one time: her skin hung down around her jaw and neck, like the wattles of a turkey. She sang 'Lead Kindly Light' over and over, swaying in time to her quavering voice, arm outstretched like the others. I never gave her any money, but hurried past, clutching Mum's hand, my face hot with shame.

She is one of the reasons I hate buskers now. I know they're singing in the street by choice, mostly, and everybody tells me how wonderfully joyful they are, but I still think of them as figures of abject misery, like that woman was.

I used to spend a lot of time mucking around in the bush or on vacant lots, playing bushrangers and cowboys and Indians with Dan Priest, my best friend at school. (Whenever we could, we slipped away from my unspeakable cousin, Jean, who always wanted to take part in our games.) The most exciting thing we did was to spy on the two-up games being played by the unemployed men in our neighbourhood.

If we were playing marbles or building cubbyhouses and we heard a rustling in the bushes near us, we would stop and creep forward to the clearing we knew the men used. We'd fall flat on our stomachs, peer through the scrub and watch. Then we saw them: a line of men furtively moving to an appointed spot. They were thin, wore hats and filthy trousers and shirts or sweaters, and sometimes smoked roll-your-owns or even bumpers.

They silently formed into a circle. 'Come in, spinner,' somebody would say quietly. A man would take the kip and a penny out of his pocket, and throw it up, and the others' heads would snap back as the penny glittered in the air and fell. The game would continue for an hour or so, and we watched. We were terrified because we thought they'd grab us if they caught us watching them playing a game that wasn't legal. We associated two-up with great wickedness, or at least I did. If anybody had as much as glanced in our direction we would have run, crashing away through the bushes.

Eventually the games stopped, the men drifted off and didn't meet any more, so we played in peace. I don't know what happened, whether they found jobs, or moved on, or just gave up in the end.

Dad was the only man in our street with a regular, decently paying job — and at least once this caused great bitterness. He decided to glass in the front verandah of the house, and put an ad in the local paper calling for tenders. It seemed that everybody in the street applied, and this upset Dad a great deal; after all, the job could go to only one person. The incident severed the friendship between Mum and Mrs Atkins next door, whose husband missed out. 'You'd think neighbours could look after each other,' she told Mum, and they hardly spoke after that.

Dad didn't offer the job of glassing in the front verandah to Uncle Clem or Uncle Harold because — miracle of miracles — they had both found work. Uncle Harold was helping to build roads in the Adelaide Hills. It wasn't much of a job, but eventually he and Auntie Margaret scraped together enough to rent a tiny little unlined weatherboard house in the seaside suburb of Glenelg. It was freezing cold in winter, boiling hot in summer, had two rooms, no furniture, a tap in the back garden with a tin tub for washing. The toilet was a primitive shed out back.

Uncle Harold had to make his own furniture, and I can still see him patiently sawing and nailing butter boxes together. I think that picture of my uncle making something out of material that was normally thrown away taught me what it is like to have nothing, nothing at all.

Uncle Clem gave up his dream of roving Australia in search of gold and found a job as a labourer in a tyre factory. But the poor man had an instant allergy to rubber. I was about eight when I saw him come home from work for the first time, and I didn't recognise him. His face was swollen up to twice its size, and was a frightening dark blood colour; his hands and arms were puffy and the pallid colour of sausages. He could hardly speak. But there was no question of his giving up the job. He had to keep it.

A year or two later Uncle Clem applied to join the Army, as soon as they began calling for recruits. His entry depended on his learning trigonometry, and night after night Dad gave him lessons on the kitchen table. When war came, Clem went overseas, to the Middle East, where he fought well and rose to the rank of lieutenant. I think that probably satisfied his desire for adventure!

Mum and Dad and Nan were great ones for picnics. Like most people, Dad didn't own a car, but he occasionally borrowed a Ford roadster from work for the weekend. He christened her Jemima, and a splendid beast she was. Jemima never went very fast, even downhill, but she had one unvarying trait: she knew exactly how to find flints or sharp pieces of glass on the road. More often than not, Dad would say, 'Damn and blast!' as one of Jemima's tyres went down and we rocked around. Mum, Nan and I would pile out of the car and sit on the edge of the road while Dad jacked up Jemima and changed the tyre. Car trips were quite exciting.

Occasionally we took one of Mum's friends with us. Sometimes this was Patricia Coverdale with whom Mum had grown up. She made wonderful rabbit pie for our picnics and talked a lot about England, which she had visited extensively in the 1920s before her husband lost all his money. Imagine: she had actually been in the same room as the Prince of Wales! (This accomplishment lost a bit of its lustre after the abdication, but the reflected glory of knowing somebody who Knew Royalty was quite impressive.) I always thought Patricia was nice, but slightly affected.

However, the person I loved most dearly outside the family was Patricia's friend, Gusta Lomax, who sometimes came with us too. Gusta ran a boarding house in Kensington Park, 'a good suburb, deah', and was a woman with a great booming voice and enormous bust, who went in for long, flowing green gowns — not short dresses to the knee like everybody else. She was allowed to, because she was artistic. Whenever she came with us, she brought an easel and canvas and paints, would plonk herself down in front of a vista of gum trees in the Adelaide Hills, or a seascape at Henley Beach, and proceed to paint it. I thought I had never seen watercolours as beautiful as hers. I still have one somewhere — a landscape with a very blue river and a very green, strategically placed gum tree. Gusta also painted china, and Mum was the grateful recipient of saucers with pansies or robins on them, every Christmas.

Moreover, Gusta had written Books. 'What sort of books?' I asked her curiously.

'Nothing that would be suitable for you yet, deah,' she said. I think she wrote tracts for the Bible Society. 'All about God and salvation.' I lost interest in her literary career immediately. Writing things about God was like writing hymns, dull, and I couldn't bear the thought that Gusta wasn't wonderful.

She was terribly kind to me. Though she had never married, she adored children and always brought some coconut ice or toffee she had made especially for me. She called me 'the boy' in a voice that suggested great significance. 'You are going to do Great Things,' she said solemnly. 'I can see it in your hand.' Gusta read palms to bring in a bit of extra money. 'You will make the hearts of men open and heed you.' Though I was anything but a demonstrative child, I never used to mind Gusta hugging me, which she often did. I can still smell her perfume and remember being pressed against her enormous bust.

We went to the beach, to Glenelg, particularly after Uncle Harold and Auntie Margaret rented a house there. I never went in swimming for very long, no matter how hot the weather, because of the sharks. The beaches were not netted then as they are now. Although Adelaide's beaches are hardly famous for their thundering surf, and the water was blue and clear, I knew that dark shadows were hiding.

On Saturdays during the summer, if there was a shark in the water, a small plane would sweep low over the beach and drop a bomb about the size of a golf ball with a black casing full of holes. It made a very satisfying noise, between a pop and a bang, and that was the signal for everybody to scramble ashore.

Once I saw the shark plane have an accident. For some reason I was by myself on the beach, watching the plane. I heard the engine cut out. The plane lost height quickly. The nose swung round. The pilot seemed to be trying to land on the beach. He didn't make it and turned to the road leading to the beach. Then the plane suddenly upended and crashed on its nose. I couldn't believe how quiet, how quick, how *ordinary* the accident seemed. I wasn't afraid, not even when people ran over and I saw two bodies being taken out of the plane. I knew those men were dead but it didn't worry me particularly; the whole episode seemed completely unreal.

It was a fairly ordinary childhood, I suppose, or certainly not unusual for those times. I'm afraid I was not a particularly sensitive little boy; I didn't grieve much over the miseries of other people because everything seemed so normal to me. It's like that with kids, you know; they can accept, mainly, whatever happens to them. It's just the way life is.

"ATHELSTANE"
ARNCLIFFE

Keeping up appearances was terribly important to us

Keeping up appearances was terribly important to us

The doll's name is Susan. She is a large, jointed china doll with a skin of the most delicate pink; her dark-lashed eyes are a staring, bright blue (for she was made in the days before dolls had eyes that closed), her red mouth is a perfect Cupid's bow, her dark ringlets are still glossy. A very demure and elegant young lady she is, to be cherished, not scolded or slapped in games of mothers and fathers.

'She was imported from France,' says her owner, Kate Turner. 'She wore a frilled organdie dress and pantalets and little boots with real black buttons. Beautiful craftsmanship.' But Susan has come down in the world. After suffering the attentions of two further generations of little girls, her fine little feet are now bare and she wears nothing but a plain, blue cotton shift with nothing underneath.

'Dad gave Susan to me when I was very small,' says Kate. 'She belonged to his mother. He always told me to take care of her, because she's quite valuable. Susan is the only present he ever gave me.'

The first thing I remember is walking to the station in Kyneton with my mother, sister and brother, to catch a train to Melbourne. This was in 1932 when I was three. The others had gone on ahead, carrying suitcases, and I toddled behind them, clutching Susan and sniffing because I thought everyone had forgotten me.

I had been told that we were getting into a steam train to visit Grandpa and Grandma in the city. 'Daddy isn't coming with us,' Mum had said, 'but we'll see him soon.'

I didn't know then that Mum was taking us to her parents' house to borrow some money, and that we would never live with Dad again.

Mum's family were very wealthy, having made a lot of money out of a road transport company. Mum, who had never worked in

143

her life and whose education had consisted of learning a little French, some music, and reading carefully selected English classics, had married Dad, a charming solicitor. Dad's family were comfortably off, but not in Mum's league.

What Dad had was an almost unlimited capacity for spending money. I don't remember our house in Kyneton, but I was told that it was the grandest in town: far too large for the needs of a couple and three children, especially as Dad did not consider it necessary to earn a living. Far better to live off capital, as the nobility did. Dad believed he was descended from a Scottish earl, but he was unable to claim the title because descent was through the female line, not the male. Photographs show him looking rather aristocratic himself, in a Ronald Colman style: tall and slim with a clipped military moustache.

When my sister Vera, who was seven years older than I, announced to him just before we left that she would like to be a secretary when she grew up because she liked the idea of working in an office, he turned on her. 'How dare you think you'll ever have to work!' he said.

Delusions of grandeur are dangerous things when the world around you is beginning a depression. And Dad couldn't afford them. His reckless spending on 'the good things of life' — French champagne, imported clothes, concerts in Melbourne, whisky — meant that he ran out of his own money and had to use Mum's. She owned our house in Kyneton, in fact. And when he developed a gentlemanly addiction to gambling and Mum could no longer pay his debts, she had to go to see her own parents in Melbourne.

For years I didn't know how much Mum hated going back to her family, cap in hand — I understood when I came to know her family better — but that day, going to Kyneton station, I knew something was wrong with the world.

I remember my brother, Charlie, who was nine years older than I, asking, 'Mum, if Grandpa doesn't give you any money, will Dad have to go to gaol?' and Mum replying sharply, 'For God's sake, Charlie, keep quiet! Things are bad enough without your questions!'

Grandfather's chauffeur met us in the Bentley at Flinders Street station, and drove us to my grandparents' house in Toorak. A completely new life began.

The Toorak house was the biggest I had ever seen, with huge and chilly rooms. I think I considered we had come to live in a cathedral; the place had the same echoing emptiness. It was a house for adults, not children. Long, bleak corridors led to reception rooms, the dining room with its huge cedar table seating thirty-six, and the glassed-in conservatory beyond, where my grandmother used to sit on a little stool and water the plants every day. Several rooms, with names like 'the red room' and 'the blue room' were swathed in ghostly dust sheets. The three of us had our own rooms. Mine overlooked the sculpted garden at the back of the house, and contained an enormous bed with slippery cold sheets, a mahogany washstand with basin and ewer, a carved wardrobe (which I was convinced was the home of the Bad Banksia Men from *Snugglepot and Cuddlepie*) and a bookcase, also elaborately carved, which was completely empty except for an ancient copy of *Hymns Ancient and Modern*.

All the time we lived in that house, for almost four years, I felt like walking around on tiptoe and whispering. And I clung desperately to Susan, who seemed to be the only friend I had.

Soon after we arrived at the Toorak house, there was a meeting of aunts, uncles and cousins. Mum was the youngest of nine. Most of the uncles had lost their jobs because of the Depression but, like Dad, they lived off their wives' incomes. The amount Grandpa had made out of road transport was phenomenal, and Mum's sisters and brothers were still living off their investments and shares.

I don't remember very much about the meeting, except that I was forced to meet a whole lot of people I had never seen before, but I gathered later that the subject of discussion was: What Shall We Do With Amy (Mum)? I now know that Mum's brothers and sisters, especially her elder sister, Pauline, told her about Dad's debts, those he had incurred both before marriage and during it (I think they actually went to the lengths of employing a private detective) and persuaded her that Dad was no good, and that she should not return to him. They would pay his debts this time on one condition; that she sold the house in Kyneton, arranged to have the contents packed up and left him only a few possessions.

So poor Mum, who was small and vulnerable and who dressed beautifully on very little money, was forced to make a decision she had never intended to make. She had intended to return to Kyneton, and to Dad, as soon as the money had been settled. But she never did.

I found out that we had left Dad through my cousin, Jane, Auntie Pauline's daughter, who was eight, four years older than I. Jane had many more dolls than I did (I only had Susan, after all) and they were all beautifully elaborate confections, their dresses, hats and coats made in silk and lace and velvet. Jane had a doll's house that I coveted, too; it swung open from the front and had a real stove with tiny tin saucepans with handles. I particularly loved this because the Toorak mansion was so chilly and splendid, and this was such a contrast.

Jane said, 'You're not allowed to play with those any more.'
I was stunned. 'Why not?'

'Because you haven't got a real daddy, not like us,' said Jane.
'And he's never coming to see you again.'

When you're only four and uncertain about what's going to
happen to you, this really hurts. 'Yes he is,' I said. 'He's coming
to live with us soon.'

Jane looked smug and said, 'No he's not. My mummy told
your mummy that he wasn't any good, and she'd better face that.
So there!'

I dropped the tiny saucepans and ran to Mum and asked her
if what Jane had said was true. But all she said was, 'Darling, I
don't know.'

Nothing was safe. I couldn't depend on anything. And life in
the Toorak house was so difficult, mainly because there didn't
seem to be any rules you could learn. I always seemed to do the
wrong thing. I didn't stand up straight enough, or I chewed with
my mouth open or I used the wrong fork. ('Good heavens, Kate,
you should have better manners than *that*,' said Aunt Kath.)
Uncle Ronald used to grab my elbow and jam it down, hard, on
the table if he caught me eating with my elbows out. And all this
was, obscurely, Mum's fault.

Vera and Charlie suffered too, Vera because she was ten and
just beginning to have opinions of her own, so was regarded as
'cheeky', Charlie because he 'always had his nose in a book'. They
had both started school, 'good schools', and I didn't see them
very much. I was very lonely, and Mum seemed preoccupied with
her own troubles, so she didn't play with me much.

Poor Mum. She really suffered from her brothers and sisters,
especially Auntie Pauline. I remember hearing Auntie Pauline
saying to Mum, 'You have no right to claim Great-uncle Walter's
desk. He left it to *me*!' This was sheer greed: Auntie Pauline had
more than enough furniture in her elegant house at South Yarra.
She could have written on a different desk every day for a week if
she had wanted to. But Mum, who felt she had made a dreadful
mistake and let the family down by marrying Dad, and who was
dependent on her family, always gave in for the sake of peace. Yet
she did not look like a drudge: she was pretty and elegant, always
the best-dressed woman at bridge parties, or receptions. This was
remarkable, considering how little she had.

Grandpa and Grandma, who owned the house at Toorak,
must have been very old when Mum, Charles, Vera and I were
foisted upon them. They were the only bright spots in my existence
for some time. In photographs they look like King George V and

Queen Mary, but I never remember them like that. My grandmother had warm hands and a sapphire ring. After dinner, which
was served in the chilly dining room (with two maids waiting on
the seven of us), Grandma went into the withdrawing room and
sat and embroidered huge traycloths with poinsettias and roses.
At least one was big enough to cover a billiard table. I used to
love to watch her needle darting in and out of the linen; I thought
she was the cleverest person I had ever met, and she didn't mind
my sitting and watching her for what seemed hours. She also had
a jam room, off the kitchen, and when I was very little one of my
delights was to help her stir the rich fruit. The huge vats and pots
bubbled and hissed over their own special gas jets.

Grandma always wore a white apron over her dress to make
jam, which I knew was a very serious business. Yet it puzzled me;
who ate the pots of apricot, strawberry, raspberry and plum jam?
In fact, Grandma made jam to give away at the door to the
dozens of unemployed men who knocked, looking for work, their
numbers increasing as the Depression worsened.

Nobody was ever sent away empty-handed: even if there was
no work, Grandma always saw that men got at least a cup of tea
and a biscuit. And she always bought whatever people were
selling door to door: little cases with perfume bottles, matches,
buttons.

Grandpa used to let me sit on his knee while he told me
stories or sang songs about the Grand Old Duke of York who had
ten thousand men, or about being on Ilkley Moor without a hat. I
loved visiting him in the pigeon house. He kept homing pigeons in
a separate enclosure out the back, at the end of the garden, and he
was often there during the day, talking to the birds as they
swooped in and cooed and strutted up and down on their perches.
There seemed to be hundreds of them, though there could only
have been about fifty or so. Grandpa and I had great fun making
up stories about them: we called them Gloria and Jean, and
Leicester Square and Thames Embankment, and Bertie and Jeeves.
The pigeon house was cool, and safe, and soothing. And I suppose
that Grandpa was a sort of father substitute for me. I hardly
noticed the absence of my own father after a while.

We did see him a few times after we moved to Toorak; he
took a flat nearby for a while, and we visited him on Saturday
afternoons. He was blustery and angry, and didn't seem at all like
the kind man who had given me Susan. Once he insisted on
having his photograph taken with us, in turn, and I was afraid: in
the photograph I look as though I am straining to get away.

It was really difficult then, because Mum and Dad were still fond of each other, at least for a while. They still hugged when they met, and at parting. And Mum never tried to turn us against Dad; I was very thankful for that.

Years later I learned from a family solicitor that he had said to Dad, 'Now look here, if you want to see your children you had better support them.' But Dad was not prepared to do that. 'Oh,' he said, 'they'll be all right. They'll get enough from the old man' — Grandpa.

When I was about twelve, and we had long left Grandpa's house, Mum and I were shopping in Bourke Street. She grabbed my arm and hustled me into a nearby furniture shop. 'I thought I saw somebody,' she said. I now know that that 'somebody' was Dad. They had not seen each other for seven years and Mum was frightened that he would find her. Their estrangement had become total. Dad could easily have found us if he had wished to do so, but he never did, and Mum had no intention of telling him where, or how, we were.

Yet, though they were separated, they never divorced. The family would never have stood for that.

When I was almost seven Grandpa and Grandma both became ill at the same time. They were in their eighties, so I think they were just wearing out. I didn't know what a turning point that was in our lives until later. Grandma's room was upstairs, Grandpa's on the ground floor, and there seemed to be nurses everywhere. Mum helped look after them too, and she seemed more tired and drawn than usual.

Grandpa became terribly angry during his illness. He would refuse to take the medicine Mum tried to give him, and his face would go purple with rage. In despair Mum sent me into his room one day to 'see what I could do'. For some reason I seemed to calm him down, and after that I played marbles and draughts with him, talked to him about all sorts of things, told him how the pigeons were getting on without him. When he became really ill, I chased imaginary people out of the room for him. (He kept seeing his little brother Henry, who had gone to sea, and whom he apparently had never liked; 'Henry! Stay away!' he would yell. But Henry would never go until I said, 'Yes, Henry, go away,' and hurried him out of the room.)

Grandpa died a few months after he became ill; Grandma followed three weeks later.

In no time at all, it seemed, the aunts and uncles were congregated in the drawing room, talking about shares and debentures and falling values. Uncle George, Mum's eldest brother, dominated the family in money matters, and he was about to make a decision. George, who was a solid-looking man with a very strong sense of his own importance, was the head of the family after Grandpa's death. He had a habit of making very ordinary statements in a particularly serious voice, but what impressed me were his shoes. They reflected the sun, glistening like polished coal.

He said that all family members should sell their shares in Grandpa's transport firm; the value had gone down as a result of the Depression, the family company had amalgamated with another. Everybody agreed. This was extremely unwise; when the war came the value of the shares went sky-high. If everybody had held on for only another three or four years, they would have had no problems.

George had apparently been supposed to organise the family money into a trust, which would have made it exempt from death duties. But as well as being pompous, he was a very bad money manager, and he hadn't done this. Consequently, nobody in the family had the money they thought they had from Grandpa's will. Death duties made appalling inroads into the estate. Some members of the family, like Mum, were living on their capital; some of the others were still managing to live off returns from their investments. But as the Depression worsened, their money dwindled. The house in Toorak was eventually put up for sale, and it stayed empty for years, until after the war, when it was pulled down. (A service station stands on the site now.)

None of Mum's sisters and brothers talked about being in difficulty, then or afterwards. But I noticed that my cousin Jane talked a lot less about the wonderful clothes and toys she had; Auntie Pauline, too, spent much less time going to concerts and having little dinner parties at home. When her elder daughter, Juliet, was about to 'come out' — very important in Pauline's social circle — Pauline was reduced to making all her daughter's clothes.

Vera, Charlie and I were all aware that we lived on the fringes of an extremely wealthy society, in the same city as the poorest of the poor. From the window of the Cadillac in which I was taken to ballet lessons in Collins Street, I saw dirty, pale men in dyed Army coats loitering around the streets, as well as sprawled on benches in the Exhibition Gardens, with empty bottles at their feet. And there were Mum's family, worrying about the quality of the silver, and telling me that it was impolite to use an ordinary knife to eat fish!

Keeping up appearances became almost a family religion. After Grandpa and Grandma died and the house was put on the market, Mum, Vera, Charlie and I had to find somewhere else to live. There was yet another family conference, this time about us.

Uncle George didn't see any problems, he said. I would be sent to a boarding school, as befitted my social standing; Vera was already attending a girls' college in Melbourne.

Mum was horrified. 'But George, I can't afford it,' she protested. 'Vera's expensive enough, and Charlie!' But Uncle George raised his eyebrows and announced that he would pay my fees, and that was that.

I was only seven, and when I was told that I was being sent away I burst into tears. What would I do without Mum and Vera and Charlie? I couldn't imagine life without them. But no. It was settled, and Mum and I went shopping for strange clothes: beige gloves, which I'd never worn in my life, a felt hat for winter, a straw for summer, each with the school ribbon around it, a blue serge tunic and blouses, a blazer and a cloak with a hood. All English winterweight clothing; nothing for summer. And all in the smallest size available for I was tiny for my age.

So there I was, a small, forlorn little creature being sent to the mountains a long way from Melbourne. The classic picture I suppose is of Jane Eyre, poor little orphan. Well, that wasn't my experience. I adored school from the moment I walked into the building. For the first time in my life I had a place. I was Kate Wright, in first class, with teachers, and bells to obey, and things to do. There were no aunts ordering me about or criticising me, no confusing messages about Mum and Dad. I looked the same as everybody else, and I loved it; the beauty of school uniforms, I think, is that they tend to level out or nullify social class.

And I found I was good at some things. The day I really felt I was worth something, the day I stopped feeling like a parcel being pushed around by adults, was when I went down the hall to Mrs Dwyer with my school reader (it had a picture of a red motor car on the cover). Mrs Dwyer was the second class teacher, and I was being sent in to read to her, to show her how well I could do it. I read a story about a little girl and a dancing bear without stumbling over a single word. It was the proudest moment of my life!

Every day after school in that first year we had to leave the classroom singing: 'Merrily, merrily, shall I live now/Under the blossom that hangs on the bough.' Ten little seven-year-olds in blue tunics and black stockings and shoes, skipping out of the classroom like little penguins. I think it's rather nice to go hop, skip and jump out of school singing, 'Merrily, merrily...'

At the end of my first year I won a prize for being the youngest child in the school. I stumbled up the steps on to the stage of the school hall, and was given a copy of *The Wind in the Willows* by the archbishop's wife. She bent down and whispered, 'Good on you, Kate-o!'

The three years I spent at boarding school were the happiest of my life. I felt safe and secure for the first time. Then, at the end of third class, when I was ten, Mum came to take me back to Melbourne. I cried bitterly all the way to the city.

It turned out that, as he had promised, Uncle George had paid for my tuition: for the first year. Then he had forgotten, or was unable to afford the fees, so Mum was forced to pay for the ensuing two years herself. God knows how she afforded it, but two years was her limit. She was almost cleaned out. I've often wondered since why she didn't do the sensible thing and take me away from school after the first year, when it became obvious that Uncle George would no longer pay for me. I like to think that she couldn't have borne to take me away from the only real security I had known, but I think, too, she suffered from the feeling that she had to keep up appearances.

I returned to find Mum, Charlie and Vera living in a boarding house at St Kilda. Like so many houses at that time it had once been a mansion and was now broken into little flatettes, share kitchen and bathroom, all separated by prefabricated walls. Our boarding house was called Wendover and was run by the Misses Huffell, two middle-aged ladies who were always cheerful and friendly.

Miss Ida, who was about fifty, got around in a dressing-gown that had seen many better days (and many egg stains down the front), smoking cigarettes whose ash spilled down to join the mess on her gown. She wore lipstick all day, even at breakfast, and her aim was unsteady, for her lipstick line never quite coincided with the shape of her mouth. I have no idea what she did during the day: I don't remember seeing her out of her blue chenille dressing-gown, even when I came home from primary school at three in the afternoon.

Miss June, the other Huffell sister, wasn't around very much. 'She plays a lot of bridge,' Miss Ida said vaguely. I had a confused impression that Miss June knew a great deal about girders and arches and struts. Miss June had a clear skin, pale clothes, dark, very clean hair, and she wore no make-up. She was the younger Miss Huffell, but she bossed her sister around terribly.

Both sisters had high, fluty, very refined voices. But sometimes at night, if I lay awake in the room I shared with Mum, Vera and Charlie, I heard them quarrelling — and their voices were loud and harsh and deep. They scared me.

Nevertheless, most of the time I was blissfully happy at Wendover; we all were. Mum still had a bit of family money — I don't know where it came from — probably some shares she hadn't known about. Gone was the influence of the aunts and uncles, whom we hardly saw except at Christmas. I noticed that when we visited Auntie Pauline and Uncle Dennis, quite valuable bits of family china, including two Meissen figurines I'd always admired, were missing from their rosewood sideboard in the dining room and that the paint on the living-room walls and in the hall was peeling quite badly. The small window in the bathroom was cracked too. There was obviously not enough money to have these things repaired or replaced — yet Auntie Pauline still persisted in pitying us. Poor things, I could see her thinking. Poor Vera and me, wearing made-over dresses that had had the hems let down so often there was no more material, so Mum had sewn on a strip of a different-coloured material at the bottom. This was a badge of poverty. You saw girls wearing similar clothes all over the city, but I didn't care.

Charlie had a job with Burns Philp because of family connections. It wasn't much, but he was thankful to have it. He was the office boy, and I think his job consisted mainly of buying sweets for the managing director who was particularly fond of Columbine caramels, and making a cup of tea from time to time. Charlie had become a wireless fanatic, and he strung wires all across our large room at Wendover. Sometimes it was downright dangerous to walk in. 'Careful!' Charlie would yell frantically. 'Don't move the wires!' I often had to stop dead to prevent myself being decapitated; Charlie always rigged wires at exactly my neck height, it seemed to me. He was also very keen on short wave. At night he would turn on the huge set he had made himself, which was bristling with wires (I have never known the reason for the name 'wireless'), and tell us all to be quiet and listen. All we heard was 'oooweee, oooweee' for minutes on end, while Charlie twiddled knobs and moved aerials and wires. Then a voice would be heard, advancing and receding through a cloud of static. 'That's Russian!'

'Congratulations, dear,' said Mum politely. 'Can we continue with a conversation in English, please?'

After finishing her third year at high school (alas, the fee money for Vera's private school had gone, just as mine had done), Vera fulfilled the ambition that Dad had scorned for her, and managed to get a job as a secretary in a Collins Street office.

I was happily going to primary school, eating Oslo lunches from the shop across the road, learning tables and spelling, walking down to St Kilda beach with my best friend, Sandra Richards, after school. This was not encouraged — the area still had its fair share of drunks and unemployed — but we knew when to avoid the pubs and the men staggering out in their black and grey clothes. We sat on the beach, taking it in turns to draw pictures in the dirty sand with a piece of stick. We made tiny shell and seaweed gardens, and had weddings and parties for our dolls. Later, we told each other the plots of movies.

We were happy in St Kilda, where we lived for some years. You see, we didn't have to pretend any more.

We all knew that war was coming

❖*We all knew that war was coming*

David Jenkins still owns his Boy Scout badge; it's in a cardboard box in his study with a Sam Browne belt about the right size for a twelve-year-old boy, and a silver whistle. A careful, neat person, he remembers how to tie knots, build fires in the bush, and the other skills he learned as a member of the 1st Stanthorpe Boy Scout troop. He was born in the granite country of Queensland in 1925.

Throughout my childhood, the Movietone newsreels at our local picture theatre fascinated me more than all the other films that were shown. Oh, I enjoyed the usual things, the Tarzan serials and George Wallace and Gary Cooper and Jimmy Cagney, but I knew they weren't real — I found facts, reality, much more interesting.

So I watched the flickering pictures of thousands of men goose-stepping at Nuremburg, their swastika armbands and their huge flags and the unbelievable numbers of people cheering them, and Hitler standing on his dais mouthing words below his silly toothbrush moustache, his right arm raised in salute. I also watched Il Duce, Mussolini, with his absurdly jutting jaw, reviewing thousands of Italians wearing berets and carrying rifles.

Though the Nazis and Fascisti certainly looked warlike enough to be dangerous, they were in Europe, thousands of miles away from us. I don't think I ever worried about the Germans invading Australia, for instance. The Japanese were a different story.

At the time of the Manchuria campaign, I saw newsreel film of enormous troops of Japanese soldiers marching past, huge, grim, with their bayonets. These were completely different from the little yellow men that people laughed about; the soldiers in Manchuria had to be taken most seriously. Some people thought that when the Japs had finished with Manchuria, they would attack the Dutch East Indies and sweep into Queensland and thence the rest of Australia.

Quite a lot of other people considered that the Japanese weren't funny. Once, when I was walking through the main street of Stanthorpe, a car backfired nearby. Everybody within earshot jumped. 'Watch out!' yelled somebody. 'The Japs are here already!' Nobody laughed.

People in town took the threat of war seriously. For instance, the local militia had never disbanded after the first war. It consisted mostly of young men, blokes who had not been old enough to fight. As time went on, every second man in town joined a militia unit. They were part-time soldiers who drilled and led parades. And we had our Light Horse troop right through until 1939: men who gave tent-pegging exhibitions at the local shows.

'What'll I join if war comes?' I asked my father. He said, 'You should join the Light Horse. It's a *good* troop.' Like many others, he was convinced that this war, like the last, would be fought on horseback.

I wasn't so sure. The Japanese were an efficient land army: they didn't use horses. If they came down, I was sure there would be guerilla warfare. And I had worked out exactly how I would defend myself.

Being a keen Boy Scout, I decided I would hide in the bush and live off the land. I knew exactly what I would take to survive. Firstly, my swag — these were the days before haversacks. A sheet of heavy waterproof canvas would do for a groundsheet, six feet long by three feet wide. Then I'd get two blankets, lay them on the ground with the groundsheet underneath, and put a spare pair of socks and underwear on top. My toothpaste and toothbrush would go in a cloth camping bag with a piece of Velvet or Sunlight soap for washing myself and my clothes. I would roll the lot up into a long sausage and fasten a leather strap at each end to hold it together, with one strap in the middle, looped for carrying the swag.

I'd use a fruit tin with a cut-off top, holes punched in the sides and a handle made of fencing wire for cooking: much cheaper than spending one and sixpence on a billy. And I'd make two other billies the same way, one for tea and for boiling water, the other for vegetables. The largest billy would be for stews which I'd make from kangaroos killed with my .22. I hadn't really worked out where I'd find the vegetables, but I thought that raiding Stanthorpe's market gardens would ensure a supply of potatoes and carrots and onions for a while.

If I met a Japanese patrol in the granite hills behind Stanthorpe, I would pick them off, one by one, with my .22. I would move so silently and swiftly that they wouldn't see me, and of course I knew the surrounding country pretty thoroughly.

I didn't discuss my plans with anybody, nor did I worry about what would happen to my father, my mother and my sister, Margaret. I suppose I thought somebody would look after them — or else that the whole of Stanthorpe's population would be in the hills with me, fighting the Japanese and living off the land in the same way as I would do.

Though I knew that war was a dreadful thing, I had a sneaking wish that the Japs *would* invade and let me prove myself. It would be quite an adventure!

We would all be able to last for years, I thought, until the British came down and rescued us.

As things turned out, of course, I never had to carry out my survival plans. And when I joined up a few years later, in 1942, being a soldier was a very different thing.

WORLD WAR II:
1939–1945

To be perfectly honest, I was sorry when it finished

*T*o be perfectly honest, I was sorry when it finished

'What sort of kid was I?' Tim Murphy echoes the question, puffs thoughtfully on his Benson and Hedges and sits back to think. He is a man of medium height and slight build, with fair hair and a long, bony nose. 'A cheeky little bugger!' His bright and lively brown eyes laugh, and you can see exactly what he means.

"I wasn't bad, though,' he adds. 'Not malicious. And, mind you, coming from a family like mine — they were all mad — I had to do what I could to keep up the tradition, didn't I?

'I know the war was dreadful for many, many people, but for us it was anything but. It was a lot of fun, really.'

On 3 September 1939, the day Australia entered the war, I was eight. Mum, Dad, my sister Norma and I were living in the Sydney suburb of West Ryde. I spent that Sunday doing what I normally did during the school holidays; mooching around with my best mate, Richard, playing cubbyhouses, swapping Speed Gordons and Tarzan comics, making catapults from twigs, inner tubing and bits of leather. I stayed at Richard's for tea, as arranged, and came home when it was dark.

I suppose I was a bit late, but instead of saying. 'Where have you *been*?' Mum and Dad scarcely seemed to notice my appearance. With Norma, they were listening intently to the white bakelite radio on the dresser. All Mum said was, 'Sssh!' I obediently shushed, and heard a solemn voice, an ABC voice, saying: 'Ladies and gentlemen, the Prime Minister of Australia.' Then the soothing tones of Mr Menzies came on the air, announcing that, because Germany had persisted in its invasion of Poland, Great Britain was at war and that, as a consequence, Australia too was at war.

'Gosh!' I said, feeling that an appropriate remark was necessary. 'Sssh!' said Mum again. I subsided, and somebody came on air to tell us that war had been inevitable, was a good thing, would check the menace of Nazism, etc. But I wasn't listening. I was absolutely frozen with panic.

This had nothing to do with what Mr Menzies had said, or not directly. About two weeks before, Richard and I had sent a letter to the *Sydney Morning Herald*. In our best printing we had said we thought Mr Hitler was a nice man and that there was too much fuss about war. Even though the letter had been signed 'Two Friends', what if the military police picked us up for *treason*? (From reading comics I knew the police Had Their Methods.) What would Mum say if I had to spend the rest of my life in handcuffs?

I never breathed a word about this to Mum and Dad, or to anybody else — but for the first couple of months of war I was convinced I was about to be carted off every time there was a knock at the door.

I had very little idea about what war meant, except that men had to go off to France, put on tin helmets and shoot Germans from trenches, as Mum's elder brother, Uncle Ken, had done in the first war. Either that, or men would shoot at each other from aeroplanes, or gallop towards each other on splendid horses, wearing plumes in their slouch hats.

Germany was a mystery to me. I knew it was a large country in Europe, a long way away, with dull-looking purplish and green stamps which I'd seen in my cousin Laurie's collection. As well as writing and posting a lot of letters, Germans were air aces: I knew that because of the serials in *Champion* magazine, but they never won because the British were better.

> Zing! Pow! Zow! Crack! Bullets rained through the cockpit. Sweat bedewing his brow, Vernon Alverstoke Fortescue could see the evil leer on the face of Fritz the Hun in his death-dealing Messerschmitt. 'By the living jingo, I'll shoot you down,' vowed the British hero as he hurled his trusty plane in a screaming half-circle. Fritz fell in a plume of smoke, but Alverstoke Fortescue had failed to see three more of the enemy lurking nearby. Biff! Kapow! With two bullets he shot two down and then, summoning up his reserves of courage, he dived over and below the third enemy plane, deafened by the screaming rush of his tortured engine...

Well, I thought, Australia might be at war, but obviously the British would have the job of disposing of the Germans. They were much closer, after all.

'Will you have to fight, Dad?' I asked. I knew he was probably too old, he must have been at least forty, but I wanted to know if he was going to dress up in a slouch hat and rifle. But Dad said, no, he was working as an engineer at Homebush abattoirs, so they wouldn't send him. He was in a 'reserved occupation'. I was quite put out, because that meant nobody in our family was going to be a soldier. Some of the other kids at school had elder brothers or cousins who had been given NX numbers and who were dying to get on troop ships and go over to the Middle East.

The papers started to sprout maps of North Africa, with the names of some places spelled out. Arrows and dotted lines became very important, to show where the Australians were. 'This is history,' said Mr Gardner, my teacher, and like everybody else in the class I cut out the maps and pasted them in my social studies book. Names like Benghazi and Bardia didn't mean much, because they were foreign.

Then Mr Gardner took us to a Red Cross exhibition of things the Australians had captured in the Western Desert. This was much more exciting than maps with peculiar names, and besides, I had the chance to travel into Sydney on a proper electric train, something I'd only done a few times before. With Richard I gazed, thrilled, at things I'd never imagined; real Lugers and Beretta pistols, Italian water-bottles, banknotes, goggles. Some of the things were decorated with a strange broken cross that Mr Gardner told us was called a swashticker, worn by Germans to show they were evil Nazis. I was dying to pinch a ceremonial dagger I saw, glinting wickedly in its case. Just the thing to impress the other kids!

Then the Prime Minister, whom my Auntie Molly called 'that nice Mr Menzies', wasn't Prime Minister any more. He had been replaced by a thin-faced man who wore round glasses and whose name was Curtin. This meant that the dreaded Labor Party was in charge of the country — and, according to Auntie Molly, we might as well give up any hope of winning the war. Curtin, she said, was 'common', a drunkard who hadn't had the decency to fight in the last war. 'He showed the white feather,' she said ominously. (I thought that made him sound like a cockatoo.) Mum either agreed with what Auntie Molly said or kept quiet — Auntie Molly could spend a quarter of an hour telling you why she was right about almost everything — but Dad became a little irritated sometimes. I now think he was a secret Labor supporter; certainly he defended Eddie Ward when Auntie Molly got stuck into him.

Towards the end of 1940, the *Sydney Morning Herald* started printing more maps than our social studies books could keep up with. There were new places to learn about in Asia. And for the first time the arrowheads and dotted lines pointed threateningly towards us. Suddenly the Japanese were the enemy, not the Germans at all.

I found this hard to believe. What? The Japs a threat? Funny little yellow men who said 'ah so' like Frank Watanabe on the wireless? Everybody knew that whatever they made fell apart in five minutes; cheap paper umbrellas, matches that didn't light. If Richard and I bought a balsawood glider set that didn't fit together properly, it was always 'Made in Japan'.

But now it seemed the Japanese had real planes that did work, and the papers taught us their names, with recognition diagrams: Zeros mainly. At recess in the playground we all zoomed around with our arms out going 'ackackack'. The goodies were Spitfires or Wirraways or Mosquitoes, the baddies German Stukas or Japanese Zeros.

Our local council started taking the Japanese invasion threat very seriously. Because the local water pumping station was considered to be a really prime target, they got men to cover it with black and green camouflage paint so the Japs wouldn't see it from the air. Then the obvious thing to do, they thought, was build a dummy one which the Japs would bomb instead. This was all right — but they built the dummy tower only about half a mile from the real one. 'And you know the real cunning?' said Dad, who had followed this story with glee, 'they're going to build a road from the dummy pumping station that'll go *nowhere*. So when the planes bomb it, and the pilots land, they'll be lost. Good idea, eh?'

A couple of weeks later, Norma came home late from the local technical college where she was taking typing and shorthand lessons.

'It's nine o'clock and your dinner's spoiled,' complained Mum crossly.

'*You* try coming home in a blackout when they've changed the names of the stations!' said Norma, just as annoyed.

The government had excelled themselves. All up the northern line they had erased station names from seats, indicators and boards. Every station looked exactly the same as every other one. 'I only knew I was getting off at West Ryde because I knew where the station steps were!' said Norma.

Dad had a lot of fun with this. 'I can see it all,' he explained, between chuckles. 'When the Japs get on at Town Hall — and I bet they won't pay their fares either — and go up the northern line, they'll have battle plans that will tell them to invade Concord West. But they won't see the name on the indicator, *and they'll really be at North Strathfield*. These war planners are clever bastards.'

Then there was the memorable day of the great air-raid drill. We all watched it on the way home from school. Near the pub at West Ryde the wardens had drawn a large circle, supposed to be a bomb crater, and various people were lying around in injured positions, ready to be looked after. It worked wonderfully — until the bus came in from Parramatta.

A warden leapt in front of it, wearing his tin hat and blowing his whistle. The driver pulled up.

'You can't drive across here!' shouted the warden. 'Can't you see it's a bomb crater?'

The driver said, 'Looks like a bloody chalk circle to me, and anyway, it's on my route.'

'Go round! Go round!' shrieked the warden desperately.

'Be buggered,' replied the driver, and drove his bus right across the bomb crater. The warden nearly had a stroke.

Shortly afterwards, a utility drove up pretending to be an ambulance. Out leaped several efficient-looking men who started preparing the bomb victims for hospital. (Some of them were groaning feebly, getting into the spirit of the thing.) One bloke grabbed a man with a red-ink-splashed bandage around his head. 'Give me a hand here, Fred!' he shouted to his mate. 'Righto,' said Fred, and together they lugged the bandaged man to the utility, which was open, hurled him in feet first, and shut the door — on his head. The poor chap had to be taken to hospital.

But Dad's favourite joke concerned the local minister's wife. 'I always carry a cork,' said Mrs Durrant. 'You never know when you might need it.' She meant that when the bombs dropped, she would put the cork in her mouth so that her teeth wouldn't shatter from the pressure. Dad said he wondered if she'd need it somewhere else!

At school we did our bit too. Air-raid drill, for instance. One day we came to school and found that trenches had been dug in the sandy-soiled playground. Mr Sewell, the headmaster (known to Richard and me as Droopy Drawers), explained at assembly that a siren would sound unexpectedly during the day, and we would all file out of our classroom 'in good order' and dive into the trenches. We would stay there until the all clear signal went.

Well, we could hardly wait. The most dreary arithmetic lesson suddenly became exciting because we just didn't know when the siren would go and we could drop everything.

The first time it happened, Mrs Harris, our class teacher, was giving us a geography lesson. Off went the siren.

'Get into line! Get into line!' she called, as about twenty ten-year-olds, boys and girls, rushed for the doorway, pushing and shoving and paying off several old scores with the odd dig in the ribs. We burst through the door and raced for the trenches. This was it! Really something! In we went, scrambled down and crouched, as we'd been shown. ('Get off my hand!' I yelled at Joyce Doughty.) There we stayed, arms folded about our heads, knees bent, waiting. I imagined I could hear anti-aircraft fire and machine-guns all around and didn't want to lift my head in case a Jap fighter plane got me...ackackack...

Eventually — it seemed like hours later — the all clear sounded. We dragged ourselves out of the trenches, emptied sand from our school shoes and washed our hands.

One time we almost lost a child, a tiny little girl in first class. It had been raining and the trenches were half full of water — but we had to do drill as usual. Poor little kid slipped into her part of the trench, lost her balance and was under water before anybody noticed. Fortunately her friend screamed: 'Carolyn's drowning!' and she was pulled out.

Air-raid drills cheered me up considerably. My only regret was that the Japs never happened to be hovering obligingly overhead to watch.

We had first aid classes, too. Ladies from the Red Cross came out to tell us about the best way to bandage ourselves and each other. We were told that all the classrooms could be made into relief stations in case there was a bombing attack — something that puzzles me now, because the school wasn't far from a couple of small hospitals. Obviously the Red Cross were taking no chances, though.

They also ran class competitions for the best first aid kit. The trick was to put in as many different things with a possible medical use as you could find — not just obvious things like bandages, or safety pins or tweezers ('for removing flying shrapnel') but whatever you had in your medicine chest at home. My finest hour came when the nurse noticed I'd put some tinea ointment in my kit. 'What's this for?' she asked.

'Trench foot,' I told her smugly. I won the class prize that day.

Richard and I had a lot of fun being mock patients. We thought the bomb drill by the pub had been feeble and the adults hadn't really put their hearts and souls into it. We bandaged each other until we looked like mummies, then got red paint or Mercurochrome and splattered it all over our bandaged arms and legs and heads. Richard loved this. His favourite trick was to get me to bandage him after school and totter, groaning, into the local Moran and Cato grocery shop, lurch up to the counter and collapse on the floor, causing the mums who were getting their groceries to scatter.

Mr Rogers, the grocer, was never impressed. 'Hello, Richard,' he said, as he continued to weigh out sugar. Later in life Richard became a well-known radio actor.

Then it was February 1942, and the Japanese had gone

through Hawaii and the islands and had bombed Darwin. Darwin! On Australian shores!

Auntie Molly and Uncle Harold came to visit us on a Friday night just after it happened. 'This may be our last visit for a while,' said Auntie Molly. 'The Japs might be here and we won't be able to travel.'

Dad suggested gently that, if the Japs were actually in Sydney, which didn't seem terribly likely just then, worrying how to get from Penshurst to West Ryde would probably be among the least of Auntie Molly's problems. But she wouldn't have it.

'I've told Harold that, if the Japs come, they won't take us alive,' she said. 'Everybody knows they torture innocent women and children, and...' She was about to continue, but remembered that I was there and these sorts of conversations weren't suitable for the ears of a young boy.

'So Harold and I are going to take cyanide,' she said. 'After we bury all my jewels.'

'You going to be in this, Harold?' queried Dad.

Uncle Harold nodded, not quite firmly.

'Well, that'll certainly show the Japs,' remarked Dad, lighting another cigarette.

He stopped joking in the ensuing weeks, though. When we went to the pictures on Saturday afternoons, the newsreels (always a few weeks behind the news we heard on the radio) were frightening — they showed towns and villages in Asia being bombed, planes dropping bombs, lines of desperate people making their way through the ruins of their houses. The propaganda posters showed fearsome warriors with cunning faces, not funny little yellow men any more; people started to leave Sydney for places inland, which the Japs would find more difficult to capture.

One of Norma's friends, who had gone to a Catholic school and who still kept in contact with the nuns, told her that some of them had moved to the Blue Mountains, west of Sydney, until the war was over, since everybody knew that the Japs raped nuns. Mum's best friend, Auntie Shirley, told us quite matter-of-factly that when the Japs invaded she intended to throw herself off the Ryde Bridge, holding her two daughters by the hand, so that all three would be drowned. Her husband was away in New Guinea and she was alone. 'I'd rather kill myself than be caught by those little yellow so-and-sos,' she said. 'And the thought of what they could do to Anne and Julie...' She didn't really need to say any more. There had been too many reports in the paper of atrocities: the Japs were known to have cut off women's breasts and tortured children in unspeakable ways.

We stopped playing Wirraways and Zeros in the school playground; that had suddenly become bad taste because the threat was getting more real all the time.

'Shouldn't we build an air-raid shelter?' I suggested to Mum and Dad. There was a lot in the papers about the Japanese plans for bombing Australia; they wouldn't invade until they had knocked out hospitals, electricity plants, and so on. My friend Richard's uncle was busily constructing a shelter underneath their garden shed.

'No, that's probably not necessary,' said Dad, who appeared to treat the whole thing with great calmness. 'We can go under the house.'

I wasn't sure about this. Underneath the house, which was solid enough, was full of old broken wringers and damaged chairs and bits of furniture that had come from Grandma's house after her death eight years before. It was cobwebby and sinister — and I couldn't make up my mind whether being bombed was preferable to being bitten to death by a funnel-web spider. But Mum thought we should do something, so we spent a whole weekend clearing a space among the dusty sideboards and old pictures that nobody wanted any more. In the end we had an area with four spare chairs, a table, kerosene lamps and tinned food. 'Don't forget the tin-opener,' said ever-practical Mum.

Then came the night in May 1942 when the midget subs slid into Sydney Harbour. We drew our blackout curtains and waited in the dark silence, hearing distant wailing from sirens and ships fifteen miles away. We knew that the harbourside suburbs — Maroubra, Bondi, Rose Bay — would be more likely to be hit than we were; Dad had explained that the Japanese artillery would hardly be likely to reach West Ryde.

It was very dull sitting in the living room, and for some reason everybody was whispering.

'Shouldn't we go and hide under a table?' hissed Norma.

'What for?' demanded Dad reasonably.

'Well, that's what the Defence Department says you're supposed to do if you're being bombed.'

'But we're not being bombed,' said Dad.

'Not yet, but we could be,' said Norma.

'But we aren't . . .'

'But we could be.'

In our family this sort of conversation was apt to continue until everybody got bored with it. Dad was bored already, but Norma insisted.

'Look,' said Dad eventually, forgetting to whisper, 'there is no point in doing anything. The Japs won't get us. There is nothing we can do.'

We sat in the dark for about another half hour. Eventually Mum said, 'I'm going to bed.' So we all did.

The next morning we found out that the subs had been destroyed. That appeared to be that: and I felt reassured. If the Japs couldn't organise a simple submarine raid, I thought, not much danger could be expected from them.

I started becoming a little bored with the war. 'There's a war on' was a phrase generally used by adults to justify your doing something you didn't want to do, or to stop you having fun. Everybody had ration books. There weren't any sweets, except chewing gum. Norma, who was now working in a city office, said she couldn't find any new clothes and getting stockings was impossible.

Norma was beginning to irritate me. She was eighteen, seven years older than I was, and when she was at home she spent her time gazing soulfully into the mirror trying to look like Rita Hayworth, putting her bristly dark hair in pin curls and reading the *Women's Weekly* and other magazines that told you how to be attractive to men. She mixed up horrible glop and slathered it all over her face to improve her complexion. ('Is that what all that stuff's for?' asked Dad. 'I thought you were going to swim the English Channel.') Most annoying of all, she was trying out a new laugh, a sort of swooping 'hahaha', which reminded me of a knife scraping across a plate. She accompanied this with a backward sweep of her hair, just like Veronica Lake. I wasn't yet old enough to shave, of course, so I watched with interest while Norma attacked the hair on her legs with a razor blade (difficult to get, these were, there was a war on). Her legs were nicked and scraped all the time, it seemed, and I thought that if I couldn't do better than that when it was my turn to start shaving, I'd grow a beard.

Our relationship hit rock bottom when I saw her slathering a horrid mixture of coffee essence and liquid make-up on her legs. The idea was, apparently, that you gave your legs a nice tanned matte finish, and then drew a pencil line from the middle of the ankle to your upper thigh to make you look as if you had stockings on. She had asked me to help her draw the line because I had a pretty straight eye.

I looked at her thoughtfully. 'Norma, why is your left leg darker than your right one?' I asked curiously. She threw her eyebrow pencil at me and didn't speak to me for the rest of the day.

I was delighted that the Japanese weren't going to invade, mostly because I thought it was probably my duty to protect the family. I didn't mind protecting Mum from rape and torture (though strictly speaking, she was Dad's responsibility), but the thought of protecting Norma made my blood run cold. I'd rather run away.

It came as no surprise to me that the answer to the Japanese menace was the Yanks. The English were better people, but they had quite enough on their plates, and the Americans were probably okay. They had a good record for saving people; I knew that from watching Westerns. They even saved French people sometimes (I was besotted with all things French after I saw *Beau Geste*) so it stood to reason they'd give us a hand.

Even Auntie Molly admitted, grudgingly, that 'common' Mr Curtin probably knew what he was doing when he said that Australia looked to America for help. 'I'd rather it was the Mother Country,' she said, 'but I suppose beggars can't be choosers.'

According to the movies, the Yanks had more planes than anybody else, including the Germans, and probably the Japanese as well. Their general, Douglas MacArthur, looked like a movie hero in all the photographs I saw, or like Rockfist, the hero in my old comic books. You couldn't get anybody better.

Suddenly the Yanks were here. The papers were full of them. They all seemed to have big mouths and square teeth, and came from places I'd never heard of, like Omaha, and Nebraska. I kept my eyes open for a few who might drift around West Ryde, but it didn't seem to be on their beat. (This wasn't too surprising; the Japanese hadn't made any effort to attack West Ryde, so presumably the Yanks weren't needed to save it.)

Some of the boys at school started doing American accents, just to keep in trim. We were in final year of primary school now, and terribly sophisticated. Richard, of course, did the best one. All he had to say was, 'What tahm duh yew come home frahm school?' and we fell around laughing. He sounded much funnier than the Yanks in the pictures.

Gregory Turner, the most sophisticated boy in our class, turned up at recess with some real chewing gum. 'My sister's got a Yank boyfriend,' he said nonchalantly. Real gum! The stuff we were used to was in small ridged packets, each piece white and pillow-shaped. But Gregory showed us long, grey strips packed in silver foil. He didn't offer it round, just let us look at it. I had loved my PK and Juicy Fruit because that was practically all you could get in the way of sweets. Now I felt like a tugboat owner confronted by a battleship; completely outclassed.

Gregory's chewing gum was yet another reason to get annoyed with Norma. If she had any sense, I thought, she'd find a Yank for herself. Then I could flash packets of real chewing gum around at school, and look very smug, just as Gregory was doing. If she was any sort of loyal sister at all, she'd do me a favour for a change and help me increase my status, which could do with some increasing.

Then, a few weeks later, Norma asked casually at tea, 'Can I bring a friend home for dinner next week?'

Mum was onto this like a hawk. 'A girlfriend?' she asked.

Norma hung her head so a curl drooped over her right eye. Veronica Lake. 'No, it's...well, actually it's an American soldier I met...' Mum was about to ask her where, but she said quickly, 'I thought he'd like to have a good home-cooked meal. He's very nice. *No*, Mum, we haven't been up to anything.'

'Hmm,' said Mum. 'What's his name?'

'Henry Sorensen. He's from the West somewhere.'

I asked, 'Does he have a ten-gallon hat and ride a horse?' chortling at my own wit.

Norma gave me one of her looks. 'He comes from the Midwest, and his parents are Swedish.' Mum frowned. Not only an American, but a foreigner as well!

'Look, Mum, I'm almost nineteen, and I do know what I'm doing,' began Norma.

This was an old, familiar theme, and to cut her off Mum said, 'All right, he can come.'

Norma beamed radiantly, like Loretta Young. She always did when she got her own way.

It was settled that Henry Sorensen would come to dinner the following Saturday evening. I kept out of Norma's way that week. She was unbearable, giggling in her new way whenever you asked her anything, bursting into tears if anybody challenged her. Like when Dad asked her: 'Aussie boys not good enough for you, eh?'

I couldn't quite understand Dad's attitude. For the first time in months I was pleased with Norma, generally speaking. She'd done the right thing, hadn't she? Then why did Dad seem to think that Henry Sorensen wasn't quite good enough for us? I heard him say to Mum, 'You shouldn't have given in so easily over this Yank, Marge.' Dad apparently just didn't like Americans.

I could hardly wait to meet him, to ask him questions about aeroplanes, Hollywood and movie stars.

Mum said loudly, often, that she wasn't going to cook any-thing special, but I caught her in the kitchen more than once, with Norma, poring over a *Women's Weekly* article called 'Dinner with a Yankee', which mentioned all sorts of American delicacies like California Chocolate Pie (chocolate? We couldn't get it!) and Fish Chowder. I think it got too complicated in the end. But Mum had heard from Auntie Shirley, whose husband was in New Guinea, that Americans could eat anything they wanted, even chicken and beer, in the jungle. Chicken and beer! We simply couldn't compete. So Mum settled for what Dad called 'good wholesome tucker'.

Saturday came. Mum had dinner ready as soon as Dad came home at six, though Norma and Henry Sorensen weren't expected for another hour. Dad was sent off to change into his best and only blue suit, and he didn't like that. 'He's only a bloody Yank,' he mumbled. I wore my first pair of long trousers, which I knew made me look older, at least fifteen, and I had my hair slicked down in wet grooves with Californian Poppy. I felt as if I'd been scalped. Mum in her best green dress (made over from one of Norma's, who was slightly larger) flicked invisible crumbs from the tablecloth.

She'd made shepherd's pie, which wasn't easy; I'd had to go down to the grocer's that morning and queue because potatoes, as usual, were scarce. Barley broth, my favourite soup, was the first course. Mum said that she had wanted to do something a bit more exotic (I think she felt she was letting Australia down) but nobody else seemed to mind.

Knock, knock. There they were at last. 'I'll go,' said Dad. There was a murmur of voices in the hall, with an odd accent. I heard Norma's well-known annoying giggle. Then Dad ushered in Norma, who had at least a pound and a half of make-up on, and a tall young man with sandy hair who clutched a bunch of carnations. Mum couldn't believe it. How did he get hold of carnations? At that time of year, with a war on?

Giggling in a way that made me long to trip her up, Norma presented Henry Sorensen. 'How do you do, ma'am?' he said, very politely in a slow drawl, presenting Mum with the flowers. 'And I thought you might like these,' he added, producing a flat packet that had some brown, streaky stuff inside.

Mum gasped. 'Real nylons! Thank you very much!'

'Henry gave me three pairs,' said Norma.

Henry gave Dad three packets of Marlboro cigarettes. 'Thanks, mate,' he mumbled. Dad was a very enthusiastic smoker who, like everybody else, was always complaining about not being able to get cigarettes. They weren't rationed exactly, just impossible to find. Dad usually made do with roll-your-owns, keeping the bumpers — the ends — in a spare tobacco tin, and rolling them carefully into new cigarettes when he ran out. Three packets of Marlboro were treasures indeed, and I could tell that Henry Sorensen was well on the way to winning Dad's heart after all.

Well, I thought, what do I get? With a firm, sincere handshake, Henry Sorensen presented me with three — three — long packets of real chewing gum. Wonderful!

After the present giving was over, and Mum had said she hoped he was enjoying his stay, and he said he was enjoying

'Ahstralia' very much, I had a chance to take a really good look at Henry Sorensen.

He looked magnificent, the smartest soldier I had ever seen in my life. All the Aussies wore baggy khaki or jungle green uniforms that didn't fit properly. I didn't mind that our boys looked a bit scruffy: they were in uniform to fight, after all, and there was a war on. But Henry looked extremely neat. His dark beige trousers were so well pressed you could have cut your finger on the creases. His drill shirt was clean and unrumpled around the collar, and his pinkish-brown tie was spotless and new, the end tucked into the shirt. He clutched a neat little forage cap in one hand and his crew-cut blond hair bristled. He had the regulation standard American square white teeth, and his shoes were black and glossy. But his chief glory was his jacket. *Three* rows of ribbons! He must have been incredibly brave. This even made up for the fact that he wore scent, which was only for girls, I thought. (Actually it was aftershave and hair oil.)

Dinner was not a relaxed meal. None of us quite knew what to say and I sat, head down, chomping away diligently. Henry Sorensen didn't use his knife to eat with, just cut up his shepherd's pie and shovelled it in with his fork. He also asked for a glass of water with the meal. Norma, for once, didn't have a thing to say, and she ate much faster than usual.

Dad really tried. 'Where are you from, Mr Sorensen?'

'Call me Henry, sir. Well, I'm from a part of the Yewnited States called the Midwest. I guess it's some of the best grain-raising country around,' he said. He followed this up with a lot of statistics about grain yields in towns around places called Minneapolis and St Paul. All Dad could say was, 'Really?' 'How interesting. I didn't know that,' and 'Mmmmm'.

Norma, who'd never previously had an interest in wheat, hung on every word Henry Sorensen said. She was being Loretta Young again.

From wheat, Henry Sorensen moved to General MacArthur, Guadalcanal, the infamy of Pearl Harbor and how well the Americans were doing. This made Dad and me a bit cross: he made it sound as though Australians hadn't been anywhere in the area.

'So I guess that'll be fine,' said Henry Sorensen, scooping up the last of the vanilla ice-cream. 'That was a mighty fine meal, ma'am. Yes, I can hardly wait to see some action.'

'But you've already been in action, haven't you?' I asked.

He flashed those extremely white, square teeth. 'Why no, Junior.' (*Junior!*)

I gazed incredulously at his beribboned chest. 'What are all those ribbons for?'

He smiled modestly. 'Well, that one's a good conduct ribbon, and that's for rifle shooting, and that's for fatigue parade. . .' He told me what every one of those ribbons was for and *not one* had been gained in battle.

I was outraged. This Yank was a fraud! He was soft! He was a fake, not a real soldier at all, worse than a choco! I felt like returning his chewing gum to him, unused.

I could tell from the look on Dad's face that he agreed with me. After the meal, though, he asked Henry Sorensen to join him in a bottle of beer. This was a great honour: Dad had been saving two precious bottles for weeks.

Henry Sorensen accepted with enthusiasm. While Mum and Norma cleared up, he and Dad continued to sit at the table and Dad poured out the precious fluid, slowly and carefully. Henry Sorensen tilted back his head and poured the first glass down his throat without blinking. Dad looked surprised — beer wasn't something you disposed of lightly then — and swallowed his own beer cautiously. Henry poured the next glass down his throat at about the same speed as his first. Very soon both bottles had gone, and at a rough guess I would say that two-thirds was drunk by Henry Sorensen.

'That sure is powerful beer, hoo-ee!' he said enthusiastically. I noticed that his face was a lot pinker. Instead of telling us about the grain harvests in Minnesota, he started relating a lot of pointless jokes. Dad laughed politely, with side glances at me, but I didn't understand any of them. Then Henry fished a flask of whisky out of his back pocket and insisted on sharing it with Dad, who agreed and sipped tentatively. Not so Henry Sorensen, who began singing some of 'the ole songs I grew up with when ah was young'. They seemed to consist of commands to bring in the harvest and milk cows. Dad hummed along politely, obviously nonplussed.

Henry Sorensen was in tears after another twenty minutes. His songs became stories of lost loves on May mornings and misery and woe. Then he grabbed Dad's arm and kept saying to Dad that 'our General MacArthur is the greatest man in the world'. This was almost too much for Dad, who was a fervent admirer of our side, but he kept nodding politely, with a fixed smile. I was bored rigid by all this, but as the only alternative was to join Mum and Norma in the kitchen (and possibly be asked to dry up) I stayed where I was.

The evening was over at last. Henry Sorensen stood up, knocking a chair sideways, and shook everybody's hand with great effusiveness. 'I certainly am glad to have met you all,' he said, nodding many times. 'I'll have this memory of Aussie Land when I'm out in the jungle.'

Norma walked him up the hill to the station, and was back soon afterwards.

'Well, what did you think?' she asked. Dad lit a Marlboro thoughtfully.

'Not much,' he said. Norma bridled and went to her room, and that was that.

We didn't hear from Henry Sorensen again; Norma didn't mention him after that, having realised what the rest of us thought of her new beau. Dad wondered aloud whether Henry had succeeded in getting a campaign ribbon for making his own bed correctly, but that was all he said. And when the papers told us about the so-called Battle of Brisbane, when American and Australian soldiers fought in the streets, Dad said he was sure Henry Sorensen hadn't been there.

The war dragged on. Towards the end, it seemed that the Japanese probably wouldn't invade, so people relaxed slightly — though nobody was taking any chances. Things were still rationed, there were Victory Loans advertised on the wireless, and the newsreels showed Aussie soldiers slogging grimly along the Kokoda Trail and elsewhere in New Guinea; cars, when you saw them, had great soft bags of gas on top (like today's LPG gas) because petrol was so short. I carried on life as normal; the war receded until it became like a long and exciting serial — though not as good as *First Light Fraser* on the wireless.

One day in 1945, after having done the dreaded playground duty (I was in my first year at high school, and we had to take it in turns to sweep up leaves and put rubbish in the bin), I walked past the school radio, a huge tan-coloured object with a mesh-covered hole at the front, which was wheeled from room to room for school broadcasts on the ABC. For some reason it was on, muttering to itself. I heard: 'Here is a special announcement...' and stopped, curious.

On came the slow voice of Prime Minister Ben Chifley, announcing that the war was over. I couldn't believe it. I knew, like everybody else, that the Americans had dropped a bomb on Japan and the war had finished in Europe. Now the Japanese had surrendered!

I burst into the classroom, where everybody was starting a geography lesson, and yelled, 'It's over! The war's over! I just heard it on the wireless!' The teacher stopped telling everybody about the products of West Africa and walked hastily out of the room. Yes, he said upon his return, I was right.

As I went home that afternoon I felt curiously flat. Already cars were tooting and people were waving to each other, and in town I knew people were in Martin Place, dancing and singing. But I was sorry in a way. Though I knew that the war had caused great hardship to so many people all over the world, and many of our men had been killed in New Guinea and elsewhere, I had enjoyed the whole thing. I was a little sorry it was over.

❧ *We thought we were gone, for sure*

Joyce Drummond has lived in Bondi ever since she was a child. 'I love it,' she says. 'Haven't moved all my life.' Joyce is a small, fussily dressed woman with grey hair, who was ten when the Japanese submarines came into Sydney Harbour on 31 May 1942. She tells the story of that night as a joke — now it's funny and exciting — but you can still see a trace of the little girl with wide brown eyes who couldn't stop screaming when the shells hit.

Dad went to the war in New Guinea late in 1941, leaving Mum, my brother Jimmy, who was eight, and me, aged eleven. We got letters from him quite often. He was all right, he said, and made jokes about mosquitoes. He was a bootmaker by trade, and once he wrote and told us that he could probably defeat the Japs single-handed if he was captured: he'd make them boots with the nails hammered in the wrong way. I thought that was very funny.

I worried about the Japs, not in New Guinea, but here. Mrs Mills, our landlady, who lived downstairs in our block of flats, used to tell Jimmy and me that 'it's a well-known fact that Japanese make innocent women and children drink water until they burst'. And in the papers there were advertisements saying what dreadful people the Japanese were. I remember one that showed a drawing of a girl lying on her back, looking dead. It said, 'Deep in the hearts of the Japanese there has been fostered a great and calculating hate. Here in Australia the Japs will find a hate to match their own — a hate for their lies and pretences and lascivious brutality...We shall force back the Jap where he belongs.' And in capitals: 'WE'VE ALWAYS DESPISED THEM... NOW WE *MUST* SMASH THEM!'

Mum worked part-time as an usherette at the Odeon, and Jimmy and I got in for free. (I saw *Blossoms in the Dust* with Greer Garson and Walter Pidgeon five times, and cried every time.) No matter what the show was, there was at least one newsreel showing

We thought we were gone, for sure

Australian soldiers marching through mud and jungle in New Guinea. I always watched out for Dad, but never saw him. The Japs were getting closer, and they would be here soon. That's what I believed and I was scared.

So were lots of other people around us. We lived in a street that had lots of blocks of flats like ours — made of purplish brick and only about two storeys high at the most — as well as small fibro and weatherboard houses with grey paling fences around them. We weren't rich or posh; nobody around us was.

Most of the houses and flats around us had blinds of special blackout paper to put over the windows at night, and Mum's sister, Auntie Veronica, who was a nun, helped us stick strips of brown paper over the windows in crisscross patterns so that when the Japanese dropped their bombs we wouldn't be hit by flying glass. Sandbags were piled in every room of our tiny flat, and there were buckets of sand on the landings, so that any Japanese incendiary bombs could be smothered.

The beaches weren't places to play any more. Bondi Beach, as well as Bronte and Clovelly further east, had barbed-wire fences across them. Men with tractors, civilians as well as soldiers, banked the sand up into trenches, as well as building machine-gun emplacements. I thought this was terrifying, but Jimmy didn't. He used to duck in and out of the barbed-wire lines with his mates, screaming 'ackackack!' until a soldier or somebody told him, 'Get out of it, you little bastard!'

I went into town on the tram with Mum sometimes, and hated it. There were piles of sandbags outside buildings in Pitt Street and George Street, and bright red signs that directed people to air-raid shelters. All the parks had zigzag trenches, like the ones we had at school, and piles of clay were everywhere. We would fight our way down the street, dodging the crowds of Yank and Australian soldiers and girls, dashing across the street (there were no pedestrian crossings and the trams looked as though they would run you over). The whole of Sydney just looked a mess.

Dad's brother, Uncle Norm, who was a farmer at Cowra in the central west, said we didn't need to worry too much about the Japs. Like thousands of other people, Uncle Norm was an aeroplane spotter. He didn't come to see us very often, but when he did he told us about spotting, which was very important. Jimmy pestered him, wouldn't leave him alone! One time he brought his spotter's card, which showed how to identify the different aircraft.

Uncle Norm used to rush into the paddock near his house with his card whenever he heard a plane overhead, decide what sort it was, and ring the local Air Force Training Corps centre. 'You're not allowed to tell them what sort of plane you think it is,' he said. 'See, if you say it's a Douglas and it isn't, you're in trouble. You have to tell them what it is using its letters and numbers.

'Better to give no description than the wrong one,' he said. 'They can check from other posts whether the plane I've reported has been spotted by other people.'

It sounded all right, very efficient. But what if the Japs camouflaged their planes to look like ours?

'No, they can't do that,' said Uncle Norm reassuringly. I couldn't understand why he was so confident — especially after I heard him tell Mum that he'd mistaken a flight of ducks for planes in formation. I started wondering if he was any good.

Uncle Norm wasn't the only one who was confident the Japs wouldn't invade. Mrs Gale, who lived at the other end of our street and who referred to herself as 'a gay divorcee', told Mum, 'It'll be all right. We don't have to worry unless Singapore falls.' But Mum didn't take any notice of her, and neither did I, because Mrs Gale was no better than she ought to have been. She lived with her teenage daughter, Louise, in a shabby weatherboard house to which American soldiers used to come late in the afternoons. She was tall and dark-haired and pretty, with her hair rolled into big puffs about her ears, and she was the only woman in the street who had real nylon stockings. ('I know where she got those,' sniffed Mum, who had to paint her legs with make-up to make them look tanned.)

Mrs Gale thought she was too good for the street. She had been a Tivoli girl before the war and her eldest daughter, Elizabeth, had been a semi-finalist in a competition to find Australia's Deanna Durbin. Her eldest boy, Anthony (pronounced without the 'h' which we all thought was terribly affected), was in New Guinea fighting, and the day that he had a letter published in the 'Letters from Our Boys' page of the *Women's Weekly* Mrs Gale must have shown it to the whole street. I didn't like her because her daughter Louise called her 'Ellen'. *Nobody* called their mother by her Christian name!

The street didn't like Mrs Gale for yet another reason. Mr Curtin had announced that clothes rationing would come into force in a couple of months. Mrs Mills told Mum, 'You should have seen that Mrs Gale. True as I'm standing here, she got off the tram at the corner carrying a huge parcel of clothes. More than she could possibly need, even with Louise.' Mrs Gale had very selfishly bought up big before rationing came in. We had all read about the crowds of people who had besieged the shops and bought things they couldn't possibly need.

Mrs Gale said to Mum, a bit defiantly, 'Well, rationing

hasn't started yet, and I *do* work at McCathies.' As though that justified her buying so many of the clothes they sold!

Sunday 31 May 1942 was like any other day. I didn't like Sundays because there wasn't much to do. Jimmy asked me to go and play with him on the beach, but it looked like rain, and I was tired of his enthusiasm for barbed wire, tractors and sand. In the afternoon I wrote a letter to Dad, which wasn't very interesting. I'd come fourth in the class in spelling, hadn't done too well in arithmetic, and Sister Margaret at school had told me I was quite musical. The letter took hours to write, and I decided to make Dad a pyjama cord, using a cotton reel with four tacks in the top. They were all the rage at school; we called it French knitting. You wound wool in double rows round the tacks, then flicked the second row over the first, over and over again, while the knitted cord disappeared through the hole in the centre of the cotton reel. Dad's pyjama cord was about nine feet long; I didn't know how to end it off, and had to keep going until somebody told me.

We had dinner — tinned camp pie, carrots and swede turnips — and went to bed fairly early because Monday was one of Mum's days as an usherette at the Odeon and Jimmy and I had school.

During the night, I'm not sure when, I woke up with a jump. My first thought was that a lot of cars were backfiring outside; I'd never heard such loud explosions in my life. Then I heard sirens wailing, close, then far away. There were many more explosions, with the rat-a-tat of what sounded like machine-guns.

Crash! Something shattered on Mum's dressing table on the other side of the room. At the edges of the blackout blinds I could see what looked like searchlights.

'Mum! Mum!' I screamed. She was awake, listening, on her side of the room, and she came over to me and hugged me. I suddenly realised what must have happened. The Japs! The Japs were here and they were coming to get us! The Japanese were here, and I sat up in bed and screamed and screamed. I couldn't stop.

Jimmy came rushing in, and we all sat, huddled, on my bed. I quietened down after a couple of minutes, and Mum grabbed us both by the arms. Over the noise and the searchlights she yelled, 'The kitchen table!' The Department of Defence had told people to get under a table, preferably one with sandbags piled on top, if the Japanese attacked. The three of us crawled down the corridor to the kitchen and sat under the table. There was barely room for us all, but at once I felt much safer.

The noises were just as loud, and an immense 'boom', even louder than the one that had wakened me, made me wince and shudder. But at least we were all together.

We were there for what seemed like hours, while the racket went on. Then lights began to flash less frequently, the booming noises and the rat-a-tat and the 'crump' seemed further off.

Then Jimmy said, 'Where's Muggsy?' We had forgotten all about the cat. 'I'm going to find him,' said Jimmy, and crawled out from under the table before Mum could stop him. Mum and I crouched until my back was cold and my legs were beginning to ache. Mum said. 'Where's Jimmy? Should have found Muggsy by now.'

Just then, Muggsy came stalking in from the bedroom and purred against Mum's face. He had obviously been under my bed. I couldn't understand why he hadn't been scared, but he was the sort of cat who never behaved the way you expected him to.

The sounds of the shells had almost died away, and the lights were dimmer. 'Where *is* Jimmy?' Mum was starting to get really worried.

But then the all clear sounded, and as Mum and I crawled out, stiff-legged, from under the table, Jimmy came flying in through the front door. We hadn't heard him leave; we thought he was still in the bedroom.

'Where do you think you've been?' asked Mum.

Jimmy looked innocent, as only he could: 'I just went outside to have a look.'

'*What?*'

But Jimmy was far too excited to notice the expression on Mum's face. 'Mum, there were tracer bullets and Very lights, and pompoms, and searchlights, and...'

'Where did you go?'

'Up on the cliffs. And then a torpedo went off...'

'Up on the *cliffs*! You could have been killed!'

He shook his head. 'No, there were lots of people up there. Mum, it was beaut!'

After Dad had left for New Guinea, Mum didn't discipline us much: giving us whacks on the bottom for misbehaviour had been his job. But for the first time in a long while she grabbed Jimmy, whirled him round and thumped him, as hard as she could. That's when I realised how scared she had been when the Japs attacked. But Jimmy took it all, and though he sniffled a bit, probably for the sake of appearances, he had obviously had such a marvellous time watching the raid that any punishment was strictly secondary. He didn't even listen to Mum's: 'You naughty little boy. You might have been killed. How *dare* you worry me so much?'

We later found out that three Japanese midget submarines, operating from a mother ship somewhere off the coast (a ship that was never found), had sneaked in. One midget sub had been destroyed by naval depth charges, another became entangled in the harbour's anti-submarine boom, the third had escaped. The subs hadn't done much damage, we thought; it wasn't for a few days that we learned they had sunk a ferry at its moorings and killed nineteen people.

I realised that three midget subs coming into the harbour was pretty unimportant compared to what men like Dad were going through in New Guinea, but I thought that was enough. I thought we were gone, for sure, that night — and I certainly didn't want war to come any closer than it already had.

We didn't worry about the Japs . . . we had enough
problems with some of the white people

❧*We* didn't worry about the Japs... we had enough problems with some of the white people

Sandra Hardy is a pretty, dark-haired Aboriginal woman who grew up in a small Queensland community during the war. When she talks about her childhood she laughs a lot; those are obviously happy memories. 'Spoiled rotten by my grandmother, I was,' she says. But there is a wariness, a hardness, in her eyes, that does not entirely square with her words that her childhood was happy and carefree.

I don't know exactly when I was born, but my brothers, sisters and I were all registered on 5 September 1943.

There were eight kids in my family, and I was the second youngest; we were six boys and two girls. My sister was nine years older than I. We lived in the Tully—Ingham area of coastal north Queensland, between Townsville and Cairns. At first our home was a couple of dirt-floor humpies on the riverbank. Upriver was an Army camp and a bit later on all the soldiers moved away. We went to live in the Army huts that were still there — we lived in three of them and they had three-ply roofs and rubber sheeting on top.

Dad worked as a fettler on the railway, and he was never out of a job. He had a very good name as a worker even though he had to lose some time because of his asthma. He used to get awful attacks. He carried a rubber puffer with him, and sometimes he wouldn't be able to breathe. So we would have to walk a couple of miles to the house of some white people who had a telephone so we could get the ambulance for Dad. Then we walked back and my brothers would carry Dad up the road to where the ambulance could pick him up. He was in hospital for a few days at a time.

Mum's mother, my grandma, and her bloke lived not far from us. When I was two I was sent to live with her because she wanted me. She spoiled me rotten! I was very close to her, and also to my brothers who were close to me in age. Oh, Grandma made sure my brothers did the right thing by me! When I was very little I didn't want to walk anywhere — too much trouble — and everybody had to carry me. My brothers hated that because I cried and screamed and nagged them until they did what they were told!

We had a good life, carefree. We went fishing in the river for *moas* or shrimps, which gave us bait for barramundi, and on weekends we walked downriver about five or ten miles to the mouth, where we camped. We took flour, bread and syrup with us and caught lots of fish, periwinkles and mud crabs. We loved chinky apples and the wild Burdekin plums, which we buried in the sand if they weren't ripe. We left them there for a week or so until they were ready to eat. Often as not we'd come back and find that the plums were gone, and all we saw were claw grooves in the sand. The wallabies had taken them. Why do people think animals are dumb?

When I was about seven, Mum died. She died in childbirth, having my youngest brother, but all I knew then was that she went away and never came back. I lay in bed, in the Army hut, and heard Grandma wailing at her place for hours, in the dark. It was dreadful. But after a while I stopped worrying because Mum's spirit came back. See, before she went into Grandma's camp, she used to clear her throat and knock twice. We all did that, that was politeness, you always knock when you come into somebody else's home. I used to hear her, after she died, knock twice, clear her throat, and I'd look up to say hello. But her body wasn't there. She used to visit Grandma quite a lot. She still visits me, comes in and out of my house all the time.

After Mum died I spent more time than ever with Grandma, learning female things. She taught me a lot about her life too. Though she worked on cattle stations from the time she was eight years old, she was raised as a tribal person who had been promised to a tribal man much older than she was. I never knew him. Grandma often told me things, when the two of us were sitting in front of the fire, while she smoked her pipe.

She didn't have any time for white people. 'They're soft,' she said. 'Very soft. They have to go to hospital to have their babies. They stay in the hospital for days, even after the baby is born, and they're not even allowed to have their families in with them.' I agreed that this was ridiculous. Grandma had Mum on the ground, picked her up, left her with cousins, and then went back to working, gathering waterlilies, within an hour or two.

Grandma and Dad were very proud of being Aboriginal, and they made us proud too. Lots of Aborigines weren't then. They hung around in the park by the railway station in Townsville, during the day and at night too. That was their place. The whites used to hurry past, that's if they didn't call them 'ya bloody boongs' or 'Jacky-Jacky' and treat them like dirt, like they weren't even human. But Dad used to say, 'When you go into Townsville you look everybody in the eye. You're as good as they are. Don't let me catch you doing what those other Aboriginal kids do, duck your head away and look down. Just look straight back at them.'

We always did. But it made no difference how you looked at white people, or whether you looked them in the eye or not. They still treated you the same. As though you weren't fit to be on the same earth as them.

I remember being terribly worried about the Japanese coming to invade Australia. I knew that they'd probably come down through Queensland — everybody said so — and that they would kill everybody by torture or shooting.

I asked Dad, 'Will the Japs kill us?'

'No, not us,' said Dad. 'They're after the white fellers. They won't touch us.' That comforted me a lot.

Sometimes I used to wish that the Japs would invade and get the white fellers. Because we were all terribly afraid of the whites. We knew that the Protection people could take you away to Palm Island because of the Queensland Government's Aboriginals Protection Act. The Protection people could do whatever they liked to you. Beat you up if they felt like it. Not let you see your whole family, ever again.

We knew about Palm Island because cousins of ours had been sent there. We went to visit them, but we couldn't just *go* there, we had to apply for permission to visit them.

Palm Island was a terrible, terrible place. The girls were in long dormitories, separated from their brothers and their mothers and fathers. They couldn't even say hello to each other. Women used to walk around wearing dresses cut out of flour bags as a punishment for something. There was a tiny gaol where you were sent for almost anything — talking back to a white person, for instance. (My cousins never did that, but they told me about other Aborigines who did.) They also said the food was very bad, no fruit, just porridge and bread and a few vegetables.

We couldn't even talk privately to our cousins when we visited them. Too many white people around. And they couldn't do anything, even go away, without permission from the Protection people. My cousins didn't get away from Palm Island until they were eighteen. They were there, some of them, for more than ten years.

We hated going there; we thought the whites would say, 'You have to stay and you can't go back home.' Fortunately they never did. We were lucky. I don't know how we escaped, because we knew lots of people who were sent there. Probably we were all right because we were quiet, kept to ourselves, and Dad had a regular job.

We all went to the local state primary school, twelve miles into town by bike. I stayed there until sixth class. There were about forty kids, I suppose, and we were the only Aboriginal family there on a permanent basis.

We did all right. We had a very good teacher, a white bloke of course, called Reginald Faulkner. He told us that we had to learn to read and write and speak English well to succeed in life. He taught me that it wasn't enough to be as good as white people, we had to be *better*.

At school I was very good at spelling and reading, and was mad about history. We didn't learn anything about the war at school. Nor, of course, about our own culture. Just about Captain Cook and how he was speared by blacks at Endeavour River. The white kids used to get at us about that. 'Boongs! Abos!'

'You're all wops and reffos,' we said. 'We were the first people here. We were here before you.'

But mostly we got on all right with the white kids, who were nearly all from farming families around the place. We didn't have shoes or socks, and we brought our damper and golden syrup for lunch instead of the white kids' neat little sandwiches. Our clothes were a bit raggedy, but we were used to that. If any of the white kids tried to chiack us, we'd punch them out straightaway. We were the fastest runners in the class, too.

I never felt like two separate people, an Aboriginal split between my culture and the white culture. I guess I knew I was as good as they were, I knew things they didn't, and I was as bright and good at school as anybody else.

❧ *I always felt there was something missing from my life*

'I think people are so secretive about war because it's such a dehumanising thing,' says Jack Hudson. He's a man of medium height, with dark hair and thoughtful eyes, and he sips quietly at his beer before continuing. 'If you've seen a bit of it yourself, which I did in Vietnam when I went over as a reporter, you don't really want to bring it back in any way.

'I didn't find out what had happened to my father for a long time. I didn't have any point of reference. I didn't know what to ask and, in any case, kids were not encouraged to ask questions then. We relied on hand-fed information, like most kids do.'

I don't remember when Dad enlisted. I was born in 1937, and he went into the Army from his job as a bank teller when the war came. But he joined the militia — he was a choco — and became a victim of the system whereby men who really wanted to fight were often the last sent overseas. So he stayed in the reserve, and was sent to Tenterfield army camp in northern New South Wales, where he was appointed regimental sergeant-major, a training officer.

We were a family of four: my parents, my younger brother Colin and myself. While Dad was at Tenterfield we lived at Kempsey, on the coast. That's the town where Mum and Dad had done their courting. We saw Dad whenever he could get away.

Dad was tallish, thin-faced, with glasses and sandy hair. He looked like John Curtin, I think. He was a good rifle shot, and his glasses must have been to correct long sight, not short sight which is more common. When I was very little, our house at Kempsey was often full of soldiers; Dad's mates from the camp would come over to sink a few beers with him. They were pretty loud sometimes, it was only a small house, and occasionally I had trouble

I always felt there was something missing from my life

getting to sleep, but they weren't really big drinkers, and they were good blokes. Mum never joined in with them much; they talked about the war, which was men's talk.

I remember one particular holiday we had at Yamba. Dad normally didn't talk to me much — I was only six — but this day we had a conversation on the beach. Dad had just given me a corner of his handkerchief to wipe my nose with and he suddenly said: 'If anything happens to me, look after your mother, will you? And be a good boy.'

'Yes, Dad,' I said, a bit puzzled and wondering if there was more to come. We looked at each other for a moment or two, then he said: 'That's all,' and we went back to Mum and Colin.

I forgot about that then. Not long afterwards, Dad went back to camp and we went down to Sydney to visit some relatives. We were staying at a lovely old rooming house near Waverton, called Charing Cross, a house attached to a convent. (Mum was a Catholic though Dad was not.) A man in a uniform came to see Mum.

I was sitting on the front lawn, playing marbles. Next thing Mum came running out of the house, dashing this way and that, frantically, screaming and screaming. My Uncle Leo, who was with us, caught her by the arm and led her back inside while she cried. Then he came up to me. 'Here,' he said. 'This is for you.' And he handed me a carved wooden Luger pistol that he'd made.

I don't remember who told me that Dad had been killed. All I recall is those two things; seeing my mother racing across the lawn, and running my hand over the smooth butt of the wooden Luger. And because I was only seven, the pistol was much more important to me.

Dad had fallen on a hand grenade while training his men at Tenterfield, and he died of wounds to the stomach and chest. They buried him in Tenterfield, and Mum went up for the funeral. Colin and I stayed in Sydney; adults kept children away from things like death and violence in those days.

After Dad's death we went back to Kempsey, and I started school there. Mum, who had trained as a schoolteacher before marrying Dad, went back to work. She hardly spoke to us about Dad; didn't try to build him up as a great hero, or anything like that.

But then, Mum was — and is — a very strong person. She was no looker, was very tall with frizzy hair and a big nose, but had loads of personality. Not only did she teach full-time (and she was a very good schoolteacher, who could get the kids to behave just by giving them a certain look), but as well as that she announced programmes on the local radio station, mostly music and country and western. Later on she had her own women's chat show on 2KM. I used to listen to her on the crystal set I made.

She was a bit of a loner, was Mum. Not very demonstrative. I'm not saying she didn't love us, because she did — and does. But she could manage on her own. (Mum never remarried, though I know at one stage she was thinking about it; an old friend of Dad's used to take her out from time to time. I overheard her discussing this bloke with another of Dad's mates, who said, 'No, don't marry him. What would it do to the boys?' And she didn't. Maybe she was trying to fob off her intended suitor, and we provided the excuse!)

For some weeks after Dad was killed, his mates didn't come to visit us. I think this hurt Mum; Dad had been a very popular man, captain of the local surf club. She didn't say anything about her feelings to us, of course, she never did, but when one or two did eventually call she wasn't nearly as friendly to them as she had been. They were red-faced and awkward. 'We've just come to...ah...express our condolences,' they said. They were embarrassed, didn't know what to say to Mum. And when they saw Colin and me, they always said, 'G'day, nipper, how are you going at school?' and perhaps, 'You be a good boy now, won't you, like your dad would have wanted.'

The only time Mum expressed any bitterness was the time she told me about going to the butcher to collect our meat ration just after Dad died. She apparently asked for too much, and the butcher looked at her and said, 'Lady, don't you know there's a war on?'

Nobody else at West Kempsey Primary School had a father who had been killed in the war. This didn't mean Colin and I were distinguished in any way: like the other kids we swam in the river and went barefoot (I didn't wear shoes till I was twelve; shoes were for sissies). I played with Kim, my kelpie, who used to sit outside the school all day, waiting for me. From the verandah of our fibro house, I used to signal in Morse code to a friend across the road. We went to the pictures on Saturdays, with the other kids, but not with the Aborigines who lived out of town: they were segregated from the rest of us at the picture theatre, and we hardly saw them normally. Mum earned a reasonable salary, enough for us to have a woman to come in and 'do' a couple of days a week; she also earned enough money for me to be given a Speedwell bike for my birthday. It cost eight pounds, which was a lot of money.

'Think yer smart, doncha, just because yer mum's a teacher?' said some of the kids, and I got into quite a lot of fights. It's not easy being a schoolteacher's son. I wasn't a bad fighter, which helped, and I had my own gang at school; sometimes I got the other kids to do my fighting for me. The other teachers singled me out, not because I was particularly bright, but because, being Mum's son, I was supposed to behave better than the other kids, which I did not. I was caned more than most; fifty-four times in one year. If you multiply that by six, because every caning was six cuts, that's a lot of thumping. I knew enough to cover my hands with lemon juice beforehand so the caning wouldn't hurt so much.

I don't think I was worse than other kids, and I didn't feel hard done by. I just seemed to get caught a lot, that's all. I was a stoical kid, on the whole. We weren't a particularly demonstrative family.

But I do remember resenting the attitudes some adults had towards Mum, my brother and me. 'Poor things, they've had a hard time,' sums it up. And I didn't think people had the right to pity me just because I didn't have a father. I went to several parties given by the local Catholic church people — little Christmas parties in the church hall for 'the kiddies whose fathers were killed in the war'. A whole lot of boys and girls, about my age, gathered there from all over the district and we just looked at each other dumbly. We had nothing in common except lacking fathers, and we ate our sandwiches and scones and drank our lemonade in silence. I detested these gatherings; adults were always looking at me with kindly pity, and I loathed them. What did my life have to do with them, anyway? How *dared* they feel sorry for *me*?

All the same, I felt something was missing from my life. Mum never spoke to us about Dad. She looked after us, and I know she cared for us, but she wasn't given to displays of affectionate behaviour. Colin and I were good mates — but his feeling for me was much more that of a younger brother for the elder than a wish to have a father substitute. Or that's the way it seems to me now...it might have been different in his own head. He's told me since that he felt the lack of a father dreadfully; he couldn't even remember what Dad had looked like. He was missing a man of whom he had no memories, none at all. But I didn't find out how he felt for years. We didn't do much talking, Colin and I.

So the three of us went along, each with our own thoughts and memories and feelings, which we never discussed. Once Mum, Colin and I went down to Taree by train. It was a very slow trip and we were all tired for some reason. Colin dozed off in a corner of the compartment, Mum put her head on my shoulder and went to sleep. I still remember how odd that felt: I wanted to put my arm around her, to protect her, and tell her I loved her. But I stared through the window at the gum trees and cows and the grass outside as the train clunked along. I could never have told Mum how I felt about her at that moment. And I never did.

I might be wrong, but I think things would have been different if Dad had been alive.

Nobody talked to us much about the war; there were very few men in uniform around Kempsey. I remember coupons, and rationing, but I had only the vaguest idea of what was going on. We did war history at school, but not of the war we were fighting: one of the teachers, Fred Archer, was a Gallipoli veteran, so we heard all about the brave Aussies and how proud we should be of them. The legend was well and truly alive; Fred Archer talked about it incessantly. It bored us all rigid, I'm afraid, because it seemed to have so little to do with us.

In sixth class at West Kempsey Primary School, we had a teacher called Dave James, who had been a bomber pilot over Germany for a year or so before being wounded and sent back to Australia. He never talked to us about what he had done or seen, just taught school mildly, as though the war had never been. Another teacher had also been a bomber pilot, and he and Dave James were, I think, good friends. But Dave's mate was a very difficult man, a complete drunk. You'd see him at recess down at the bottom of the playground, drinking Scotch out of a bottle. Neither of them ever mentioned the war; they acted as though nothing had happened. We knew that Dave's mate had a 'drinking problem', but that was okay: just another of the funny quirks grown-ups had. I certainly didn't think it had anything to do with the war.

Many years later I became the military correspondent for a national newspaper.

For a long time I'd been bothered about *why* Dad died. I had a lot of mates at Victoria Barracks in Melbourne and I got hold of their records to try to find out more. I already knew that Dad had fallen on a hand grenade while he was instructing soldiers, that the grenade had bounced off a tree, and that he had fallen on it. This had troubled me for years: hand grenades don't bounce.

What exactly had happened to Dad? Was the grenade threatening his men, and did he, as their officer, feel he had to jump in front of it to shield them? Or was the grenade faulty, and did it explode in his face?

The records didn't help much. I asked an old mate of Dad's who had been in Tenterfield with him for more details, and he agreed that the basic story was true. But he didn't say much more.

Dad left behind a wife and two boys, and that's not really a good thing to do. I've sometimes wondered whether he thought about us in the split second before he copped it. Probably not; people only have thoughts like that in the movies.

Not long ago I happened to be in Tenterfield, and I drove

out to the camp to visit his grave for the first time. I got to the cemetery and sat in the car looking at the graves for a long time. Then I turned the car around, and went away, drove off without seeing where my father is buried. I don't know why. Perhaps I had just closed him off.

Life got difficult when Dad came home

❖ *Life got difficult when Dad came home*

'I was a real daydreamer,' says Rob Davenport. But there is nothing remotely vague about him now: he's perceptive and articulate, with thoughtful blue eyes and a wry sense of humour. As a boy he might have spent a lot of time up in trees, shooting imaginary enemies with his (unloaded) .22, but he was obviously the sort of child who didn't miss a thing.

I was born in 1939. When I was small, there were only two sorts of men: very young and very old. The very young were delivery boys and newsboys, the very old were my grandfather and his mates. There were no men in between. They were all away at the war, including my father.

Dad joined the Army a year or so before war broke out. He became a corporal in 1939, and was very proud that his Army registration number was NX 162, making him the hundred and sixty-second person who joined in New South Wales. He was soon promoted to lieutenant, went overseas and, like thousands of other Australians, he was captured in Greece in 1940. He remained in POW camps in Germany for the following five years.

Of course, I didn't know much about him, or about the war, when I was very small. I knew a lot more about the first war, because my grandfather — Dad's father — had been a mustard gas victim and took great pride in his German war relics, which he used to show me. He had postcards and coins he'd picked up in Belgium, but his prize possession was an Army tunic with a sleeve patch showing the Sacred Heart. A Belgian nun had sewn it on for him when he was in hospital in 1917. The badge had no combat value, of course, but he cherished it, despite the fact that he wasn't a Catholic.

Mum, who had got her Leaving Certificate and was therefore very well educated, worked at the Gas Company when I was small; she was only twenty-three when Dad left. Like most women of the time, she didn't have much social life while Dad was away. It must have been pretty hard on her. We went to see her sister, to whom Mum was very close; Auntie Jenny had married a curly-headed wonder boy who disappeared to New Guinea and never came back. He wasn't heard of again. Nobody talked about that.

We visited Mum's friends a lot when I was little. Nobody had a car then, of course, though I do remember one uncle who owned a Whippet with its seat covered in flour bags. Nobody could afford leather-covered seats.

But mostly Mum and I visited Dad's parents, who had a chook farm out of Sydney at Chipping Norton. Getting there was quite a feat; from our house in the southern suburbs we had to take three buses and change trains twice.

Grandma was a tough lady. Because she kept chooks, having chicken for dinner wasn't a great luxury for me, as it was for other kids. Gran grew grapes for a while too, until she discovered the temperance movement and ripped up her winemaking vines and replaced them with eating grapes, purple and green.

To hear her talk, she and she alone was responsible for the Australian effort in two world wars. Not only had her husband been a mustard gas victim, but she had sent two sons to the second war. She knitted more khaki socks than anybody else in the district. There was never any doubt in her mind that everybody should treat her with enormous respect because of this, and she tended to remind people very often, especially my mother. Mum herself didn't have much to do with the war effort, except for a little gentle knitting and sending letters and photographs to Dad. She never joined the Women's Land Army, for instance; that was only for women who were no better than they ought to have been. Mum was far too respectable for that.

Grandma was the only person I knew who had an air-raid shelter. 'When you know as much about war as I do, you need one,' she used to say grimly. She was convinced that Australia was going to be invaded. 'I've never trusted them communist Japanese,' she said. The shelter was in the orchard, near the peach trees and not far from the dunny. Like the dunny, it was almost completely covered in wisteria vine, which held it together after the wood rotted. The shelter was an old shed with fruit boxes for seats and makeshift shelves, also of wood, and absolutely crammed with Fowlers Vacola bottles of preserved nectarines, peaches and vegetables. Naturally, it would have been absolutely useless if the Japs had attacked. But, being a thoughtful woman, Grandma had cut an emergency exit from the shed to the dunny, so that if one became too terrified when the invasion came, relief was at hand. (The shed later came in handy for exploring the anatomy of my young cousins.)

The dunny held an important place in family mythology. Like most first children, I was photographed incessantly, and black and white Box Brownie prints were sent to Dad all the time he was in German camps — when Mum knew where he was, that is. Dad received dozens of photographs of me: young Rob smiling, yawning, crawling, learning to walk, playing with toys. He must have wondered why on earth so many were necessary: why get a dozen photographs today when he got a dozen yesterday? For some loony security reason, Mum always photographed me up against the dunny door at Grandma's. If Dad's German guards ever saw the pictures, they must have thought that Australians lived in small wooden houses without windows.

Apart from visits to Grandma's and staying with her during the holidays, Mum and I sometimes went to the pictures in town. Mum wore one of those flat, pancake hats women had during the war, and carried a handbag like a little leather suitcase. (One of those street photographers took a picture of us — and it got sent off in the next batch to Dad in Germany.)

Going to the pictures gave me a very clear idea about the war. I remember seeing a newsreel of Australian soldiers sitting on a log in the New Guinea jungle, wearing their uniforms, rolling cigarettes, chatting and *eating condensed milk out of a tin*. Wow! This was luxury beyond my dreams, because my passionate ambition in life at the age of three was to eat an entire tin of condensed milk, which was impossible to get. If being a soldier meant you could get all the condensed milk you wanted, I thought, being shot at by the Japanese was a small price to pay.

I remember clothes rationing and hearing dark hints about a black market in all sorts of goods. But there were no real shortages, as far as I remember (apart from condensed milk), though there were definitely profiteers. Mum knew women in our street who seemed to have more meat than the rest of us, and there were a lot of lewd jokes about butchers and meat, which I didn't understand. Butter was rationed; nobody would touch margarine, which was dreadful, oily whitish stuff. You never ate that unless you were very poor. You could buy copha, which was a substitute, but I don't recall that being used for anything much except chocolate crackles. (I once made myself spectacularly sick at a party gorging on these ghastly things, which consisted of copha, cocoa and rice bubbles, and I can barely look at Kellogg's Rice Bubbles now without shuddering.)

There were some very tense mornings when Mum read the casualty lists in the *Sydney Morning Herald*. She explained to me that there were several categories: missing believed killed, killed, missing believed wounded, and missing. (That 'missing' always irritated me — how could the Army lose an entire person?) Mum found out where Dad was from these lists; he was moved around various camps in Germany, and a letter would always arrive telling her *after* she had read about his whereabouts in the paper. The Army was like that. People found out if their relatives were killed in the papers before they got an official letter with 'We regret to inform you...' It must have been hell for women. I didn't know what Mum went through, every morning, looking for Dad's name, until I was much older.

When I was three or four, somebody gave me a .22 for my birthday, which now strikes me as an extraordinarily lethal present. I can't remember wanting one, but I was delighted with it, even though Mum specified that the bolt had to be removed so it couldn't be fired. I sat up in our peach tree in the backyard, 'blamming' all the people I didn't like into eternity.

We knew the people we didn't like. My grandmother had Italian neighbours, who had lived next door to her for about thirty years. From the time that war was declared, she refused to speak to them. They were The Enemy, coming from the same race as that dreadful Mussolini.

Down by the creek at the back of our place lived an old hermit whom June next door and I were convinced was Hitler's brother. He was one of those strange men who seemed to exist in a welter of tin cans and rotting wooden boxes. He had several very fine apricot trees, however, and June and I were sure that our patriotic duty was to raid them whenever possible. We did, very successfully, except once. Hitler's brother came roaring out to find us in mid-raid, and he fired saltpetre at us from a shotgun. I arrived home with no apricots and a burning rear end. Mum was frantic, but I didn't worry about it too much. No sacrifice was too great to make in defeating Australia's enemies!

Most of the kids around our place were girls, for some reason. We were all in the same position; not many of us had fathers at home, and those who were at home we never saw. They were probably at work all day, in exempted jobs.

So, for the first six years of my life, I was very happy indeed. I had a mother and a succession of female relatives who doted on me, keeping all my drawings, photographing me and repeating all the clever things I said. I was learning to read, and making friends of my own age. Being a great daydreamer, I was happiest climbing in the peach tree, which was a gun emplacement or a galleon or a mountain peak. I sensed, really, that Mum was unhappy, but that didn't worry me much: I was far too taken up with my own life.

Then Dad came home.

VE Day had come and gone. I remember it mainly because Mum kissed the greengrocer in the general excitement, then became terribly embarrassed and apologised. Then it was VJ Day. Still no word from Dad. This must have been sheer torture for Mum. The war was over, but Dad could have been shot by the Russians, when they came through the German camps, and she wouldn't have known for months.

Then in 1946 we got the letter. Dad was coming home.

I still remember the day he returned. It was a typical late summer Sydney day, hot, grey and still, with flies everywhere. Mum got us breakfast in silence — most unlike her, she was usually chatty and bright. I got into my best grey trousers, a clean white shirt, and socks and sandals, and then sat on the bed and watched Mum standing in front of her dressing-table mirror, trying on her absurd pancake hat, first this way, then the other. She took a long, long time to get ready, worrying about lipstick, whether her shoes were polished, if I had a clean handkerchief. She said very little. The tension was so terrible that my shoulders and neck were aching.

We went to the wharf by train and bus to meet Dad's ship. The journey took an hour, and I spent the whole time trying to be excited. 'Isn't it wonderful?' Mum's friends had said. 'Isn't it wonderful that you will meet your father?' I had nodded and smiled politely, but I couldn't imagine what it would be like. All I knew about Dad was that he was a sort of guardian god whose blurred, dark photograph was on Mum's dressing table. Mum had read bits of his letters to me — 'Give Rob a hug' — but they hadn't meant much. There was too much talk of camps, and I hadn't been particularly interested in them. Now I was going to meet this person, my father, I felt vaguely curious, but nothing more.

We finally got off the bus at the wharf and trudged for miles over concrete, Mum holding my hand very tightly. After a while we seemed to be part of a crowd of what seemed like thousands of loud, eager people pushing and shoving each other. I pressed close to Mum, out of range of shuffling, stamping feet. Then I looked up and saw the side of a ship, with a gangplank leading down to the wharf. And down came a mass of men in khaki uniforms. Everybody went mad, waving and cheering.

'There's your father!' cried Mum. 'Come on, Rob, *wave!*' She pointed. '*Look!*' I stared. But where was he? There were four hundred of my father; I hadn't the faintest idea who I was looking for. The world was composed of waving arms, and shrieks, and cheers. I had no idea what to do, so I stood quietly, hoping somebody would tell me. *I'm going to see my father*, I thought. It came out flat and dull.

After a long time, Mum and I moved into a tin shed and waited some more, while nothing happened. I was numb and hot and tired, and badly wanted to go to the toilet, but Mum had hold of me so tightly that I couldn't have got away, even if I'd known where to go.

'Well!' A strange man stood in front of us. He and Mum hugged for a very long time, then he bent down and scooped me up. But he didn't feel right. 'How are you, son?' he said. His arms weren't used to holding me, and they felt stiff and awkward. I wriggled, and he put me down.

'Hello, Dad,' I said.

The dark-haired, sharp-nosed man standing with Mum seemed to have nothing to do with us. I felt peculiar and somehow cheated. He didn't even look like his photograph.

Then the three of us, the Davenport family, walked out of the shed, with me holding Mum's hand, and nobody saying very much. We took a taxi (a taxi!) home, and a new life began.

It was bewildering. I had been allowed to shout in the house, slam doors, say and do almost exactly as I pleased. My life had been full of adoring, approving people, friends and relatives, and everything I said had been greeted as the words of a young genius. Mum had sung around the house at all hours, one of her favourite songs being 'Mockingbird Hill'. Now all these things stopped. I had to learn a new phrase: 'Don't annoy your father.'

And Dad annoyed was dreadful. For no reason at all, it seemed, his face would become smaller, tighter, his black eyes furious, his mouth thin. His hand could move faster than a striking snake. Once I brought him his breakfast and said, 'Dad, the yolk's yellow, isn't it?' and he picked up the whole plate and threw it at my head. I couldn't understand how or why these things happened; why we had a violent stranger in the house. I went around in a state of shock.

Looking back, I can understand something of Dad's feelings. After five years of intolerable boredom in the POW camp, he had come back to meet somebody whom he'd married a few months before he embarked, and to get used to a son who hadn't even existed when he left. He didn't know where he belonged.

And it must have been dreadful for Mum. She had spent five years worrying, wondering, sending letters and photographs to a man she hardly knew, and now she had to set about being a wife to someone she found she didn't have anything in common with. And she had no alternative. Nobody divorced in those days.

Dad stayed in the Army after he got back. He remained there

for twenty years, until he died. That was another source of frustration for him. All the men who had gone into the Army when he did, one of the first intakes, had risen to higher ranks very quickly. If he hadn't been captured, he would probably have risen much higher. As it was, he stayed a lieutenant. The Army had been his one chance to make something of himself, and he hadn't done so. He was ashamed of having been captured; it wasn't as though he'd been in Changi, for instance, because he would have belonged to that community of men who had overcome incredible hardship to survive, and had been admired for it. He felt as though he was a failure, and he didn't know how to cope.

The only people he felt at ease with, the only people he could talk to, were the men Mum referred to, tight-lipped, as 'your father's Army mates'. There seemed to be dozens of them, and they met in the pub up the road. Like Mum, I learned to dread the sound of their boots, coming up the concrete path to the back door most nights after six o'clock closing. They were all probably quite amiable blokes, but they sat and drank beer around the kitchen table for hours, getting loud and red-faced and stupid. I remember one in particular, Snow, a balding, fair-haired chap who had been a choco and who told lots of stories about life at Singleton army camp. He took a shine to me for some reason, and used to grab my arm and draw me into the group of sweaty, guffawing blokes. 'Lissenna this, sonny...this'll rip ya,' he said, before launching off into some yarn about hand grenades or jungle training. I was always bored and embarrassed.

Mum couldn't tell Dad how she felt about his friends. She probably felt that, after five years in German POW camps, he needed to make new friends, to relax a bit.

I now realise that Dad and his mates were, really, arrested adolescents. Some of them had joined the Army after leaving school, or after being unemployed for a long time, like Dad. They had spent five years away, at a critical time in their lives, and they were, in a way, frozen in their attitudes. They hadn't really *had* their young manhood.

They did a lot of juvenile things. Once I saw Dad and his mates outside the pub, playing trains. A couple of dozen men in their twenties had their arms around each other's waists, stumbling in line along the footpath yelling: 'Choo, choo, whooo whooo!'

Dad never said a word to me about the war nor, as far as I can gather, did he talk about it to Mum. To us he pretended that it had never happened. But his attitudes sometimes came out very clearly.

For instance, he loathed Germans to the day he died. 'Krauts' he called them, and 'squareheads'. At the same time, he obviously admired their efficiency. 'You have to hand it to those bastards, how they've recovered since the war,' he used to say, grudgingly. But this did not mean *we* could have anything to do with them.

When I was eleven, a German boy moved into the street, and Hans and I became friends. We played cricket and football together, went on hikes, built billycarts and talked constantly. Mum said, 'You know your father has a thing about Hans Keller...just play with him where your father can't see you.' Dad said, 'You're not allowed to play with that bloody reffo Kraut.' But I dug my toes in, and made a point of ensuring that Hans and I were kicking a football in the street when Dad came home. Dad called Hans 'young Adolf' to his face, but I stood firm. It was my way of standing up to him: God knew I couldn't think of any other way. I was terrified of my father, and I think defying him over Hans was the bravest thing I ever did.

Hans, who was a nice, blond, straightforward kid, was bewildered by Dad's attitude, which wasn't the only example of prejudice he had encountered in Australia. Being one of the first wave of post-war immigrants, he, like the Italians and Greeks, was treated with suspicion and contempt. This he couldn't understand.

'Why do you Australians hate Germans so much?' he kept asking me. 'Australia didn't suffer in the war. Not like Germany did. You didn't have your big cities bombed, like Cologne and Dresden were.' I couldn't say anything, just kept playing cricket with him in the street.

When Dad came back, he and Mum started what amounted to a second family. My brother Dave was born in 1946, my sisters, Sally and Geraldine, in 1951 and 1953. I was very much on the outer: my relationship with Dad grew worse and worse, and Mum had three other kids to look after. Married to a man she didn't know, she devoted her life to us. I didn't have anybody in the family to talk to, so I just led my own life. My friends and I roamed around the creek beds, went to school, threw rocks at the Catholic kids every now and again. But above all, I retreated into books. I became an absolutely avid reader. Mum gave me a copy of *Newnes Encyclopaedia*, which I read until it fell to bits, especially the articles on history. Because I was becoming known as the family intellectual, well-meaning relatives gave me 'the classics', but I couldn't get excited by *David Copperfield* or *The Three Musketeers*. I was into comics in a big way, and I first came across Dickens, Dumas and Robert Louis Stevenson in the *Classics Illustrated* comics series. They were great.

My brother Dave was Dad's favourite. Dad told him things about the war he didn't discuss with me, and he even did fatherly things, like taking him to football matches. Dave and I didn't get on at all — there was too much of an age difference between us, for one thing — and I couldn't understand why Dave wasn't punished for doing things that inevitably earned me a belt over the ear. It took us a long time to become friends and to understand each other, but we get on well now.

Dad and I never became mates, but we eventually did learn to tolerate each other. And when I was about sixteen he astonished me by showing me drawings he did in the POW camp. He told me he had written poetry, too, but Mum had burned it (probably because it was erotic). I still have some of the drawings. They're not badly done, sketches of soldiers and guards playing cards, lining up, eating meals, and so on. But there is one obsessively recurring image: German guards burning Russian prisoners. Always flames, burning, shrieking bodies and guns, guns, guns. Dozens of pictures of the same things. Yet Dad never spoke to me about what he had seen, just showed me these drawings. I think that, like so many Australian men, he was more sensitive and perceptive than he was allowed to be, or than he could permit himself to be.

But if he'd talked to me, if I'd seen those poems and drawings when he first came back, I would have understood him better.

THE 1950s

There were definite rules and life was pretty stable

*T*here were definite rules and life was pretty stable

Jenny Rockwell's handwriting has not changed since she learned how to angle the alphabet correctly at primary school by careful use of a slope card. Here 'd's and 't's are still shorter than her 'l's and 'b's. 'At least it's legible,' she says half-apologetically. 'Writing was one of my best subjects.' A neat and careful person with sandy hair and a wide smile, Jenny has worked as an accountant for some years.

My two sisters and I grew up in an old house in one of the outer bush suburbs of Sydney. Dad bought it when he came back from the war. It had rats' nests in the walls, and Mum cried a lot when we moved in. But I loved it. We always had modern furniture, chairs with sloping backs and pale wood arms, patterned grey and yellow and red kitchen curtains, laminex in the kitchen and an Early Kooka gas stove. All bright and shiny and new.

Except for the Japanese sword.

This was the first foreign object I ever knew about. It lived on top of my parents' pale walnut wardrobe in their bedroom, next to the dusty suitcase that contained their wedding photographs. I enjoyed climbing up to look at pictures of Mum in her long white dress and train and Dad looking smug and spruce in his Army uniform. But I never looked at the sword. It lay cocooned in a white cotton sheath printed with black marks. I had been told this was writing, but never believed it; writing didn't look like that. 'That sword's sharp enough to cut your arm off,' Dad said.

He told me he had taken it from a Japanese soldier on Balikpapan. As I understood the story, the little yellow man (one of the swarming millions who had tried to invade Australia) had stood with it poised to chop off the head of an innocent Australian. Up came Dad and blew the Jap to smithereens. Dad had calmly stepped over the body, picked up the sword, brought it home, married Mum and put the sword on top of the wardrobe.

Not for many years did he admit that he had won the sword in a Melbourne two-up game.

Like most men, Dad never talked about the war. Perhaps he thought that, with three daughters, it wasn't an appropriate subject for conversation. We knew he had been in Borneo, a place I imagined as covered in morning-glory and lantana and bamboo, like the stuff that grew around the septic tank down the back.

Apart from the Japanese sword, there were a few other legacies of the war in our house. For instance, none of us was allowed to wear rubber thongs when we were growing up. 'They're bad for your feet,' said Mum, but we knew Dad hated thongs because they reminded him of the footwear the Japanese had worn in the jungle. (To this day my father has never owned a Japanese car.) On 25 April every year, Dad went into town, returned after we had gone to bed and was grumpy and red-eyed the next morning. And a highlight of our birthday parties was the lolly chase. Mum sewed paper bags of sweets on the chest, back and arms of Dad's Army jacket, and he would run all over the lawn, pursued by greedy, shrieking little girls trying to leap up and snatch Fantales, Columbines and chocolate bullets.

I didn't know a great deal about the war. I knew that Churchill had saved Australia, but I didn't know about the Japanese midget subs in 1942 for many years. Nor did I hear the name of Curtin mentioned: as far as I was concerned, Robert Menzies had always been Prime Minister. But the war had finished two years before I was born; how could I have known anything about it?

One of my earliest memories is dancing to some very serious music that came over our radio in the kitchen. I jumped from red squares to white ones on the lino, trying hard not to step on any of the borders, while still keeping in time to the music (which was easy because it was slow and quiet). Mum's mother, Nan, came into the kitchen and, in a shocked voice, said: 'You naughty little girl! Stop that! Don't you know that King George is dead?'

I stopped immediately; I could tell by her face that I had done something bad. But what? At the age of five I couldn't have cared that King George VI had shuffled off this mortal coil. To me he was an incised profile on one side of a penny (a lot of money) with writing around him. 'GEORGIUS VI REX' it said, but partly because the 'U' in 'GEORGIUS' was written like a 'V', I always read it as 'George Gives Rex'. Because my grandmother appeared to think I shouldn't be cheerful about the death of George Gives, I obediently decided to feel sad. I said to myself, 'The King is dead', for the rest of that day without any effect on my emotional state.

George Gives was replaced by a lovely new Queen, who was much younger, prettier and more interesting. *Her* pennies were bright and new. We all became very keen about her, particularly because she was coming to visit us, the first time a real king or queen had set foot on Australian soil.

That was in 1954, when the new school year had just begun. In second class we fingerpainted the Union Jack and the Australian flag over and over again. The stars in the Southern Cross always caused me great trouble; there were so many and I could never get the points even. I drew a picture that Mrs Prentice, my teacher, said was excellent. It showed a fairy princess with frizzy hair, an enormous crown and carrying a sceptre with a star on top, talking to a little girl. That was the Queen talking graciously to me without my glasses.

Jeannie Coates came to school carrying a white mug with the Queen and Duke of Edinburgh staring balefully at each other on one side with 'GOD SAVE THE QUEEN' underneath in *real* gold. It was glorious. I couldn't compete, so I had to make do with a hanky that had 'E II R' printed on it in dye that came out the first time it went into the copper to be washed. Jeannie Coates was not impressed. 'That's nothing,' she said. 'Everybody's got those.' She was right, they did.

At home I practised curtseying. Left foot behind right foot, knees bent together making sure they didn't lock, hold out the skirt (even though this was summer and we were wearing shorts and plastic sandals and blouses), incline the head graciously, and count: one two down, three four up. This was just in case the Queen noticed me. I used to wish I was a boy. No curtseying business for them, just a neat bow, feet together, bend from the waist in a snappy, no-nonsense doubling up, right arm across the stomach, left arm across the back. Quick and neat.

My parents took my little sister, Matty, and me to see the Queen and the Duke drive along Moore Park Road, near Centennial Park. It was a hot February day and I was aghast: I had no idea Sydney contained so many people. Somehow I pushed myself into a position where I could see the road in front. Where were they? Heads moved, people began saying excitedly: 'Here she comes!' I jumped up and down, waving my Union Jack as loyally as possible. All I saw was part of a car, a white glove, a pink hat and dress. 'She looked straight at you, darling,' said Mum. I tried to believe her.

Despite the fact that I hadn't been able to demonstrate to the Queen how good I was at curtseying, I was very keen on England for years. Everybody knew that anything with 'Made in England' on it was miles better then any equivalent article with 'Made in Australia'. I deeply respected my best friend, Julie Clayton, whose mother had actually been *born* in England. (Julie would have been, too, but her parents got on the ship to Sydney before she had a chance.) Julie's vowels were sharper than mine, and Mum was always praising her for 'speaking well'. I was cross that Mum thought Julie did something better than I did. The other kids at school didn't agree. Bill Lindsay used to screw his face up like a prune: 'Hey, Julie, this is what Poms look like when they're saying "actually". . . "ektuelleh".' The others would giggle applause, and Julie would look depressed.

Julie's mother made me uncomfortable. Like her daughter, she was long and pale, with stringy hair. She had a lined, weary face and smoked Ardaths constantly. Whenever I went to tea at the Claytons (and it wasn't tea, it was supper, Mrs Clayton explained, because tea was at four o'clock, not at six, in England) I mentally straightened my back and folded my hands. Mrs Clayton never spoke to me in the kitchen while she was cooking chops for supper; conversation was carried on in the front room with the dark green holland blind pulled down on the sunniest days. She always asked me about school. Did I like English? 'Very much, thank you. I like compositions.' I used to wish that she would go to the kitchen and put something on the stove, as other mothers did when you came to visit. But the only thing that interrupted our dreadful, stilted sentences was the appearance of a blowfly in the room. Mrs Clayton would tense, excuse herself, march to the kitchen and return with a Mortein tank-and-plunger flyspray. Whoosh, whoosh, whoosh, she pushed it frantically, covering the fly and me in a mist that made me feel sick. Whenever this happened, Mrs Clayton said, 'They don't have huge flies like this in England,' as though it was my fault.

Mrs Clayton was always complaining about biting, stinging insects, bluebottles in the surf, and the snakes that occasionally turned up in the backyard rose beds. Unlike other mothers, she wore shoes and stockings at home, instead of sandals, and she was the first person I ever saw wearing white cotton gloves and a hat in summer 'because this sun ruins the complexion'. Julie was her only child, christened Anthea Julia Clayton, but called Julie 'because you Australian children wouldn't get the name "Anthea" right, would you?' Mrs Clayton had a point, I suppose, but I couldn't help thinking it was a bit pretentious to call your child by her middle name instead of her real one.

On balance, though, I agreed eagerly with Mrs Clayton that Australia was a second-rate place. I knew that Christmas should be cold, and that it was silly to have minced pies and chicken and hot plum pudding when the temperature was over ninety (even though I loved that sleepy feeling of having eaten too much in the heat). Julie and I used to get *School Friend* and *Girl's Crystal*, illustrated papers that came out every Thursday and were full of midnight feasts in the dorms, hockey and 'bowling out' troublesome prefects. When I read Julie's complete collection of Enid Blyton's Famous Five and Secret Seven books, I wished passionately that our house had a secret passage that led to a cave where treasure was buried.

Family life was far too humdrum in Australia. Mum stayed at home all day, doing boring housework; Dad drove into town to sell electrical appliances for a retail chain; my sisters and I didn't play together much because they were much younger than I. School was all right, but it lacked romance.

When I was nine, I decided that I had only come into my own family by accident. When I was a tiny baby in the hospital, a nurse had swapped the name tags (as had happened to the current heroine in my *Girl's Crystal*, Myrtle Thompson, heroine of the Fourth Form, who was really a Russian princess). I had been sent to the Rockwell family when I belonged in a much more glamorous, perceptive and intelligent house. My real family were the Harrisons.

Carolyn Harrison and I had been friendly enemies since the first day we started school together; she had led the Methodist or 'methylated spirit' faction in the playground; I championed the Anglicans. (There must have been Catholic kids at our primary school, but I don't remember any.) Carolyn had been given a real two-wheeler bicycle for her birthday while I was forbidden one because 'you'll be killed on the road'. She had promptly fallen off and broken her arm, but that was glamorous too; we queued up to autograph her plaster cast. Carolyn was allowed to have chocolate-flavoured straws with her milk at recess. These were expensive and made drinking school milk much more palatable; it had been dumped in crates on the hot asphalt well before school started, and was turning bluish by eleven o'clock. But the greatest favour Carolyn could confer was to share her piece of cake with you. Mrs Harrison made the most superb chocolate cake with peppermint icing. It beat iced vovos hollow.

After we had all lined up and were given our Salk vaccine injections for polio, Carolyn asked me, 'Would you like to come home and play with me after school?' I looked at her suspiciously. What had prompted this? I decided that she had admired my cool courage in not crying out when the nurse had jabbed the needle home at the top of my arm. Anyway, I was determined to go. Instinctively I knew I was a Harrison.

'Of course I can,' I said.

'Do you have to tell your mother?' asked Carolyn.

'No.' This was a lie, but I wasn't going to risk Mum's saying

I couldn't go. Carolyn would have had to come home with me and I wasn't about to let her see Mum with her hair up in pincurls and a scarf tied in a floppy bow on top.

'All right.'

After school, Carolyn and I walked to her place. We had to go right past our front fence, and I mentally said 'hello' to my parents and sisters as though they were distant and not particularly pleasant acquaintances.

I think Mrs Harrison was surprised to see me, but she made me welcome. She was a small, pretty woman with a turned-up nose and laughing brown eyes, very different from my slim, grey-eyed mother who was often bad-tempered. Carolyn and I played knucklebones and pickup sticks in her room, and I admired her dolls, then we went into the backyard to swing on the old tyre her father had attached by a rope to the branch of a tree.

I was enjoying myself thoroughly — *much* more my sort of place, this — when Mrs Harrison said, 'Is it all right if you stay to tea?'

'Yes,' I said, 'I've asked Mum.' Without a qualm.

Tea was cocktail frankfurters, great luxury, with mashed potato and salad, followed by the famous chocolate cake with peppermint icing. The perfect meal, I thought.

It grew dark, and my conscience started nagging me. Perhaps I should have told Mum and Dad where I'd gone. After all, I hadn't left them forever, not yet. I probably would when I'd talked the Harrisons into having me on a permanent basis, but not for a week or so. (Besides, I still had to go home to collect my clothes and my prized collection of matchbox lids I was going to lacquer and make into a coffee table top eventually. If I didn't, my sister Matty would get her hands on them, and I wasn't having that.)

Most unwillingly, I said, 'Thank you for having me, Mrs Harrison. I'd better go home now.'

She smiled. 'Thank you for coming. Will you be all right? Perhaps you'd better wait until Mr Harrison comes home. He can drive you.'

But I wasn't going to involve Mr Harrison at that stage. If Mum was cross with me for not telling her where I had gone, he might decide I was not a responsible person and be put off adopting me.

'No thank you, Mrs Harrison,' I said. 'I don't have far to go.' I managed to persuade her that I'd be all right, and I set off. It was quite dark, but I wasn't afraid; the main road was well enough lit. I was just wondering how I could persuade Mum to make chocolate cake with peppermint icing instead of her usual boring raspberry jelly, when a tall man in a peaked cap and shiny buttons came looming over me.

'Are you Jenny Rockwell?' he asked. I nodded cautiously, but not in fear. I knew that policemen were your friends.

'Your mum's been worried sick about you,' he said, sounding very cross indeed. 'She called us out to find you.' I was scared. My first thought was that the policeman had found out about my ambition to be adopted by the Harrisons, and had been sent to punish me for it.

'Come on,' he said, taking me by the hand just as if I was a little girl instead of being nine years old.

All the lights were on at home, and Mum burst into tears as soon as she saw me. 'Promise me you won't run away again,' she said. This irritated me considerably. I hadn't run away, I insisted. I was just playing. But Mum and Dad didn't believe me. Though I promised not to run away, just to stop Mum crying, I secretly vowed I would if life became boring again. Just let them try to stop me, I thought, I'd go to Broken Hill and they'd never get me back.

The next day Carolyn asked me whether I had got home all right. 'Of course,' I said, and I never told her, or any of the other kids at school, about my first brush with the police.

The year I turned ten, Dad finished building a one-bedroom granny flat at the back of our house. It wasn't much, and we weren't encouraged to play in it: just a living room, tiny kitchen, bedroom and bathroom. Then Dad advertised for tenants in the local paper. Next thing we knew, the Lorenzinis had moved in.

There were three Lorenzinis: Giuseppina, Aldo and Roy. They were my first New Australians. Aldo was in his early thirties, I suppose; a thickset, morose man with more black hair on his chest than I had ever seen. He spoke very little English and worked for the railways; sometimes in the early morning I saw him going off to catch the bus, wearing his blue overalls and carrying a metal lunchbox. He rarely spoke to us, and we saw him mainly on weekends, which he seemed to spend lounging around the tiny living room of the flat, listening to the races on the wireless (which intrigued me: he didn't speak much English, so how could he possibly follow the race descriptions?) and speaking very little. Giuseppina, his wife, whom we called Josie, was plump and pretty and curly haired. She occasionally helped Mum in the house. We all liked Josie because she was good-natured and made attempts to learn English. Mum spoke to her very slowly and loudly, as though she was deaf as well as Italian. Josie giggled at everything, which convinced me she was stupid, and she spent an incredible amount of time in their flat doing the washing or the ironing or the cleaning. Their flat, about one-third the size of a normal house, was spotless, and Josie spent her whole life making it even cleaner. But I couldn't believe it was really shiny and sparkling, because it smelled of garlic. Josie never went out, as far as I knew; Mum did her shopping for her. (They solved the communication problem by Josie pointing to empty packets or jars and nodding vigorously to indicate she wanted replacements.)

Roy, who must have been about four, was a dead loss. A real sook, Matty and I thought. He had silky blond curls and dark eyes and a sulky mouth. Spoiled rotten. Josie adored him, and he always wore little embroidered shorts, much shorter than those other boys wore, pale-coloured shirts, long socks and sandals. What's more, he was a sissy who refused to climb the sugar gum in the front garden. He cried, which boys were never supposed to do. But Roy learned English very quickly — we never knew how, because he stayed at home with Josie all day. We didn't think he was very clever, though. Anybody could speak English.

Though Mum made eager attempts to learn a few Italian words from Josie, which enabled her to agree that the weather was fine, or not, and that it was eleven o'clock in the morning, these were token efforts. The rest of us didn't even try. Though we were polite to the Lorenzinis, we didn't have much to do with their lives, so we found out very little about them: where they came from, how long they were staying, whether they were happy. (Of course they were happy: they were in Australia, weren't they?)

The fact that they were Italian disappointed me. I was just reading stories of the brave Romans in Arthur Mee's *Children's Encyclopaedia*, and I couldn't connect Josie, Aldo and Roy with the steely-jawed warriors I was finding out about. If the Romans had had to depend to Aldo Lorenzini to keep the bridge instead of Horatius in the brave days of old, I thought, the enemy would have overrun Rome within minutes.

The Lorenzinis stayed in our granny flat for about a year, then left to buy their own house somewhere. We never saw them after they departed. They weren't nearly as exciting as the other event that occurred that year; the coming of television.

Because Dad worked for an electrical retail chain, we were the first people in the street to have a set of our own. It was a huge twenty-eight-inch Admiral on four solid legs, with a fearsome array of shiny knobs under the screen. It arrived in about June 1956, a few months before television transmission officially started.

I'd already seen TV at the Royal Easter Show that year. It hadn't particularly thrilled me because the pictures had been so small *and* only in black and white, instead of glorious Technicolor like the movies. But having our own set was really something. Matty and I could afford to sneer at the people who lined up in front of the display windows of H. G. Palmers to look at the test pattern.

Matty quickly established her bargaining position at school: 'You can come and watch our TV set if you let me have one of your baked bean sandwiches,' she said. I wasn't as keen about the TCN 9 test pattern, the constantly repeated shows featuring an English pianist called Kay Cavendish, or songs sung in French by Lilli Palmer.

One reason for my lack of enthusiasm about television was that our reception was so temperamental. We never knew when the screen would start rolling hypnotically, or break up into a series of black and grey wavy lines. Matty and I suddenly had new jobs: aerial-movers. We seemed to walk around the living room for hours, with the rabbit's-ears aerial above our heads, or out in front like a tray. One step this way, two steps that way, while Mum or Dad frowned at the set and said, 'No,' or 'Come over here. I think that's made it better,' or 'Back a bit.' They never said, 'That's good, right there,' unless I was standing over in a corner, my arms aching, my back to the set so I couldn't see a thing.

The Admiral was bundled back to the department store, and for the official opening of television in September 1956 Dad was allowed to borrow a really splendid set. It was huge, square and walnut, and gloriously combined a cocktail cabinet with a glass back and a plastic ballerina that twirled around in a pink gauze tutu to the tune of 'Für Elise', a record player with an automatic turnable for spinning the new Microgroove LP records (including Mum's favourite Carmen Cavallaro), and a twenty-one-inch television set, which could be hidden from view by closing carved wooden doors across it. Matty and I gazed at this object in awe. We thought it was the most beautiful piece of furniture we had ever seen.

But the actual opening of television from 'TCN Channel Nine, first in Australia' was a bit of a frost. A young man in a dinner jacket made a speech declaring the station open, there were more speeches, and then a bit of singing and dancing. That was it. The programmes seemed to continue as before, except that there were more and more advertisements. I liked the Rothmans ad that showed cigarettes pouring out of packets by themselves and encircling the globe, and another that told us, incessantly, that TV stood for 'Take Vincents' headache powders.

Matty, who was three years younger than I, was very keen on

TV, and became a fan promptly and forever. She refused to come outside to play Robin Hood or hold my skipping-rope when the cartoons were on in the afternoons. It was very frustrating to see a small blonde girl with her eyes fixed in glassy concentration on the screen. 'You'll rot your brain,' I told her virtuously, but she took no notice. At night she developed very effective fake earaches that necessitated her coming into the living room to summon Mum or Dad, and somehow settling down with them to watch *I Love Lucy* or *Sergeant Bilko*.

The sophisticated kids in my class at school weren't nearly as keen on the box. Jeannie Coates, for instance, let me know pretty smartly that only vulgar people had television so soon, and it was even *more* vulgar to boast about it. The real people, such as the Coates family, would buy a set at exactly the right moment, not an instant before. 'Dad doesn't want us to have one yet,' said Jeannie smugly. 'And anyway, he says TV is only for stupid people.' Coming from Jeannie, who had great difficulty in reading a book that had words of more than two syllables, that was pretty good, but I let her get away with a certain amount. (Jeannie Coates was the sort of child who would be your best friend until she grew tired of playing with your birthday Pedigree doll that bleated 'mama' when you tilted it forwards. Then she would throw you out in favour of somebody who had been given a Davy Crockett nylon coonskin cap.) Basically I didn't entirely disagree with Jeannie's attitude. I still preferred radio.

Somebody in the family should be loyal to the wireless, I thought. It had been neglected by everybody else. So, to make a pompous point, I ostentatiously took the radio from the kitchen after school and retired to my bedroom to listen to the Argonauts and, later, serials such as *Hop Harrigan*, *Biggles*, and comedy programmes *Yes, What?* and *Life With Dexter* starring Willie Fennell. Sometimes I crept into the kitchen at night while the tinny TV set was blasting away in the living room, took the radio from its shelf above the stove, carried it carefully into my room, plugged it in and switched on *Lux Radio Theatre* or one of the other 'showcase' radio plays. Lying in the dark under the blankets. I terrified myself almost to death one night listening to *The Tell-Tale Heart* by Edgar Allan Poe. Kerdup, kerdup, kerdup...I knew that if I poked my nose out even an inch to breathe, the Tell-Tale Heart would leap into bed with me and *never stop beating*.

But there was no way radio could compete with television when Olympic Games fever hit at the end of 1956.

Having seen pictures of Australia's athletes on bubblegum cards, newsagents' brochures and special colour supplements in the papers and the *Women's Weekly* ('WIN A TRIP FOR TWO

TO MELBOURNE!'), the Games came to us directly when the Olympic runner with his torch came down the Pacific Highway. We watched him from Pearces Corner, in front of the Peter Rabbit Kindergarten (scene of some of my greatest triumphs in taking naps and fingerpainting).

There was very little traffic on the highway. Men with loud-hailers ordered the crowds back, back, so the runner could pass through on the way to Melbourne. Everybody we knew was there, including the woman of whom I was most scared in all the world: Miss Boland, who lived next door to us. She had a nutcracker nose and chin and drove a horse and sulky down to the shops, which made her a local identity who was periodically written up in the local paper. I was scared of her because Dad's Chevrolet had caused her horse to shy on the road one Saturday morning, and she had threatened to tell the police about him. We all waited, while it grew dark, and nothing happened.

Presently, a weedy young man wearing running shorts, shoes and a shirt ran along the highway. I had envisaged a giant in a toga carrying a huge blazing brand; what I saw was a dispirited plodder with a smallish torch that looked as though it would go out at any moment. It was disappointing. Nevertheless, on Mum's instructions I committed the incident to memory as one of the things I would remember all my life, privately thinking it wasn't half as interesting as seeing Jack Davey roar past in the first Redex Trial the year before.

We listened to the Games on radio at first, because the TV transmission from Melbourne wasn't particularly reliable. But the TV film, a couple of days after the events, was thrilling. There was my heroine, Betty Cuthbert, tendons standing out in her neck, her head jerking from side to side, legs relentlessly pushing, running past the finishing line. Marvellous! I also admired Lorraine Crapp and the Konrads kids and Dawn Fraser and Murray Rose because they were such splendid swimmers. They were really something. And, like everybody else, I was terribly proud when Australia won *thirteen* gold medals.

The Olympic Games, of course, were a once-in-a lifetime event: even more exciting, because we could become involved on a daily basis, was tennis. We followed Lew Hoad and Ken Rosewall with immense enthusiasm, mainly through the newspapers and the radio. For a while, all the kids at school abandoned hula hoops and Coca-Cola yoyos and skipping-ropes. At recess we brought out our Slazenger tennis racquets (stringed with gut if your family was wealthy, nylon if it was just average) and cardboard boxes containing white tennis balls with a length of frail elastic attached. We put the end of the elastic under a half brick and hit the ball, which bounced back. After about a week of this, the headmaster, Mr Edwards the First, forbade us to use tennis balls in the playground, especially after John Fanshaw, demonstrating his super-Rosewall backhand, swiped Susan Taylor in the eye. Her face came up in an awesome purple lump; she cried so much that she had to be sent home, and her mother marched up to the school the following morning and had a ding-dong row with Mr Edwards the Second, Susan's class teacher. But we persisted. Before school, during recess and lunch and after classes were over, lines of us stood facing the brick walls of the school buildings, bashing tennis balls against them, thok thok thok.

Both Mr Edwardses were school characters. Mr Edwards the First was built like a Grenadier Guard: tall, slim and very straight. He had a ferocious moustache and a stiff right leg, the result of a war injury, I think. When he took assembly, marching down between the class lines like General Montgomery reviewing the troops at El Alamein, he swung his leg out in front of him in a half goosestep. Then he bellowed: 'Right and left...HURN!' and we all wheeled obediently and marched off to our classrooms. We were terrified of him.

Mr Edwards the Second, however, was completely different. My teacher in fourth class and close to retiring age, he was short with mild, brown eyes, and fingers yellow-brown with nicotine stains. He was almost bald with tufts of grey hair in his ears, which fascinated me, and a man of real enthusiasms, one of which was politics. Whenever he could, he introduced political vocabulary into spelling classes ('Spell "referendum". Who can tell me what a referendum is?'). For the first time in my life I heard words like electorate, constituency, senate and Democratic Labor Party.

Most of them went right over my head. I wasn't politically aware at all. As far as I was concerned, Australia had always had a kindly Prime Minister called Menzies, who ran the country through the Liberal Party. His opponent was Dr Evatt ('Not a *real* doctor,' my mother said), who ran the much inferior Labor Party. The Labor Party approved of the Reds, they organised strikes, and they weren't keen on anybody making much money. People who belonged to the Labor Party were usually Catholics, which meant they said 'haitch' instead of 'H'. Workers, who were Catholics and therefore Labor Party members, didn't wear collars or ties or have television sets because they were too poor. I didn't like the Labor Party, one reason being that John Fanshaw in my class boasted that his father was a worker. So what? I thought.

Mr Edwards the Second was insistent on the importance of voting. This guaranteed democracy, he said. Voting was a citizen's duty as well as his right, and we were very lucky that voting was compulsory in Australia. We had gained this inestimable privilege without bloodshed. This didn't impress me. Voting meant that, on a Saturday every three years or so, people stood around the school with leaflets, handing them to everybody who was twenty-one or over so they could vote properly. What was special about that? I knew from my parents that voting was a great chore; Mum and Dad always complained bitterly about having to do it and they rarely bothered to go to the school until about five minutes before the booth closed at eight o'clock in the evening. 'How did you vote?' I asked them, but I always knew the answer. (Years later, Mum confessed to me that she *almost* voted Labor in 1961, during Menzies' credit squeeze.)

I first heard about the Petrov affair from Mr Edwards the Second. It had taken place three years before he became our teacher, but as far as he was concerned, the whole thing could have happened the day before. 'It was inhuman to treat Evdokia Petrov like that,' he told us gravely, showing us the newspaper photograph of an anguished woman — wearing a suit and one shoe — between two large grim men in suits. Sitting behind our much-carved wooden desks, we stared at him blankly. The episode had nothing to do with us. The Russians were bad, we all knew that. I remembered an episode of *Night Beat* on the radio in which Randy Stone fell foul of some Russsky spies, who had thick accents and were out to destroy 'democracy as we know it', in other words the American Way of Life. I knew from Mum and Dad that the Russians were dying for the opportunity to take over Australia. It was only a matter of time before they did, unless the Yellow Peril beat them to it.

But you had to admit the Russians were clever. This was proved when they sent a space capsule into orbit with a dog on board. Matty's eyes used to overflow if anybody mentioned that poor little dog. 'I bet they didn't even feed him,' she sobbed. 'Poor thing.' She came home from school with a painting she had done, showing a dog (traced from the cover of a His Master's Voice record) sitting in a rocket with lurid yellow and purple flames spouting out the end. Mum was very proud of this and attached it to the refrigerator door where it stayed, brown and tatty, for months. We also told Sputnik jokes: 'Knock knock.' 'Who's there?' 'Come quick.' 'Come quick who?' 'Come quick Sputnik.' There was a school craze for Sputnik ice-creams, phallic-shaped, chocolate-coated things in vanilla and strawberry on a stick.

More than anything else I longed to be grown-up. I was sick of being a kid. But before that could happen, I would have to be a teenager, or, in the words of our minister at the Anglican church 'one of today's Young People'. Me a Young Person? One of those girls who wore rope petticoats and teased her hair and listened to Elvis Presley and Big Bopper records on jukeboxes in milkbars? Why couldn't I just skip that and get on with real life? But there was no help for it. In 1959 I moved with my family to Adelaide and the 1960s.

❧ *Looking back, it all seems crook*

Mickey Butler is tall and thin. He doesn't say much; most Aborigines don't, and he probably wasn't ever a great talker. When he tells you about his 1950s childhood in a camp north-west of Rockhampton, there are long pauses between sentences. Having been a kid who kept out of trouble as much as possible, he is working out what he thinks should be recorded, and how he should express himself.

I don't remember where we came from in the beginning. All of us, all the people in the camp, had been moved in from the west, I think, because the back country was wanted for something else. But nobody talked about what life had been like before the camp.

It was a sort of gaol really. It had a big wire fence around it. We weren't allowed out unless we had passes, and if you mucked up you wouldn't be allowed to have one.

Some of us lived in wooden huts, and there were iron shacks too. Down away from the rest of us were a lot of shacks for people who had bad lungs. TB, I suppose it was. There were also people who had leprosy, I think, but they were taken away fairly quickly.

A lot of white people ran the place. The boss was a little fat man, and I suppose he was friendly, but none of us liked him. The white people lived in bungalows, and we used to work for them. They used us as servants. My mother cleaned the boss's house. We looked after the whole place, growing vegetables and milking the cows. One of the white men would tell us what to do and we had to do it.

I don't remember how many of us there were. Seemed to be hundreds. I had six brothers and two sisters. My mother and father didn't say much. My father spent time with the other blokes; they'd get bottles of port and drink them. Every night they'd do that.

Drinking was mucking up. You'd lose your pass for that. Black people weren't allowed to bring drink into the camp at all.

Looking back, it all seems crook

But we knew that a white man brought a car full of bottles of booze to a place near the camp, and that my dad and his friends — whoever had a pass — would go and get the booze and bring it back into the camp. There was trouble if they were caught.

We were frightened of the cops; the camp had its own cops. All black, but not the same people as us. They were big men who kept to themselves. I heard they were criminals from up north, mainly tribal murderers who were working out their sentences. They were there to frighten us because they were killers, and they did frighten us, too. But they didn't stop the blokes drinking. When I was about twelve I started to get drunk myself.

Looking back it all seems crook, but it wasn't that bad. At least we had the rodeo. That was the big thing.

Every year, there was a rodeo in the camp. All the black people would ride and the white people would come from miles around. It was real rough, real rough horses, brumbies they were, and not many rules. But if you could ride well, you got cheered, and people remembered you.

Looking back, I suppose we didn't ride all that well. Dad's best mate Chicka would try every year, and fall off, and try again. He had terrible falls, and was cheered a lot. By the white people mostly. I remember the whites up on the slope above the riding ground drinking beer and cheering. There were newspaper and radio people, too, and they took pictures and talked to us. Once they took a photo of Chicka on the ground after he'd been thrown.

All us kids were dying to ride in the rodeo. Because of Chicka, who I thought was great, I wanted to be a champion rodeo rider. I could have been, too, I think; when I was twelve I was tall and skinny and Chicka told me I had good hands. All I know was that I could stay on longer than the other kids. But that wasn't too hard because the horses they had around camp were pretty quiet, not like the brumbies they brought in for the rodeo. Anyway, that year, I decided to have a go.

There was one particular horse, a really mean, brown bastard with rolling eyes. Dangerous. The white man who brought him in was betting that none of us could ride him. 'Go on,' said Chicka, so I walked up and said I'd have a go.

'Okay,' said the man. He brought out this horse and I climbed onto the fence and then onto the horse, bareback, gripping with my thighs. Stayed on for about five seconds, and then the horse pigrooted, threw me right up high in the air. I must have gone very high, because I remember looking down from up there and seeing the horse still pigrooting below me. Then I came down across the fence and hurt my back. I couldn't move. The white people and my own people too were cheering me. Then they carried me over to the truck and took me off to hospital in town.

That was the last I saw of the camp, nearly. One of the nurses who worked at the hospital got to like me — I was there nearly six months — and asked if I would like to live with her and her husband. I said yes, because I didn't really get on with my own mum and dad. The nurse fixed up the papers and I went to live in town. I went to school there. I was lucky, and became a clerk in the public service, which I still am. The life in the camp and that horse ride seem to have happened to somebody else now.

After a while, my dad died and Mum went away. I didn't see my brothers and sisters again for years. But I went back to the camp last year, just to have a look.

It was all different. There weren't many black people there, just a few, but they were allowed to keep their bottles in the huts. Not like before at all. And there were only a few white people, a white cop and an administrator and a couple of others. There was no camp police force, and no passes: all that had gone.

You know something funny? I tried to talk to the white people a bit, remember the old days kind of, and they seemed sort of nervous and didn't want to say anything. I suppose they thought I was writing an article for the newspapers.

I won't bother going up there again. One thing I did notice, though; there were a lot of kangaroos around the camp. Now, there were never kangaroos when I was there, because lots of our people had rifles and were always going out and shooting them. Often they'd eat parts of them, but mainly they just went shooting for fun. There were no kangaroos within miles of the camp.

Now it was all different: nearly all the people had gone and the camp was nothing like the old camp, but the kangaroos had come back.

&*I* knew that, to survive, I had to be better than the other kids

Nicholas Kallergis runs his hand over the warm red bark of an angophora as an expert will handle a piece of rare jade. 'Australia has so many beautiful trees,' he says. 'That's the first thing I noticed when I came here as a kid. We had very few trees on Cyprus.'

Words don't come easily to Nick, a barrel-chested stoic who takes pride in being practical and who has always respected logical thinking and method. When he is talking about his own feelings, things he cares about, he takes his time. And he always means what he says.

Our village in Cyprus was small, at the foot of a stony hillside. It consisted of our house, my uncle's house across the road, a cluster of small cottages, the church and my mother's aunt's house a little way up the hill. People kept pigs and there were a few olive trees which were very valuable. Everybody respected ownership of olive trees. When I was three, a Model T Ford, the first car I had ever seen, plunged over the side of the bridge into the stream at the bottom of the hill. We rushed down to have a look. I saw a black car and two dead bodies.

I was an only child. My sister wasn't born until I was four. A neighbour's son and I used to play together in the hillside caves where the partisans had hidden during the war. One day this boy, who was a year or two older than I, stooped down and picked up an iron nail. 'Here,' he said, handing it to me. 'You will need this when you make your boxes to take to Australia.'

I hadn't the faintest idea what he was talking about. What or where was Australia? Nobody in our house had mentioned the word. Dad was still riding the island; he used to go around Cyprus on his bicycle, buying pins, netting, rope, whatever he could get cheap in one place, and selling these goods for a small profit somewhere else. I don't know, now, how he managed to support Mum and me. But times were hard for everybody then, just after the war.

I knew that, to survive, I had to be better than the other kids

One day, my father and uncle weren't there. They had gone to Australia, with other men from Cyprus, to work on the Snowy Mountains Hydro-electric Scheme. Mum and I stayed on Cyprus for another eighteen months, and during that time my sister, Poppy, was born.

I didn't have any idea what was happening to Dad. Not until years later did he tell me how bad life had been on the Snowy Scheme, how the Australian workers refused to talk to the Greeks and how he and the other Cypriots, who spoke no English at all, could communicate only with each other. During the first winter in the Snowy, it was so cold that Dad and the other migrants scavenged newspapers to wrap around themselves to keep warm. He never mentioned such things in the rare letters he wrote to Mum; like most of the Cypriot men, he sent back money rather than words.

When I was five and Poppy was a year old, we left the village with Mum. We went down to the sea and boarded a ship, to join Dad in Australia. I remember stepping off a pontoon that was bigger than our house and looked like a floating cutting board, then going into a place that wouldn't keep still, a long, long house without normal windows or doors.

I don't remember much about the trip. My mother, I know, was very seasick and spent a lot of time lying on her bunk. There didn't seem much I could do about this, so I spent a lot of time up on deck, just watching the sea and nodding to the other Greek families on board. There were many, bound for Melbourne as we were, but we didn't become friends, not really. All the women spoiled Poppy, who was the youngest child on board and very pretty, with curly hair and brown eyes, and who was just learning to walk. I was supposed to look after Poppy, but I didn't do much of a job. She bored me slightly.

On a cold, grey summer day, the ship docked in Melbourne. With Mum and Poppy I stood on the top deck, straining my eyes to find Dad among the thousands of people who were waving and calling on the wharf. Suddenly my mother started to cry and call out 'Andreas! Andreas!' A tall, thin man at the back of the crowd was waving and grinning. Was that Dad? I couldn't remember him well, but was sure my mother wouldn't blow kisses and wave at a stranger. Hours later we filed down the gangplank with the others, collected the luggage and Dad and I greeted each other. He was absolutely overjoyed to see us.

Dad had left the Snowy Mountains Scheme by then; he and my Uncle Costas had set up business in Rutherglen, a small Victorian town, running the cafe there. We went back from the dock to the station, and caught a train to Rutherglen.

At Rutherglen, my memories suddenly focus. The first thing I remember about the place is the smell of the eucalypts. And the cafe, and the house we lived in.

Our house was about a mile from the cafe, a two-bedroomed, tin-roofed place. It was nothing special, but I was enchanted by the fact that it had a refrigerator. I used to go into the kitchen and open and close it, fascinated by the cold air that came out. How could a metal box keep things cool? Mum used to scold me about that. She was fanatical about cleaning the house, sweeping, scrubbing, washing, day in, day out. She spent hours boiling Dad's and Costas's grease-splashed shirts in the copper, drying them, ironing them with a heavy flatiron Dad had picked up from a local shop. I used to stand and watch her, but real life wasn't at home. Real life was in the cafe.

Dad and Uncle Costas, who was fatter and jollier than ever and smoked more cigarettes than anybody I had ever met — ran the cafe from early morning until late at night. I used to take Poppy there for breakfast on the way to school. It was a magical place; the heavy smell of frying sausages, bacon, eggs and tomatoes (Australian food, Uncle Costas called it scornfully; we had moussaka, lamb and vegetables at home), the long, gleaming counters and the Formica tables. Poppy and I used to play houses under the tables and on the long benches when there were no customers; as soon as they appeared, we scuttled through to the kitchen. So much food was being prepared: tomatoes sizzling in frying pans much bigger than the one we had at home, stacks of white bread for toast, enormous slabs of bacon.

I was the only non-Australian kid at the school, which didn't worry me for some time. When I was very small, the kids called me '*Ushi*', which is Greek for 'Giddyap!' This was because I was a pretty strapping kid with a broad back and the other kids used to jump on my shoulders and demand to be galloped around the playground. 'Giddyap!' they yelled, and because I didn't speak any English, I echoed them in Greek: '*Ushi, ushi!*'

I don't remember a time when I learned to read English. It wasn't hard, because I learned at school, just as the Australian kids did. I hadn't learned to read the Greek alphabet, so I didn't have to cope with another system of letters: we spoke Greek at home, we didn't write it.

I never spoke English at home. Dad had some knowledge of the language, picked up on the Snowy and at work in the cafe, but Mum had none. (She still has very little English.) My Uncle Costas, who was very sharp and who spoke English with great fluency, frowned at me if I started talking English to him. 'You are not Australian, you are Greek,' he said. I gradually worked out that, while learning English and speaking it to the other kids at school was necessary to survive, Greek was the language they liked at home. I easily stopped speaking English the moment I walked in the front door.

At least Dad, Uncle Costas and I were mixing with Australians, with other people, whether we enjoyed it or not. It was different for my mother. There were no other Greek women in Rutherglen, so she had nobody to talk to. Her life was cleaning the house and looking after two children, one of whom — me — was at school most of the day. She had two men and two young children to talk to, and I think she must have had a very lonely life. On Cyprus, much of her day had been spent chatting and swapping information with the other women in the village.

When I was seven, my Uncle Costas was betrothed to a girl who had been found for him back in Cyprus. She was sent out to Australia to marry him. It was understood that the newly married couple would make their home with us — but my new Aunt Angela didn't get on with Mum. Mum was very scornful of Angela, who she said cared far too much about her appearance and hadn't done a stroke of work in her life. She spent a lot of time putting on make-up, or walking around Rutherglen in her best clothes. She didn't see much of Costas, who was working in the cafe most of the time. She didn't want to work there herself. Dad couldn't understand this. 'If your wife has no children to look after,' he said to his brother, 'why doesn't she work?' And even if you *did* have children, he implied, women should take jobs whenever possible, so the family would gain two incomes. That was how you got on, how you made money.

One day Mum burst into tears and told Dad that she couldn't stand living with that useless Angela any longer. She wanted to move, or make Angela go away. This caused great problems between Dad and Uncle Costas, but eventually it was decided that we would move. Uncle Costas, who had mates all over the place, it seemed, arranged for Dad to work in the cafe at Shepparton.

Shepparton was the town where I really grew up, I suppose. It was much bigger than Rutherglen, and a farming town. Opposite our house were a dairy and some paddocks. Poppy and I used to beg peas, or cabbages, or potatoes at the end of the season, just before the tractors ploughed the last of the crop into the soil. We were usually allowed to take what we wanted. My job was to go to the dairy and get milk for breakfast and dinner. I enjoyed watching the milking and collecting a billy full of white, foaming milk.

At school, life changed. I was no longer Ushi, the kid who let the others ride on his back. I was Greek, different from the other kids. There were other migrants at Shepparton Public School:

Italians, Yugoslavs, a few Polish boys and girls. But the overwhelming majority were Australians. For the first time I heard myself being called a wog, not always affectionately. I was bewildered. Why did they call me this? I looked the same as they did, learned composition and tables and the primary products of Australia, just as they did. So what was so different about me?

The Australian kids weren't actively cruel. They just didn't include me in everything. Birthday parties, for instance. Sometimes on Mondays the other kids would have leftover birthday cake for playlunch, from Darrell Smith's or Margaret Gilroy's party. I didn't even know it had taken place. I tried not to care. After all, I could get free lollies if I really wanted them, from the cafe.

I became very self-reliant. I made up my mind not to worry about how the other kids treated me. I was better than they were.

To survive I knew I had to be better than the others. Fortunately, I was good at marbles and I soon became playground champion. I'd often go to school with empty pockets and return with a whole fistful of alleys and catseyes to show Mum. She had no idea what these strange glass balls were, but they were important to me, she knew.

I was a great playground fighter, too. Not because I was bigger or faster than the other kids, but because I would never give up. I would slug and kick and punch, even if the other kids thought I was beaten. I would try and heave myself up from the ground to dislodge a kid who had attacked me and was sitting on my chest. I learned that the secret was to get in before the other kid could bash me first. This didn't come easily. I'm competitive, I suppose, but not really aggressive in that way. But I knew I had to hit first. Being belted was the only thing a couple of those kids understood, and I had to learn to speak the same language.

In front of the dairy near our place were the three tallest pine trees in Shepparton. The bravest thing you could do was climb them all. One afternoon, after school, I didn't play marbles as usual, but went to the first pine tree and started to climb it, without telling anybody. It wasn't easy, but I did it. Nobody had seen me. Then I tackled the next tree. I made that, too, though there were some really tricky branches at the top. The third tree was really difficult; it was getting dark and my legs were aching. But I told myself I had to do this, it was necessary, so I gritted my teeth and did.

Nobody had seen me, nobody knew I had climbed those trees, but *I* did. And the great thing was that, a week or two later, one of the kids said, 'Bet you can't climb those trees, wog.' I challenged him to a competition. Because I had climbed the trees before, and knew them, I was much faster than he was, and I won. That was probably the proudest day of my life.

I couldn't tell my parents what these things meant to me. They would not have understood why I had this fierce need to prove myself in the way I did. But perhaps they might have done; after all, I was only doing what they were, in a different way. We had the same goals, after all.

Dad worked in the cafe ten or twelve hours a day. Mum had recently got a job as an assembly line worker at the local cannery. They were working to support us, to buy things, to succeed. You only got things or succeeded if you worked for them; we knew that.

Looking back, I realise that this need to work hard and to prove ourselves cost us our family life.

School mornings were very simple. Dad got Poppy and me up, made sure we were dressed (he bought all our clothes himself because he was the one who spoke English), made our breakfast and ensured that we were ready for school. Mum was never there in the mornings — she started work at the cannery at six and we never saw her before we went to school. Poppy and I would walk to school, and then take ages coming home to Mum. She was always very tired, and rather cross because of it. Her life was working long, long hours in the cannery, cleaning the house and cooking the evening meal for us. We couldn't talk to her; we were learning things at school about which she knew nothing, in a language that was strange and alarming to her. So we would do our homework, eat the evening meal, and go to bed.

The highlight of the week was Saturday, especially Saturday night. Dad had to work very late at the cafe, since on Saturdays everybody came into town and had dinner there. Because Mum didn't have to go to work the following day, Poppy and I spent time with her in the evenings. Only then did she become a person to us. She told us all about our relatives in Cyprus, and how we would all go back there when we were rich (a constant theme, because Mum hated Australia). I would marry a good Greek girl, and Poppy a good Greek man. Not a dreadful Australian.

The thrill of Saturday was Dad's return after midnight, because he brought us the taste sensation of the week. Toasted sandwiches, two kinds, ham and Kraft cheese, left over from the cafe. Eating cold toasted ham and cheese sandwiches at one in the morning was wonderful. I always ate as many as possible before Mum stopped me!

But we were a family who didn't talk to each other much. There wasn't often time.

I think I fell in love with Miss Cook, my teacher in fourth class, because she was the first adult woman I knew who seemed to understand what I was talking about. She was the only teacher I'd ever met who treated me as though I was a proper person, not a dumb wog. It was 1956, the year of the Olympic Games, and Miss Cook singled me out in class by telling the others that the people in the country I'd come from had started the Olympic Games. I could tell this was news to some of my classmates. What? Great Australians like Jon Hendricks or the Konrads kids getting gold medals because of a festival started by wogs? But Miss Cook insisted it was so.

I loved her passionately. She was small, slim and blonde, wore very colourful dresses (not like Mum's black jumpers and skirts and cardigans) and never looked tired. Whenever I did well in a test, she was pleased for me. I don't know if the other kids in the class had a crush on her, and I didn't care. Miss Cook was mine!

I missed her very badly the following year, when we had Mr Sanders. He was fair, too, but very quiet and sarcastic, and fond of using the cane.

One day, the headmaster said at assembly, 'Will Nicholas Kallergis come and see me in the office, please.' I couldn't imagine what I had done. When I got there, the headmaster, who was a nice bloke, I suppose, looked at me sternly and said, 'Kallergis, Mr Sanders tells me you have got ninety-eight per cent in a social studies test.'

I went scarlet. Ninety-eight per cent! It was the best mark I'd ever received in my life. The test had happened to be about primary industry in Victoria, something that really interested me, and I knew I'd done well — but ninety-eight per cent! Wait till I told Mum and Dad!

But the headmaster didn't look pleased at all. 'All right, Kallergis,' he said. 'Whom did you copy from?'

I couldn't believe what I had heard, just gaped at him. He obviously took this as a sign of guilt, and became very angry. 'Don't you realise what a serious thing cheating is? Why did you do it?'

'I didn't, sir!'

But I couldn't convince him. I remember thinking, what sort of place *is* this? All I had done was to show them that I was better, the way I knew I had to. And look what had happened.

Nobody at home ever knew about that incident — I didn't even tell Mum and Dad about the ninety-eight per cent. And, though I knew I had done well, and knew that they wouldn't believe I had cheated, I didn't want to tell them that I'd even been suspected of dishonesty. Mum would have said, 'This would never have happened in Cyprus,' and Dad would have looked puzzled and said, 'But why do these Australians do this to you?'

I didn't know why. It was best to ignore it, so I did.

Television came to Shepparton. We didn't have a set, nor did most of the people we knew. But when the local TV station began transmission, Kenny Harris from up the road and I were ready for it.

As soon as school was over, we would take up our positions bang in front of the window of the local TV shop, facing the pride and joy of the merchandise: the twenty-eight-inch AWA Deep Image. We watched the cartoons, and the news, and gradually a group of people collected behind us. Kenny had to go home to dinner but I was allowed to stay out later than he. I wouldn't move, just stood watching into the evening. Comedy shows like *I Love Lucy*, then — my favourite and the best show on the air — *Rawhide*. I always had to tell Kenny what had happened if he didn't see it. If one of us had to duck off for any reason, the other would hold his place.

The proudest event in the family's life, however, occurred just before we left Shepparton. Dad bought a motor car. It was a green Morris Minor 1000. Life changed dramatically for the Kallergis family. Gone were the days when Dad would take his bicycle to the cafe while we walked to school; now he dropped us at the gate. I think I found this more exciting than Poppy did; I couldn't wait to learn to drive.

But Dad wouldn't let me. After all, I was only eleven. But other kids — farmers' sons — were allowed to drive without a licence. Kids in my class had taken their fathers' Ford Customlines and pickup trucks out on the dirt roads around town and gone for a burn around the place. Why couldn't I?

But Dad refused. He made me help him clean the car — polishing its upholstery, lovingly washing the body with soap and water, polishing the tyres with boot polish until they glistened. It seemed terribly unfair that I couldn't get any of the benefits.

Especially since Mum was learning to drive. Dad decided that the time had come for her to be a bit more independent, and on Sundays he would pile Poppy and me in the back and we would go out on the roads. At first Mum was terrified, and whenever she panicked she swerved wildly to the left. 'Look out for that tree, Eleni! Aie!'

Very soon Mum forgot her fear of the car. She never drove faster than about twenty-five miles an hour, being cautious by nature, but she became a magnificently steady driver. I was very proud of her, really, though I still envied her.

And now we could go to the drive-in theatre, just like everybody else, if we had the time. We had our very own car, and our own house. We were real Australians.

❧*That terrible night is in my mind now*

Alex Lukics came to Australia from Czechoslovakia in 1952, when he was four. He's blond, short and intense with a harsh voice and bitter eyes.

This happened when we had been in Australia for less than two years.

I don't remember coming here, though I know we arrived by boat. But I remember bits of Czechoslovakia, like the time the cupboard fell on me and I screamed and my mother came running and petted me and made me feel better. I must have been about three, I suppose. I still remember that fear, the fear of being crushed under a cupboard.

We came to Sydney, to a suburb I think was Lakemba, but it could have been Petersham or Belmore. We moved around a lot in the first couple of years. Those names are all part of my childhood, jumbled up together.

There was my father, a big man with dark hair and a gruff voice, who was very strict but who sometimes laughed loudly. And my mother, who had very big breasts that I used to nuzzle against. I remember the comfort of those breasts, and I also remember being ashamed of her at school because she couldn't speak English. Nor could Dad, but he didn't come to the school. The other member of my family was Mara, but she was just 'the baby'.

One night the baby screamed and screamed and screamed. I heard that, and the next thing my mother was pulling at me and telling me to get up at once because she needed me. The baby was sick, she said, and she had to get a doctor. I was warm and sleepy and wanted to stay where I was, but she wouldn't let me. Mara was in her arms, and she was screaming. I remember the screams now more clearly than I did when I was young. They seem to have grown with time and become more terrible.

My mother was in her nightdress, and her blonde hair was

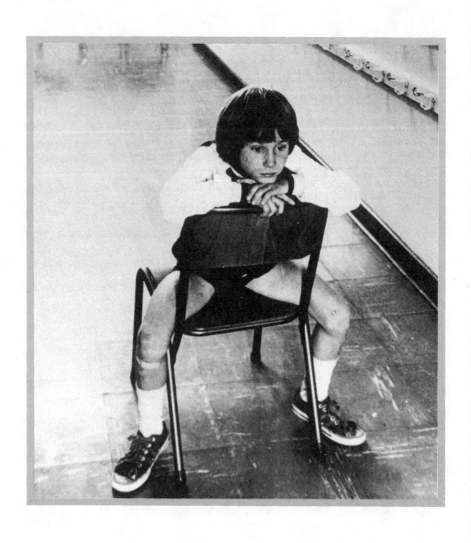

That terrible night is in my mind now

down, instead of being in a braid around her head as usual. She looked mad, and I was scared. I couldn't understand why she was in her nightdress, because she told me she wanted to go out into the night with the screaming baby, and I had to help her. She was shouting, yelling, and my mother never raised her voice normally.

My father was away. I don't know where. It never occurred to me to ask where he was; he just wasn't there.

I was grumpy and irritated with my mother, whose voice was shrill with fear and panic. But I pulled some clothes on, and she dragged me downstairs from our flat and into the street. She had no shoes on. Her hair was streaming out and she had no shoes on and she was wearing her nightdress. I didn't want to be in the street at night with my mother like that, and a screaming baby in her arms. I didn't want to be there. I was embarrassed.

A car came past and my mother screamed and waved at it. It didn't even slow down. And it was pouring rain. I remember now because I can still see the rain in front of the headlights of that car. But I don't remember getting wet.

A taxi came past, and stopped. My mother flung open the front door and shouted to the driver in Czech. The baby was still screaming. Mum tried to get into the cab. The driver leaned over and pushed her back. 'Drunken bitch,' he said. I remember that clearly because later I asked my mother what a drunken bitch was, and she slapped me.

My mother was telling me in Czech to tell the driver to take us to the hospital, and I tried, but I don't think he heard me. My mother kept shouting, and the baby kept screaming. Finally the man closed the door and drove off.

My mother started running up the street, calling aloud to passing cars. There weren't many, and they didn't stop. I kept up with her, plucking at her nightdress and wanting to say something. I didn't know what.

I was only six, and I didn't realise that she couldn't speak English. I could speak some English, and Czech, and at home I didn't know what I was speaking, but in fact it was always Czech. I didn't really understand that my mother needed me to tell somebody she had to get her baby to a doctor, and doctor meant hospital.

I don't know how long we were in the street. We ended up on the main road, with trams. I remember now, as I am talking to you, that I stood in a puddle and my feet were wet and cold. One foot was wetter and colder than the other, because I only had one shoe on.

Then another cab stopped. Thinking back, I am surprised that it did. What cab would stop for a long-haired, screaming woman in a nightdress on a wet night? But as soon as it slowed down enough, my mother pulled open the front door; this time she pushed me in beside the driver, opened the back door and got in with the baby.

'Tell him, tell him the hospital,' she said. 'The hospital. Your sister is sick.' She had thrust her head over the back seat, and her hair was in my face. I had some of it in my mouth, and had to pull it clear before I could speak.

I told the driver, in English, as clearly as I could, feeling I should apologise for my mother.

'Yeah,' he said. 'Yeah. I suppose there's no money or anything like that, is there?' But he drove off quickly; he must have been a kindly man. I cannot remember what he looked like.

We reached the hospital; I remember seeing a big light at the door. My mother jumped out of the cab and ran through a door; I followed her. The driver yelled something after me, but I couldn't understand. I think he knew he wouldn't get his fare.

Then suddenly there was a large, white room, and people in white coats and starched little hats and uniforms. My mother, in her wet nightdress and her hair in rats' tails down her back, was holding out the baby, and trying to talk to these people. They stood listening politely, without understanding. Then she turned to me, and I was telling these big, serious men and women that my mother was in her nightdress because the baby was sick. I was embarrassed. The same feeling I had when my mother came up to the school.

We sat down on a long bench and waited, with a lot of other people. The baby gradually stopped screaming and began to make little whimpering sounds. I can still hear those sounds in my head, soft and sad. Suddenly she was very quiet.

Eventually somebody came and took my mother and Mara away. I was alone on the hospital bench for a long, long time. Then I must have fallen asleep, because I remember my mother coming to wake me up. She was still in her nightdress and her hair was still down, but there was no baby.

My mother didn't speak. She didn't even seem to see me. She just took my hand, very tightly, and we walked out of the hospital. We walked all the way home, a long way. I don't think it was raining. I was tired. I wanted my mother to comfort me, but she said nothing. She was quiet for a long, long time.

My father came home the following day. He told me my sister was dead. It didn't mean much.

Then there was the funeral. I remember a small white coffin. When it went down into the ground at the cemetery I remember thinking that it should have a pipe or tube leading into it so my sister could breathe. You see, I thought of her in that coffin exactly as she had been when I knew her, a one-year-old tottering around the house, sometimes laughing, sometimes crying, sometimes falling over.

I can't say I was sad at the time. I don't think I believed what was happening.

Somehow I found out later that my sister had died because she had swallowed a safety pin and developed peritonitis. That was it. It took me a long time to realise that if my mother had been able to speak English, my sister probably wouldn't have died. She might have. But you can't help thinking.

1960—1970

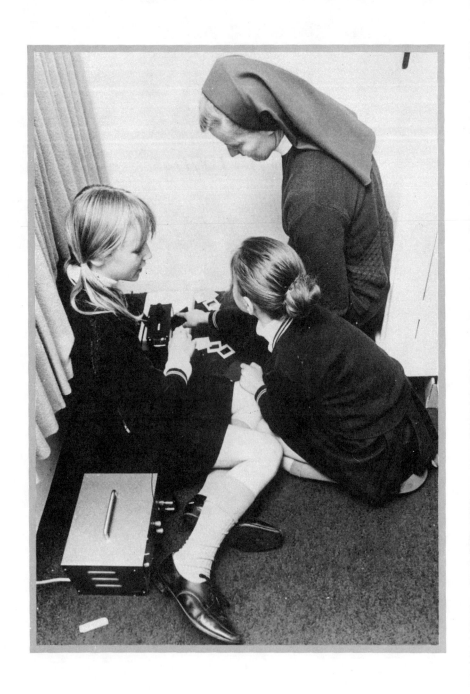

We were taught to be neat, sweet and discreet

❧*W*e were taught to be neat, sweet and discreet

'Why are you asking us about growing up Catholic in the sixties?' *asks Elizabeth Findlay. 'Nothing much happened, really.' Elizabeth* *says she was very quiet at school. She appears to be very self-contained,* *smiling rarely. When she is thinking, she runs her hands though fine,* *straight brown hair, and frowns.*

'Yeah, it was much worse for our brothers,' adds her sister, *Marion, who is three years younger. 'John and Martin had a really* *rough time. Beaten senseless and left for dead by maddened Marist* *priests every afternoon.' Words spill out of Marion Findlay; even her* *curly hair seems to crackle with energy. She was the class debater, ever* *willing to stand up in class and challenge what she was told, with six* *good reasons why.*

ELIZABETH: I was born in 1955 and started school when I was five. It was a small parochial school in the suburbs of Perth.

When I was six I made my first communion. This meant dressing up as a bride, in a white organdie dress with a little white veil. A very solemn occasion. At the same time, the school held a debutantes' ball for us. I got my hair curled at the hairdresser's and danced with a little boy from another school in a tiny dinner jacket, and kissed the Monsignor's ring.

MARION: We got dressed up as brides every five seconds, didn't we? It seemed to be what good little girls did. I remember my debut, too; three years after yours, but I wasn't nearly as elegant. My best friend Jan and I didn't like some of the other debs, who had nicer white dresses and veils than we did, and thought they were just wonderful. So Jan smuggled in two bottles of Coke just before the ball started, and we took the tops off, shook them up hard and put our fingers over the top of the bottles and sprayed the girls we didn't like. It was very satisfying!

ELIZABETH: In second class, Mum was quite sick, so I was sent to a boarding school for two weeks. I always think of it as 'the year I spent in boarding school'; it seemed to go on forever. Because I was the new girl, a late boarder and the youngest in the school, I didn't have a cubicle like the other girls did, so I slept in a bed in the corridor. That was about the time that the Moonstruck Murderer was at large; he used to shoot people at the time of the full moon. The other kids said, 'The Moonstruck Murderer's going to get you,' because, if he came through the window, he'd see me first, in the corridor. I was so terrified that I used to wet my bed, and in the morning I got up early and made my bed so the nuns wouldn't see the wet patch. Boarding school was awful.

MARION: Elizabeth and I shared a bedroom at home, and every afternoon after school we filled a small bottle full of holy water from the font at the chapel. Then, before we went to sleep at night, we said our prayers (making sure we asked everybody we knew to be blessed, we didn't want to leave anybody out), checked that the candle was burning at the foot of the Virgin Mary's statue on our bookcase, and sprinkled holy water on our beds. Then we went to sleep lying on our backs with our hands crossed on our chests. The nuns told us that would keep the devil away if we died in the night.

ELIZABETH: One of my great fears was dying at night and *not* being good enough to go to heaven. I used to feel terribly sorry for all those unbaptised babies in Limbo, denied the sight of God forever.

MARION: When I was in primary school, it seemed that every family had at least five children. I remember coming to school and seeing a little girl in tears because the new baby had died.

ELIZABETH: We were four in our family, which was not considered an excessive number. Neat and tasteful. Two boys and two girls.

MARION: We prayed for the black babies all the time. We had one baby we supported all through my primary school days. He was an Indian child, and his name was Rama. Pictures of him were handed round; he had incredibly large black eyes and a solemn face, and his ribs stuck out. We'd give our sixpences for Rama when we were told. Trouble was, Rama never got any bigger. From grade one until grade six, we were shown exactly the same photo. Ullo, ullo, I thought...bit strange!

ELIZABETH: The black babies were damned, of course, unless they were baptised.

MARION: Oh, so was everybody. We used to pray for the conversion of Russia, so the Russians wouldn't come down and overrun us.

ELIZABETH: We knew Catholics were superior to everybody else. But we were scared of the Indonesians. When Sukarno was swaggering around in the mid-1960s, he said that he'd come down and take over Australia. Sister Mary Polycarpe in the junior school told us that the communists, particularly the Indonesian communists, would come down, torture you, get you to deny Christ, then kill you. Denying Christ was the worst thing you could do.

MARION: I'd seen newsreel pictures of Jakarta, and was convinced the Indonesians would arrive on bicycles to torture us.

ELIZABETH: We knew that everybody was jealous of Catholics, because they were better than other people. But you had to watch that. In public examinations you weren't allowed to put 'JMJ' for Jesus, Mary and Joseph or 'AMDG' ('to the greater glory of God') at the tops of your papers, the way you did in your schoolbooks. We knew that the examination system was prejudiced against Catholics, and we'd be penalised. And you could always tell Protestants, because they referred to 'Roman Catholics', not 'Catholics' as we did.

MARION: The Protestants were subhuman. You went to hell if you entered a Protestant church, the nuns told us. Nobody could be friendly with a non-Catholic, so the first thing I did when I met a strange child was to ask where he or she went to school, so I could tell. We were taught to convert Protestants, to show them the error of their ways. So when we weren't sneering at them for being lower than the beasts, we were supposed to convert them, if they'd let us. They never did, not at all.

ELIZABETH: But childhood is a time of fears.

MARION: Yes. In primary school we had wall charts showing the Last Trump, with the sinners in hell at the bottom. Flames were licking around them and their hands were raised beseechingly, and an angel in white held a trumpet and was blowing hard. People in white were ascending into heaven, which was up the top of the picture. What worried me was that the world was in flames too and I felt so sorry for the poor sinners who had escaped the flaming world, only to be sent into hell. I used to worry a lot that the Day of Judgement was at hand, and there didn't seem anything much to be done about it.

ELIZABETH: I didn't worry so much about that. My fears were more personal. I was terrified of getting a vocation, for instance. We all knew from the nuns that if you were called by God, you wouldn't be able to resist it. Every year we had Vocation Week, in primary school, and a nun would come round to ask, 'Does anybody here have a vocation?' I used to think, what if God told me I *had* to be a nun? Right then? I would have to get up and be one of those people.

MARION: If you *had* become a nun, you would have been able to tell the rest of us whether nuns wore underclothes under their habits, and whether they were really men (which some of us believed; I had a nun called Sister Anne who looked exactly like Arthur Calwell), and if they had hair under their wimples...

ELIZABETH: We were terrified of them, we really were. I didn't want to be like Sister Theodore, who threw books and bits of chalk at us if we got wrong answers in mental arithmetic lessons.

MARION: That was nothing. If you believe John and Martin, who went to a parochial school too, they used to get thrashed senseless and left for dead, every afternoon, by maddened Marists.

ELIZABETH: We didn't know what was happening. When they were little, they occasionally came home with cut faces and skinned knees because they led gang wars in the playground — I think Martin led John on, even though Martin was two years younger.

MARION: I'm sure he did. See, John had a very big character change. When he was very little he was Mr Straight, a real neatness nurd. He even wanted to be a Marist brother.

ELIZABETH: Martin was hit by one of the brothers when he was about thirteen. The brother, who was a twisted old wreck, was giving a lesson on cassette, and the machine broke down. The boy in front of Martin said, 'Cassette broken, is it, brother?' in a real smart-arse voice. 'Come out here! Don't you *dare* say the word "buggered",' said the brother.

Martin said, 'He didn't say "buggered", brother; he said "broken".'

The brother was furious, and switched his attention to Martin. 'Come out the front, too! I'll cane you both!'

'No, I won't,' said Martin, who thought the whole thing was terribly unfair.

The brother actually went whack! and hit Martin across the face with his open hand. Martin sat down and burst into tears.

MARION: Dad went up to talk to the head brother, whom the boys called Brother Tojo. He promised it would never happen again; the whole thing was hushed up.

ELIZABETH: I've never really understood that. Made me realise, I suppose, how much power those brothers had. Martin and John should have been taken away and the school sued, but Mum and Dad didn't do that.

At our school things were much easier. Sometimes the nuns would hit bad girls on the legs, but that's all.

MARION: That didn't make you love the nuns, though. I was terrified of them, but my great dread was being selected to have a vision. We were always told about how joyful this was, and we heard about Bernadette of Lourdes and the children of Fatima all the time. I didn't want to see the Virgin Mary; too much responsibility. I would have had to go away from home and tell everybody about it. I didn't want to be specially chosen, to be plucked from the security of home. I knew that children who were granted visions had to mortify their flesh in some way because they had been specially chosen. The nuns told us stories about children having ropes knotted around their waists, so they could suffer for Christ, and wearing thorns in their shoes to be an example of purity. You had to offer up your pain to God, to show you were worthy. I wasn't keen on any of that!

ELIZABETH: I was afraid of having impure thoughts.

MARION: So was I, and every week I used to confess to impure thoughts and deeds. I had no idea what they were. Nobody ever told me.

ELIZABETH: On the way home, we had to walk past a barber's shop, and inside the window were various little things you could buy. One of these was a bottle opener, which was gold, about eight inches tall, and in the shape of a naked lady with ruby nipples; her feet were part of the opener itself, which pulled the top off the beer bottle. I *knew* this bottle opener represented an impure thought, so every time I went past the shop I shut my eyes. That object burned into my imagination, and I can't forget it, even now!

MARION: Yes, impure thoughts were all to do with sex, we knew that much. But sex was never, never mentioned. At junior school, we weren't allowed even to touch each other. At the age of about ten, little girls like hugging each other and going around arm in arm to show that they are best friends, but that was forbidden.

We got sex education at home, not at school. Mum and Dad, who had been brought up very strictly, hadn't had any themselves, so they were very conscious of its importance. From about the age of four, we were *told*. When I was six, I asked, 'Mum, how are babies born?' 'Right!' said Mum, and led me into the living room, where my little brothers couldn't hear, and grabbed a pencil and paper and started drawing diagrams. She was explaining something, and I listened politely, and when she'd finished I said, 'Oh, *I* see!' Of course, I didn't have a clue.

Martin said he always got confused between those diagrams and Dad's drawings of how a car worked.

ELIZABETH: I didn't know what a virgin was. I thought 'virgin' was another word for 'lady'.

MARION: In third grade, Sister Gelatine Blobs (her name was actually Sister Joseph, but we called her Sister Gelatine Blobs because she had a doughy, wobbly face) decided to tell us about the Ten Commandments. We went right through, she was droning on, we were bored to death, almost asleep. Then she got to the sixth commandment, and hesitated. She took a deep breath and said, 'Adultery is what adults do; that's where the word comes from.'

ELIZABETH: I didn't get the whole system straight until I was in my teens at least.

MARION: Nor did I. I knew that sex was wrong, unhealthy somehow. I didn't like asking too many questions, because I thought God would punish me. I worried about not loving God enough. When I was in third grade, Liz, you found me sobbing — do you remember? — you asked, 'What's the matter?' And I said, 'I love my Wiggly doll more than I love God.'

ELIZABETH: Names were very important. There were several Thereses and a couple of Bernadettes and a Veronica or two in my class at primary school. And a couple of Elizabeths.

MARION: I was born on the Feast of the Annunciation, and there was no way the nuns were going to let Mum out of the hospital without my being called Mary. She didn't think Mary Findlay was a very interesting name, and she didn't want to call me that. She didn't know what to do, and my godfather said, 'Call her Marion. It's a variation on Mary; they'll accept that.' And they did. But my second name had to be Mary, so my name's really Mary Mary.

ELIZABETH: We both took the confirmation name of Frances. I decided first, being the eldest, and chose Frances because of St Francis of Assisi, I suppose. I wanted all four of us to be called Frances or Francis; I wanted to start a trend.

MARION: No, you didn't! How can you say that! I decided on the name Francis, not you!

ELIZABETH: When Martin made his confirmation, he insisted on the name Constantine.

MARION: You have to imagine a whole line of thirteen-year-old boys being brought up, one by one, to be consecrated by the bishop, who was finicky and elderly with a sha-a-a-ky voice. Martin was fairly close to the head of the queue, and the bishop asked, 'What are you calling yourself?' 'Constantine,' said Martin loudly. The bishop said, 'Eh? Was there a Saint Constantine? I don't believe there was a Saint Constantine.' Martin stood his ground and said, 'Well, the Emperor Constantine brought religion to the East, and his mother was a saint, and Constantine found the True Cross...' This was all said in hissing whispers, and the line behind Martin muttered and shuffled. The bishop looked at the long, long queue and said hurriedly, 'Yes, well, I don't think...' Martin just continued, 'And he was a very good man, and I like the name, and I think Constantine must be a saint.' The bishop said, more or less, 'Get out!' and caved in completely. So Martin's confirmation name is Constantine.

ELIZABETH: You won't be surprised to hear that Martin's a lawyer now. When I made my confirmation, we were going through one of our poor periods at home (Dad was a freelance writer). I had the correct white bridal dress...

MARION: God, bridal dresses got a thrashing when we were kids...

ELIZABETH: But I didn't have nice black pumps like the others, so I had to make my confirmation in my brown school shoes. I minded very much.

MARION: You always were fashion-conscious when you were a kid, weren't you.

ELIZABETH: I suppose so. I had some very pretty pearl rosary beads, and was terribly proud of them. Only a couple of years ago, a friend of John, my brother, wore a set of rosary beads as ordinary jewellery, and I was shocked. Very bad taste, even though she was a non-Catholic.

MARION: Scapulars were fashion items too, sort of. There was a hierarchy in scapulars. If you bought a brown one, that was all right, but you were guaranteed one hundred days in Purgatory. A green scapular was fifty days. And if you bought a blue one — the most expensive, of course — and said certain prayers, you'd go straight into heaven. Just like that.

ELIZABETH: And there was a hierarchy of sins too. Mortal and venial. Mortal sins were missing confession for a year, not going to Mass on Sundays, murder, impure thoughts, not obeying the Ten Commandments...

MARION: Venial sins were everything else.

ELIZABETH: There were super-good saints and ordinary saints, too. We didn't really have favourites, except St Christopher.

MARION: Who's now been struck off the record. I liked St Anthony, who looked after lost property, and I remember Mum used to say whenever she couldn't find something, 'Hail St Anthony full of grace, lead me to its hiding place.' She often found it, too.

ELIZABETH: I liked St Jude, help of the helpless.

MARION: Oh, and there was Saint Maria Goretti, the little flower. She got to be a little flower because she didn't have any impure thoughts.

ELIZABETH: But St Theresa, the one who got tuberculosis, was a little flower, too. I liked her.

MARION: Lots of little flowers, there were. Quite a garden!

ELIZABETH: When I was twelve, we were sent to a much more upmarket school, and things changed. The reason we were sent there was that I came home from parochial school one day, having seen F-U-C-K written on the wall of a toilet.

MARION: Why are you being so coy?

ELIZABETH: Well, that's what I saw; those four letters. I didn't have a clue what they meant.

I said to Mum and Dad, 'What does FUCK mean?'

They looked at each other and said, 'Time to move on!'

❧ *A*ll these things seemed to be happening a long way from us

The fading colour photograph shows Andrea Kendall hugging a white Persian cat. Andrea is aged about eight, a solid child with short dark hair, a small mouth and striking green eyes. She is wearing a blue and white checked dress, short white socks and brown sandals, and she stands in front of an orange tree. At first glance, it is a conventional picture with a conventional caption: 'Snowcrisp and me, Adelaide 1963'. But there is nothing ordinary about the way Andrea is holding the animal. Instead of cradling it softly in the approved manner, she has it clutched to her like a talisman, and she is scowling at the camera.

Now Andrea smiles and shuts the album. 'I've always had cats,' she says, shooing a large tabby off the sofa. 'I think I've always loved cats better than people.'

Saturday 23 November 1963 started as an ordinary day. Dad had gone off to play golf just after dawn; Mum and my two older sisters were still in bed. I would have liked to sleep in, too, but Snowcrisp really got annoyed if I made him wait for his milk later than half past seven on any morning, including Saturday. I got up, took the milk out of the fridge and poured it into his special blue bowl. While he was lapping it up — or rather, inhaling it, because he tended to consume milk as though he had been deprived of it since birth — I switched on the radio. In our house, the 'wireless', as Mum and Dad still called it, was officially used only for the ABC news...whenever I could, I switched on to a commercial station hoping to get some music. I was after what Mum called '*that* music', particularly 'Please Please Me', the 45 rpm disc of which I'd already started requesting for Christmas.

No Beatles that morning though. Just a couple of guitar chords and a serious voice. 'Here is a news flash...President John

All these things seemed to be happening a long way from us

F. Kennedy has been shot...' with a lot of details about Dallas, Texas, motorcades, Kennedy slumping into Jackie's lap and speeding to hospital, where doctors had failed to save his life.

Kennedy shot! I couldn't believe it. Snowcrisp finished his milk and came smooching around my legs, but for the first time in his life I ignored him. Kennedy dead! I was eight, but he was the only world leader whose name I knew. I'd seen him on television, smiling and very handsome, unlike our own Prime Minister who always looked old and cross. Everything he did made front-page news in the Adelaide *Advertiser*. Women's magazines were always telling my mother and other women her age to wear little pillbox hats and short jackets and bell skirts, like Jackie Kennedy's. In *Time* magazine, there was a lot about the Kennedys and Camelot, which I didn't understand because I knew that's where King Arthur had lived. But I knew that everybody considered the Kennedys to be the most glamorous people on earth. Even our school library had sprouted a crop of picture books about Jack, Jackie, Caroline and John-John.

I raced into my sister Jo's bedroom. As usual, she was an inert lump under the bedclothes; she always needed twice as many blankets as anybody else, even in late spring.

'Jo! Jo! Wake up! Kennedy's dead, he's been shot!' Jo lifted her head and looked at me balefully.

'It's true. He's been killed!' I didn't know what I expected her to do, but nobody would want to stay in bed after they'd heard that.

'Don't be so stupid,' said Jo crossly.

'It's true, it's *true!*'

'You're lying,' she said. 'Go away and leave me alone.'

I wanted to leap on the bed and hit her hard, but I knew what the consequences would be; Jo was six years bigger than I was.

So, cursing her, I went to find Tricia, my second sister. She was reading *Exodus* in bed.

'Trish, Kennedy's been shot!'

Tricia turned a page. 'Really?' she said in an uninterested voice, without taking her eyes from the book.

Tricia was four years older than I, and easier to tackle than Jo. I tore Leon Uris out of her hands. 'Listen! He's dead!'

'Give me my book back!' was all Tricia said. 'And go outside and play.'

I hurled *Exodus* to the floor and stomped out of the room, almost in tears. Talk about unfair — I'd announced a really major piece of news, and nobody believed me. Monsters, beasts, rats! Life was miserable.

I decided not to try Mum. She hated being woken up early on weekends, and she would probably have reacted in the same way as Jo and Tricia. So I sulked all morning in the garden with Snowcrisp (who at least believed me), working out how I could possibly leave home, even though I only had one ten-shilling note and six two-shilling pieces in my piggy bank. Common sense told me that I wouldn't have been able to get far out of Adelaide with that, even on half fare.

At lunchtime Dad came home from golf. He looked very serious and carried a copy of the *News*: he never bought the paper on Saturdays. Mum, Jo and Tricia were all up by then. None of them had the decency to ask where I'd been.

'Have you heard about Kennedy? He's been shot,' said Dad.

There! It was true! I couldn't help being smug.

'See?' I said. But Mum, Jo and Tricia reacted as though they were hearing the news for the first time.

'You're joking!' Jo grabbed the paper and looked at the black headlines that took up the whole front page, with a blurred photo of Jack and Jackie in the car, and a lot of arrows and crosses showing where the shot had come from.

'I hope this doesn't mean war,' said Dad. War? He'd said the same thing a while before, when something had happened at a place called the Bay of Pigs in Cuba. Oh no, not war! I looked out of the kitchen window, expecting to see a flight of bombers swooping over our house.

'I can't believe it,' said Mum flatly. 'It's impossible.'

All that weekend, news bulletins on TV fed us more and more details, and we watched the same piece of film again and again: the long black car with Jack and Jackie waving (Jackie in a pillbox hat with a short jacket and skirt), then suddenly Kennedy putting his hand up to his head as though a mosquito had stung him and collapsing sideways into Jackie's lap. A bit later, there were photographs of a young man with a long face and three names: Lee Harvey Oswald, whom the newsreaders said had been arrested for murdering Kennedy. (I knew he was guilty; on television and in newspapers the only people who had middle names were criminals.)

At school on Monday morning, everybody was talking about Kennedy's assassination. 'I was having a shower when I found out,' said my best friend, Susan Healey. 'I'd just passed the cornflakes to my sister,' said Robert Patterson, the class goody-two-shoes. 'Well, *I* found out first and told my sisters and they didn't believe me,' I added, having no objection to blackening Jo and Tricia's names.

It's interesting, isn't it, that most people can remember exactly what they were doing when they found out Kennedy was shot. Try doing the same test with Harold Holt: few can recall exactly where they were when they heard he'd been drowned at Portsea.

The family who lived next door to us, the McIlveens, were Catholics; they were really upset about the assassination. Lucy McIlveen, who was a year older than I, told me that the nuns were practically in tears about it because Kennedy had been the first Catholic president in history, as well as of Irish descent.

School holidays came, and Christmas, and gradually Kennedy faded from my mind. I was incensed that I didn't get my Beatles record; just a lot of boring underwear, a pair of pyjamas from my grandparents and a toy piano that didn't work after about a week. But Mum and Dad did give me a pyjama case shaped like a lion, that zipped up the back. It was lovable and cuddly, and I happily crammed my shortie pyjamas into it.

I christened it 'Aslan', after the lion in C. S. Lewis's *The Lion, the Witch and the Wardrobe*. Early in February I took it to school. I hadn't counted on the fact that our new teacher for third class was named Mrs Asland. She came up to me and admired my pyjama case. 'And what have you called your lion, dear?' she asked sweetly.

I went cold all over and thought fast.

'Leo,' I said.

Whew.

That year you couldn't escape the Beatles. For the first time in our lives, Jo, Tricia and I agreed about something: we were all mad about them. We cut out magazine pictures showing the four young men in round-necked collarless jackets, with long fringes over their cheerful faces. 'They look like a group of English sheep-dogs,' said Dad, but we didn't care what he said. Adoringly we pasted pictures on cardboard project sheets which we stickytaped to the mirrors on our wardrobes. Tricia and I had furious arguments about our favourite Beatle; I liked John because he looked so sensitive, Tricia preferred George. Jo announced that she was in love with Paul and intended to go to England to meet him as soon as she could.

I knew all the words of 'Love Me Do', and Tricia did her own version of John's mouth organ accompaniment with silver paper and a comb. I deeply envied Jo, who was just starting to go to 'slumber parties' with her girlfriends and danced the Twist to all the Beatles' songs. I used to copy her, particularly doing 'Twist and Shout'...'C'mon, c'mon, c'mon, c'mon baby now... C'mon and work it on out...whooh!'

All the local shops started sprouting Beatles souvenirs. This being the era before printed T-shirts, the range of items was fairly small. I bought myself a charm bracelet with four little beetles in different colours on it: red for John, blue for Paul, yellow for George and green for Ringo. Woolworths had Beatle wigs, lengths of brown nylon hair in a fringe attached to a headband. When you put one on, you looked like a mangy chrysanthemum. 'If I catch any of you girls wearing one of those...' Mum said threateningly, but she need not have worried. We weren't tempted. Adoring the Beatles from afar was enough for us; we didn't particularly want to look like them.

Mum couldn't understand our infatuation. 'Why are you so keen on four louts from England?' she asked. 'They can't even sing. All they do is wail.' Wailing louts? Had she no soul? But we knew she hadn't really emerged from the era of Frank Sinatra. 'If you want singers, why don't you like that nice Peter, Paul and Mary?' she asked. We treated that with scorn. 'Peter, Paul and Mary are real *drips*,' said Jo, and we agreed. How could you compare the pathetic lyrics of 'Puff the Magic Dragon' to the power of 'I Wanna Hold Your Hand'?

Mum wasn't alone in her musical tastes, though. The McIlveen kids next door were allowed to listen to Peter, Paul and Mary, but they weren't allowed the Beatles. Lucy McIlveen told me with great shame that her eldest brother loved Elvis Presley. Ugh!

The Robsons over the back (Warren and his sister Lynette, the hussy who had been allowed to wear lipstick at the age of eleven) had lax parents who allowed them to listen to the Rolling Stones. We hated the Stones. They were dirty, scruffy, poor-imitation Beatles, and they couldn't even sing. Warren and Lynette thought themselves terribly superior to us. '*Everybody* loves the Beatles...all that silly yeah, yeah, yeah,' said Warren, who was sixteen and had his eye on Jo, though she spurned him. 'No style.'

Then we found out the Beatles were coming to Australia. We could hardly contain ourselves. The glory of seeing John, Paul, George and Ringo in person! In the flesh!

'I'm going to the airport to meet them,' said Jo rashly to Mum.

'Oh no you're not,' said Mum very firmly. 'You're not missing school to see those dreadful boys.' From the steely look in Jo's eye, I didn't like Mum's chances of enforcing her authority, but at least Jo had the sense not to argue any further.

Then modified disaster struck: John, Paul and George were coming, but Ringo had a throat infection and was going to be replaced by an anaemic person named Jimmy Nicholl. Three out of four was better than none, though.

They came to Adelaide, and the three of us were in torment. We were forbidden to go to any of the concerts. Jo suffered the most. 'Louise is allowed,' she wailed to Mum. 'And we'll just go to the showground and come straight home. Why can't I *go*?' Mum and Dad were firm. 'You're growing up fast enough as it is,' Mum told her. Jo's resolve to meet them at the airport had collapsed; all too difficult. 'I can't even learn to drive for *years* yet, and by the time I learn it'll be too late!' she cried. 'If I could drive, I'd go.'

We had to be content with watching them on television; at least we got better close-ups that way. I still adored John, especially when a reporter asked him if he had a message for the folks in England. Maybe for the Prime Minister? 'Ullo Sir Alec and ullo Mum,' he said. What wit!

The crowds of teenage girls fascinated me. They were all over the TV screen, chasing their heroes, screaming, running, behaving like spectators at a Grand Final football match. Who would have thought that tiny Adelaide had so many people in it?

Even when they left Australia (and Adelaide had given them their most enthusiastic welcome, we knew) we continued to love the Beatles. Tricia started building up her collection of records: by the end of the 1960s she had every record they had made. She still does, and still plays them at parties. When she got married, she said her Beatles records were her dowry!

When I was ten, towards the end of 1965, I had to learn about new money. Decimal currency. Our teachers made very heavy weather of it, explaining in enormous detail how much easier it would be to count in tens instead of twelves. 'It'll take a bit of getting used to,' said Mrs Penney, who was relentless in giving us sums about decimal money. I thought this was very unfair; it seemed I'd spent years learning that there were twelve pennies in a shilling and twenty shillings in a pound. Had I suffered dreadful long division sums with halfpennies for nothing? It seemed I had.

Grocers' shops sprouted complicated charts that told us that two cents would be worth something like 3.1214 pence. So what? As long as I didn't have to convert it, I didn't mind. At school we were bombarded with pretty coloured booklets. They promised us that pounds, tons and ounces would be replaced by other things. Pounds would be kilograms, which were bigger, tons would be tonnes, about the same size but spelled differently; ounces would be grams, which were much smaller. There didn't seem any logic in it. But the booklets also said that these changes would be 'phased in gradually' so, with any luck, I would have left school and wouldn't be forced to worry about them.

Money was enough to be going on with. What were the new coins to be called? Mr Menzies had suggested that the main unit of currency should be called the royal, and Nestles brought out a red-and-blue papered chocolate block to celebrate. But then the government decided on dollars and cents.

'Very unimaginative, just like the Americans,' commented Dad crossly. 'But at least the designs are nice.' They were, too; platypuses, frill-necked lizards, sugar gliders, lyrebirds. Very tasteful and very Australian.

On television, radio and in booklets there was a cute cartoon character named Dollar Bill, who sang about the new money to the tune of 'Click Go the Shears':

In come the dollars and in come the cents
Out go the pounds, the shillings and the pence.
Be ready now when the coins start to mix
On the fourteenth of February, nineteen sixty-six!

The changeover *was* easy, and the new coins were lovely: my only quarrel was that we couldn't have them in the Christmas pudding. 'I don't think those five cent pieces are silver,' said Mum doubt-fully. 'They may be poisonous.' We'd kept a few pudding-covered sixpences from previous years, but they looked small and mean after a while.

We started to hear about a war in Asia, in a place called Vietnam. I was twelve, I suppose, when I noticed that quite a lot of TV news bulletins featured men in loose uniforms and floppy hats walking through jungles, while helicopters hovered overhead. But the war didn't mean much to me: so what if Australia was involved? It seemed logical that we should fight the Asians, who would otherwise come down from the north and attack us. Dad said so, but didn't think there was much to worry about. This opinion was shared by Mr Braine, who owned the local grocery-cum-fish and chips shop at the end of the street. When we went down to get two packets of Kool cigarettes and a packet of Bex for Mum, he said we were fighting 'little men in black pyjamas'.

I thought everybody considered the war in Vietnam to be a mildly interesting example of current affairs; it certainly didn't occur to me that anybody would object to it. But then Jo started to go to university.

She was eighteen, and it seemed to me she changed overnight. Gone were the teased beehive hairdos and false eyelashes and winklepicker high heels she'd worn to school dances: now she grew her hair long and appeared in jeans. I admired her enor-mously, particularly because Mum and Dad seemed to object so strongly to everything she did. It took the heat off me.

Worse than the jeans and the long hair, though, was the fact that she became involved in Adelaide University's History and Politics Club. She had opinions that Mum and Dad didn't share, and therefore strongly resented.

'I don't know *why* you're so in favour of Vietnam,' Jo said to Dad one night during a particularly heated exchange over steak and beans and potatoes. 'It's a rotten, American-inspired imperialist war.'

'I suppose you heard that from your commie pinko friends,' said Dad scornfully. Dad's arguments with Jo were always like that: she'd make a statement and he'd attack her friends.

'You try and tell me why you think we should be there, supporting the Yanks,' challenged Jo.

'You're too young to know, of course, but there *is* a thing called the domino theory,' said Dad. 'And the Asians'll come down here...'

'I'm surprised you don't call them the Yellow Peril!'

'Don't you talk to me like that!'

And so on, and on. The arguments didn't vary much. I was on Jo's side in principle, because I admired her for standing up to Dad, though the whole issue didn't seem vital. They had a memorable discussion on the night Jo came home with a moratorium badge pinned to her sweater.

'What's that thing?' demanded Dad.

'You know perfectly well,' said Jo.

Dad pretended to read it. 'Moratorium! Do you know what a moratorium is? It's a legal term about delaying payment of money. What's that got to do with Vietnam?'

'So what? It's my statement that I'm against the war in Vietnam. And I don't know where you've been, Dad, but you'll find out that most *decent* people...'

'I suppose you mean your pinko friends, who can't even use words properly!'

'...most decent people are against the war, too.'

'Don't argue with your father,' said Mum.

Jo got up from the table in a rush, almost stumbling over her chair. 'I'm tired of living in this house! You're all fascists!' With which she stormed out.

The rest of us continued to shovel in our macaroni and cheese. 'Poor Jo,' said Dad. 'I suppose she's aware that the Fascists were the Italian party Mussolini led. Can't use that word accurately, either.' I didn't know why he was telling us, not Jo.

Next thing, a moratorium poster appeared on Jo's bedroom door.

'Take that thing down!' stormed Mum.

'I'll keep it up if I want to,' said Jo. But eventually she

compromised to the extent of putting the poster on the inside of the door, where visitors wouldn't see it and know that our house harboured a dangerous anti-Vietnam agitator. This seemed important to Mum and Dad.

I was pro-Jo for another reason, now I come to think about it. Warren Robson up the back, who had developed from a skinny, pimply sixteen-year-old schoolboy who loved the Rolling Stones to a skinny, pimply, twenty-year-old mechanic, was very much in favour of the Vietnam War.

'That bastard can hardly wait to get over there and start killing the Vietnamese!' said Jo furiously. Warren was still doing badly when it came to winning Jo's heart. 'Only people like Warren Robson would agree to be involved in this filthy war.'

Warren showed less delight than might have been expected when his marble came out of the barrel and he was conscripted. Just before he left to go to training camp, he came over to show us what he looked like in his resplendent new uniform. Fortunately, Jo wasn't home, but Dad was. He took one look at this skinny young man in jungle greens that appeared too large for him, and invited Warren to have a beer.

'Well, looking forward to going, eh?' said Dad, as he poured a glass of West End for Warren. 'Wouldn't mind having a go myself if I was a bit younger.'

Warren smiled politely, but didn't enter into Dad's enthusiasm. 'You want to watch those booby traps, though,' said Dad. 'Bit of a worry out there in the jungle.' From the look on Warren's face, the thought of booby-trapped villages wasn't too far from his mind. He was more silent than he'd ever been.

We heard occasional bits of news about him from Mrs Robson and Lynette when we met them down at the shops. 'Warren doesn't write many letters,' said his mother apologetically. 'But he's safe and well.'

I found it difficult to envisage exactly what Warren might be getting into. According to the news bulletins on TV, it didn't seem like much of a war. We saw films of Australians carrying rifles, marching through bits of country, helicopters hovering overhead. We saw no bodies, except Vietnamese who always seemed to lie on the ground in decorous little groups a long way from the camera. The papers told us that the American casualty figures were high. According to Jo, the US soldiers were tools of an imperialist government, and deserved to get shot or blown up.

Warren was in the fighting zone, his mother told Mum. Then we heard he had been wounded, though not seriously. 'Shot in the leg,' said Mrs Robson. 'But he'll be back in the fighting soon.'

The next report, however, was more serious. 'It seems to be a thigh wound, according to the Army,' said Mrs Robson. 'But it apparently isn't serious.' A couple of weeks later she said that it hadn't been too bad at all.

'But he's got some kind of fever, malaria, he thinks, and he can't fight,' she said. 'He hasn't mentioned his leg or his thigh, so I suppose that's better. As I've said, he's never been much of a one for writing letters.'

That was that for a while. Then, the next we heard, Warren was coming home. His family was pleased, but puzzled, especially because he didn't give any arrival date. And there had been a mysterious letter from the Army, saying something about 'in view of Pte Robson's mental condition...'

Then Lynette received a strange letter from her brother, sent from Concord Repatriation Hospital in Sydney. 'I don't know when I'll be home, but I'm all right now,' he wrote. Mr Robson fired off a letter to the hospital, demanding further information, and the reply contained the ominous word 'breakdown'.

Not long afterwards, Warren returned — only about eight months after his departure. He *looked* the same as usual, though paler, but he wouldn't say what had happened to him.

'You must be happy to have Warren home again,' Mum said to Mrs Robson down at the shops one day.

Mrs Robson's face closed up immediately. 'Yes,' was all she said. Like her son, she refused to discuss the subject any further, which was odd considering how glad she had been to tell us exactly what had been happening to Warren over there in Vietnam.

We didn't find the truth for a long time, and then only because Jo met another soldier from Warren's unit at a party.

'Yeah, Robson,' he said. 'I remember him. Refused duty and was invalided out. Nervous breakdown. He kept having screaming nightmares. Happened to a lot of blokes over there.'

Che Guevara, Robert Kennedy, Martin Luther King; all died violently. I knew who they were, of course, but their deaths didn't affect me. Dreadful things happened in the US, everybody knew that. It was full of mad people. When Harold Holt was drowned off Portsea, I was more interested, but couldn't work up much outrage or sorrow. It seemed an extraordinary thing to do, to go swimming off that beach at that time, but Holt was replaced by Gorton, and things continued as before.

I found Snowcrisp dead in the garden one day, and cried, and buried him. Then I acquired Paddypaws, a spitting, striped tom whom nobody could handle except me. That was the year I started high school, 1968. I had a new uniform and many more books to read, and life seemed jumbled and noisy. Jo was working in the public library and sharing a flat with a friend. Tricia had started Arts at Adelaide University, though she wasn't the argumentative student Jo had been. She was anti-Vietnam too, but all she seemed to want was to go to parties and dances and coffee lounges with young men from St Peter's College or Pulteney Grammar.

At the beginning of third term in 1969, when I was in second year, the whole school was summoned to the assembly hall one afternoon. The school's four television sets showed blurred pictures of history: Neil Armstrong lurching around the moon, planting his US flag on lunar rock. 'One small step for man, one giant step for mankind,' he said. The commentary was reverent.

We were interested, but, I think, not fascinated. I tried hard to be impressed, but deep down a little voice was murmuring, So what? I suppose I'd seen so many science fiction movies about moon landings that the real thing looked like a late night re-run. To hell with the fact that there were pictures coming from there *at all*: I peevishly criticised the TV reception to myself.

'This is the most wonderful scientific achievement you have witnessed in your lifetime,' declared Mrs Briggs when the pictures faded at last. 'Soon there will be people living on the moon.' I nodded solemnly, but couldn't believe her. People living up there? In a place that looked more desolate than even Sturt's Stony Desert?

That night I walked into the garden and peered through the clouds over the orange tree. 'There are men up there,' I told myself. 'I've seen them.' But it all seemed entirely unreal.

Looking back now, I find it hard to believe I was so blase — but at the time it wasn't extraordinary. Like so many other people, I'd had important events brought to me by television, and that's a double-edged thing. My parents were always saying that they wished they'd had television when they were my age, because it was a wonderful means of seeing the world. But everything, it seems to me, is reduced. My mind flattened things out, compressed them to the size of a series of small, black-and-white pictures on a screen measuring only twenty-one inches. You looked and understood, but you weren't involved. Though I remembered what I saw on televison, it seemed to have little to do with me.

I now have a four-year-old boy and six-year-old girl who watch TV constantly. I feel a bit guilty about that, in the way that conscientious parents are encouraged to, but they seem to do enough other things. They're no more addicted to television than other kids their age. They're much better informed than I was, they know more about what's happening in the world, but are they better for it? I don't know about that.

You see, they worry much more. Sandy is disturbed about the Ethiopians who don't have enough to eat. She can't understand that there are people in the same country who won't share their food with the starving babies. And the other day she came to me because she had heard about men pressing buttons that could blast the world to bits. 'What's going to happen to you and Daddy?' she wanted to know. She seemed to think that she and her brother Daniel would be all right. I had to tell her there was nothing we could do about it, the problems of the world are all too big for her, for us.

Life used to be much simpler.

Photographic sources

Australian Consolidated Press p. **208**. Australian Photographic Review p. **134**. Australian War Memorial pp. **66, 178**. Phillipa Carlyle pp. **80, 207**. Fairfax Magazines Picture Library pp. **95, 224, 238, 243, 244, 254**. La Trobe Library of Victoria pp. **18, 72, 184**. David Moore p. **228**. News Ltd pp. **114, 196**. NSW Government Printer p. **96**. *Pix* Magazine p. **122**. Geoffrey Powell p. **190**. State Library of New South Wales pp. **2, 65, 142**. State Library of South Australia pp. **30, 46, 154, 159**. West Australian Museum of Childhood pp. **1, 45, 160**.

The author and publishers acknowledge with thanks the assistance of Anne-Marie Willis in researching the photographs which appear on pages **122, 134, 190** and **228** and which are also reproduced in her book *Picturing Australia: A History of Photography* (Angus & Robertson, 1988).